KNACK
MAKE IT EASY

CYCLING
FOR EVERYONE

FUELED BY
FALCONGUIDES

KNACK

CYCLING
FOR EVERYONE

A Guide to Road, Mountain, and Commuter Biking

Leah Garcia and Jilayne Lovejoy

Photographs by Mark Doolittle

KNACK
MAKE IT EASY

Guilford, Connecticut
An imprint of Globe Pequot Press

Editorial Director: Cynthia Hughes
Editor: Lara Asher
Project Editor: Tracee Williams
Cover Design: Paul Beatrice, Bret Kerr
Interior Design: Paul Beatrice
Layout: Maggie Peterson
Diagrams by: Jilayne Lovejoy
Cover Photos by: Mark Doolittle
Interior Photos by: Mark Doolittle with the exception of those on page 116 (left): © Russ Du parcq | shutterstock; 116 (right): Courtesy of Jilayne Lovejoy, 154 (right): Courtesy of Computrainer; 155 (right): © Andresr | shutterstock; 157 (left): © Val Thoermer | shutterstock; 160 (left): Courtesy of FasCat Coaching; 163 (left): Courtesy of Alison Dunlap Adventure Camps; 168 (right): Courtesy of Tim Hancock Photography; 170 (left): Courtesy of John Miller; 170 (right): © Radin Myroslav | shutterstock; 171 (left): © Robert Young | shutterstock; 172 (left): Courtesy of Peter Cowley; 172 (right): © Sirko Hartmann | shutterstock; 173 (left): © Vaclav Volrab | shutterstock; 175 (right): Courtesy of Sven Martin Photography; 176 (left): © jocrebbin | shutterstock; 176 (right): © mudandcowbells.com; 177 (left): Courtesy of Peter Cowley; 178 (left): Courtesy of John Foote; 179 (right): Courtesy of Tim Hancock Photography; 189 (right): Jupiter Images; 190 (right): © Clay Blackburn | Jupiter Images; 201 (left): © Aaron Kohr | shutterstock; 206 (right): © Anne Keller; 208 (left): © Local Favorite Photography | shutterstock; 209 (right): © Vitalii Nesterchuk | shutterstock; 210 (right): © Michael Woodruff | shutterstock; 213 (left): © empipe | shutterstock; 213 (right): Courtesy of Jilayne Lovejoy; 214 (left): © Artsem Martysiuk | shutterstock; 215 (left): © arne thaysen | Jupiter Images; 215 (right): © yurok | shutterstock; 216 (left): Courtesy of Don Cook; 217 (right): Courtesy of Peter Kraiker/studiofstop.com; 218 (right): Courtesy of boo-creative.com; 219 (left): © Andy Gregg; and 223 (right): Courtesy of IMBA.

Library of Congress Cataloging-in-Publication Data

Garcia, Leah.
  Knack cycling for everyone : a guide to road, mountain, and commuter biking / Leah Garcia and Jilayne Lovejoy ; photographs by Mark Doolittle.
    p. cm.
  ISBN 978-1-59921-871-7
  1. Cycling. 2. Cycling—Training. 3. Bicycles. 4. Bicycle racing. I. Lovejoy, Jilayne. II. Title.
  GV1041.G36 2010
  796.6—dc22

                                                          2010001560

Printed in China

10 9 8 7 6 5 4 3 2 1

To our moms and dads for pushing us, and then, letting us pedal on our own.

Acknowledgments

This book would not have been possible without the support, assistance, and generosity of our friends and sponsors. We would like to thank our models: Ian Adamson, Chad DeMoss, Jody Proctor, Jeff Wardell, Willa Johnson, Lovedy Barbatelli, Shannon Tupa, Todd Roe, John Joseph, Gary Thacker, Norm Wawzinski, Joel Andreasen, Steve Ackerman, John Miller, Heidi and Robert Breese and their kids, and Heather Proctor and her kids. Clothing was graciously provided by Pearl Izumi, Skirt Sports, Troy Lee Design, Veltec Sports, and Marin Bikes. A huge thanks to Excel Sports and University Bikes for allowing us to use their products and shoot photos onsite. Product and photo-shoot location support came from Shimano, Wigwam, Santa Cruz Bikes, 3D Racing, Cateye, Contour Technology, Marin Bikes, Oakley, Zeal, Smith Optics, Rocky Mounts, REI, The Fix Bike Shop, and the Boulder Center for Sports Medicine. Furthermore, we appreciate those of you who provided stock photos and gave us permission for inclusion in our book.

Leah Garcia would especially like to acknowledge:

The number of memories, influences, and experiences that have transformed me into what I now consider my cycling persona and current essence is incomprehensible. I'm so grateful to have had a supportive family from the beginning. They remain my foundation.

Thanks to Antonio Balboa, a former Tour racer who taught me what it means to be a professional. I owe him a debt of gratitude for his profound knowledge of cycling. Oliver Starr took my training and racing to another level. With his tutelage, I was able to capitalize on every ounce of talent and business savvy I had. Allow me to shout out a special thanks to my fierce and early competitors. Julie, Susan, Tammy, Ruthie, Karen . . . you made me want to go faster. And to John Davis, my downhill wheelchair-blazing friend, I'll tow you up Squaw Valley anytime.

Much appreciation to Versus television for hiring me as a cycling analyst during OLN days, and production company icons Hugh Arian and Frank Matson; I'm a lucky woman to have had your support. Today Dale Henn and Mike Hays give me the tools to stay on top of my game; let's keep the momentum, guys! Finally, to Ian Adamson, my beautiful training partner, thank you for being part of my life.

Jilayne Lovejoy would especially like to acknowledge:

I owe special thanks to those who were influential at key moments along this continuing journey. Thanks to Shane McConkey, may he rest in peace, for taking me on my first mountain bike ride and making me get back on the bike after crashing—I might have hated mountain biking had he not been so persistent. Thanks to Dave Fisher for teaching me basic bike maintenance and accompanying me to those first mountain bike races. Thanks to Mark Tatum for having faith in my ability when I turned pro and teaching me how to approach sponsorship. Thanks to all the inspiring women who showed me that I could do more than I imagined, especially Ann Trombley and Kerry Barnholt, who continue to exemplify the grace of a champion. Thanks to Ira Haimann for his knowledge and support. And to every member of the Title Nine Women's Cycling Club: Never stop daring to challenge yourselves!

Most of all, thanks to the sport of cycling. Whether training, racing, commuting, exploring, teaching clinics, forging new friendships in foreign places, or enjoying the Wednesday night mountain bike ride with the usual suspects, the experiences I've had and continue to have on a bike have made me who I am.

CONTENTS

INTRODUCTION

Cycling Really Is for Everyone

Here you are, this book in your hand or displayed on your computer screen, and you are wondering, "Is this the book for me?" It could be that you are interested in getting into cycling, but you are not sure where to begin. Then again, you may already be a cycling enthusiast but have enjoyed the sport mostly alone and are trying to decide which cycling subculture suits you. Perhaps your doctor has told you to shape up, or you are a runner looking for a non-impact endurance sport to save your knees, or you just want to lose a few pounds and feel fitter. Maybe you are tired of being a slave to the whims of public transportation and would like to have more freedom moving about an urban environment. If you use a bike to get around but would like to learn more (or are a skeptic) about all the jargon and equipment that others in the sport seem unable to live without, this book is for you. This book is for you and all others who recognize how little they know about cycling but want to know more.

We have attempted to touch upon the many things to consider when starting out. This begins with an understanding of the different types of bikes; what to look for when buying a bike; basic maintenance and riding skills; and explanations of the various equipment and accessories that go along with cycling. In the latter half of the book, we will introduce you to more advanced riding skills, different types of events, considerations for cycling with kids, ideas for cycling vacations, and basic training concepts. In other words, we have covered a little bit about a broad range of topics. If you want to delve more deeply into a particular area, many other books are devoted to bike maintenance, training, or bike history, for example. We have listed some excellent resources in the last chapter to help you take the next step should you choose to do so.

The Inside Perspective

Cyclists can be an opinionated lot. The sheer multitude of choices in equipment, gearing, and accessories, not to mention different riding types, is prime breeding ground for heated debate. As a new rider, you will be subjected to lots of advice, often unsolicited, from more experienced riders who are passionate about what they think you need. As you listen to these well-intended cyclists, you may find their advice contradictory, which can lead to feeling a bit lost or overwhelmed. Just listen with an open mind and file away what you hear for further consideration as you gain your own experience and preferences. You can learn a lot from more experienced cyclists, and this is how many of us are indoctrinated into the sport. But realizing that no one source is the end-all and be-all will help you form and keep your own perspective.

Keeping all this in mind, we have tried to present the information contained in this book as objectively as possible. Just the facts, ma'am! When our experience leads us to recommend a certain method or product, we have stated so.

We realize that our readers may be British, Irish, or Australian, so we have tried to include cross-cultural terminology as much as possible. If we missed a few terms, please forgive

us. Likewise, all photos on street riding will show driving on the right side of the road because they were taken in the United States. Nevertheless, the principles of riding with traffic are the same.

Early Memories

No one starts out as an expert. Riding bikes has been a part of our lives since childhood.

On a ranch in northern California, Leah could be found bunny-hopping mud puddles on her banana seat bike. When Leah wasn't strong enough to keep up with her older brother, he'd use his roping skills to tow her the six miles to school. In college in San Luis Obispo, the bike continued to be a means of getting to and from class, as well as fighting the freshman fifteen. It was here, Leah caught the mountain biking wave and joined the boys on their Thursday night rides, ending at the farmer's market. But it wasn't until moving to Spain that Leah found her passion for racing. An 80-year-old former Tour de France racer talked Leah into doing her first pro mountain bike race, even though she didn't know the rules and thought the objective was to complete the race without placing a foot on the ground. With a new trophy and a bouquet of flowers in her arms, she was shown the national race calendar and locations for the remainder of the season. At that moment, she was determined to race her bike for real and have a reason to travel Europe with purpose.

Meanwhile, on the other side of the country, Jilayne found freedom in the form of a Schwinn ten-speed for her thirteenth birthday. In a pair of cut-off jeans, a T-shirt, and no helmet, the bicycle enabled her to escape into her own world, exploring the Connecticut coastal roads and stopping along the way to scribble poetry in a journal. That same ten-speed accompanied Jilayne to Boulder, Colorado, as her only form of transportation during the first few years of college. Her first foray into cycling as a sport, riding Flagstaff Mountain and the Morgal Bismarck race course, was experienced on that same Schwinn, much to the shock and horror of her more cycling savvy friends. But, it was a borrowed mountain bike that opened a whole new arena of cycling to Jilayne. She was instantly hooked on the prospect of being able to go anywhere on a bike. After purchasing her own mountain bike, it was not long before she tried her first race. Her fitness in those early years was gained not through high-tech training tools and well-laid plans, but by simply trying to keep up with the boys.

It was 1996 when we met on the professional mountain biking circuit. Both somewhat seasoned racers at that point, there was still much to learn. Leah traded the race bike for a microphone and camera, reporting from the sidelines of the national series. Jilayne went on to race on the road across Colorado. Both would pass along knowledge to others; Leah via her public speaking and training business and Jilayne through teaching skills clinics to new riders via a women's grassroots cycling club. Along the way, our involvement with the cycling industry would always continue in one form or another.

That's Possible?

One theme that was present in both our early cycling paths, was a certain amount of cluelessness. Sometimes ignorance really is bliss. If you don't know what you're not capable of, you're not afraid to try it. You can overprepare, overanalyze, and overthink in life. The good stories and the lasting memories come from just getting out and doing it. Sometimes it was only after we gained more experience and knowledge that we realized just how potentially dangerous our adventures were. We jumped in with both feet and often learned by trial and error.

On the other hand, a little understanding can go a long way. Some knowledge can save time and make an otherwise insurmountable-seeming challenge both do-able and safer. We hope by passing on our knowledge, whatever hurdle that might be keeping you from getting out on a bike or taking your cycling to the next level will be lowered.

After you understand more about bikes, live through the pleasure of riding with positive experiences, and surround yourself with like-minded souls, the yearning develops in its own natural way. Cycling is a sport like no other. Think about it. What other sport can fill the roles of a practical form of transportation, recreation, and top-level competition? We hope this book will show you all that riding a bike can be and that the possibilities cycling offers are truly endless. Most important, we hope this book will get the wheels turning—both under your body and in your head.

Let's ride!

~Leah Garcia and Jilayne Lovejoy

PAVEMENT

Road cycling on a smooth surface allows you to travel at fairly high speeds

It goes without saying that the bicycle's most common venue is on the roads across the globe. The bikes used to travel along roads come in all shapes and sizes. As the bicycle developed, different uses dictated the development of different frame styles, equipment, frame geometry, gearing, wheel size, and tires. Frame geometry has to do with the angles and lengths of the frame's tubing, which affects the handling and fit. This can mean that bikes that look similar from afar may ride and handle differently.

Road bikes are a broad category of bikes with drop handlebars, larger-sized wheels, and skinny tires. These bikes are used for recreation and racing but can also be used for

Road Bike—Low End

- Used for recreational riding, racing, and transportation.

- Usually has two chainrings and a cassette with eight to eleven cogs in the back for sixteen to twenty-two gear combinations.

- Uses 700c wheels, caliper brakes, and skinny tires.

- A low-end road bike will be a bit heavy and have lower performance. Parts will wear out sooner than on a more expensive bike. The price of eventual or inevitable upgrades may make it more cost-effective to purchase a higher quality bike at the beginning.

Road Bike—High End

- Used for recreational riding and racing.

- May have steeper seat tube and head tube angles for a more responsive, performance-oriented ride.

- Usually has two chainrings and a cassette with eight to eleven cogs in the back.

- Uses 700c wheels, caliper brakes, and skinny, smooth tires.

- Top-of-the-line frame and components will mean lightweight, superior performance and a hefty price tag. High-quality components mean the bike will serve you well for many years.

transportation. They are equipped to cover long distances quickly and efficiently. Road bikes vary considerably in cost, depending on the quality of the frame and equipment. Higher cost equates to lighter equipment, as well as better functioning and durability.

Time trial bikes are used for a very specific type of racing, called "time trials." These races are individual timed events in which each racer starts at a designated interval. Working together (that is, drafting) is not allowed. Time trials may be a stand-alone race, one race in a multi-day road stage race (like the Tour de France), or part of a triathlon or duathlon. Time trial bikes are designed to go fast in a straight line, and thus uses tubing and other equipment designed to be aerodynamic.

Touring bikes are really a subset of road bikes, with a few minor yet key modifications. Specific eyelets built into the frame allow racks to be attached to the bike for carrying bags or panniers. Touring bikes are also built and geared for riding comfortably with a larger weight load.

Time Trial

- Used for specific racing events called "time trials."

- Uses steeper head tube and seat tube angles. Often has aerodynamically shaped tubing.

- Harder gearing to accommodate all-out efforts on flat terrain.

- Uses 700c or 600c wheels, caliper brakes, and skinny, smooth tires. May use deep-dish rims or disc wheels.

- Time trial handlebars allow for a low, aerodynamic body position. However, this position compromises steering and bike-handling ability.

Touring Bike

- Used for touring or traveling long distances with luggage.

- May have a less-steep seat tube and head tube angle for a more relaxed position on the bike and slightly longer wheelbase. The frame has eyelets for mounting racks and is reinforced in

key spots to support cargo weight.

- Uses 700c wheels, caliper brakes, and smooth or slightly treaded tires.

- May have three chainrings or easier gearing to accommodate the added difficulty of riding with extra weight.

CITY BIKES

Riding through town can take you on interesting, safe routes otherwise missed while traveling in a vehicle

Whether in a city, town, or remote village, commuting bikes are most often used for the sole purpose of traveling relatively short distances. Generally speaking, functionality, practicality, and affordability supersede weight, efficiency, and the fancier attributes of more expensive machines. Bikes used for transportation are not always new. Many are handed down from one cyclist to another and ridden until they no longer function.

Urban bikes are simultaneously the most often seen and hardest to categorize or generalize. Common characteristics include an upright body position, a wide saddle, and durable construction. An unremarkable or even beat-up appearance makes the bike less appealing to thieves.

Hybrid

- Hybrid bikes usually have 700c wheels—the same size as road bikes.

- A more upright position enhances visibility for both the rider and others, making your commute safer.

- Gearing may vary, as will the style of brakes. Most hybrids will have a wide range of gears.

- Some new hybrids have a short-travel suspension fork and disc brakes.

- "Hybrid" is really a catch-all term for bikes that don't fit into any of the more specific categories.

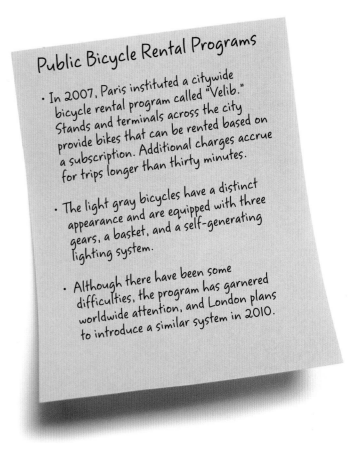

Public Bicycle Rental Programs

- In 2007, Paris instituted a citywide bicycle rental program called "Velib." Stands and terminals across the city provide bikes that can be rented based on a subscription. Additional charges accrue for trips longer than thirty minutes.

- The light gray bicycles have a distinct appearance and are equipped with three gears, a basket, and a self-generating lighting system.

- Although there have been some difficulties, the program has garnered worldwide attention, and London plans to introduce a similar system in 2010.

Cycling is the most energy-efficient means of transportation that is widely available. Traveling at a low to medium speed requires an energy expenditure similar to that of walking. In spite of a push toward the use of automobiles, the bicycle is still the most common form of transportation in many developing nations. Conversely, some Western developed cities have instituted programs and policies to get more people out of their cars and onto bikes to reduce traffic congestion and air pollution, as well as to improve the general health of the population.

Cruiser

- Used for cruising around town and looking cool.

- Most cruisers have an upright position with wide, sweeping handlebars.

- A cruiser may have several gears in an internal hub or be a singlespeed with coaster-style brakes.

- Compared with urban or city bikes, cruisers are heavy and do not have modern front suspension.

- The old Schwinn cruisers provided the inspiration for the invention of the mountain bike.

Step-through Frame

- Frames with a lowered top tube have traditionally been called "ladies'" bikes and were designed for women wearing long skirts.

- A step-through frame is still handy for persons who may have trouble swinging their leg over a horizontal top tube as well as for anyone wearing a long coat.

- By design, step-through frames are not as structurally rigid. Because the triangle is the strongest geometrical shape, the bicycle frame developed in the form of two triangles.

OFF-ROAD
Riding off-road means less traffic, access to nature, and a variety of terrain

Although people have been riding bicycles off-road longer than we might realize, the advent of the mountain bike in the 1980s created a whole new discipline of the sport. Mountain bikes enabled cyclists to enjoy the peace and challenges of the mountains, backwoods, and other remote locales.

The technology of the mountain bike evolved quickly.

Mountain bikes needed to be light and strong and able to take a beating. Gearing needed to accommodate a wider range of ascending and descending pitches. Tire tread needed to be designed for varying types of terrain surfaces from wet, slippery roots to dry, ball-bearing-like rocks. The motocross world provided a huge source of crossover technology, most

Cyclocross Bike

- Used for cyclocross racing and riding on dirt roads and nontechnical trails.

- Compared with road frames, cyclocross frames have a higher bottom bracket, more clearance around the brakes for mud, easier gearing, and a slightly more relaxed geometry.

- Most commonly uses a double chainring, but some cyclocross riders run a single chainring.

- Uses 700c wheels with knobby tires. Cantilever brakes are most common, but disc or V-Brakes may also be used.

Hardtail Mountain Bike

- Used for off-road riding of all kinds.

- The term "hardtail" refers to a rigid frame combined with a suspension fork.

- Typically has a triple chainring and nine-speed cassette, providing a wide range of gear options.

- Uses 26-inch wheels with knobby tires and cantilever, V-Brakes, or disc brakes.

- Mountain bikes can make excellent commuting machines by replacing knobby tires with slick, narrow tires.

notably in the form of suspension and disc brakes. A whole new industry boomed in a short period of time, driven by soaring sales from first-time buyers throughout the nineties.

As mountain bikers pushed the envelope of what could be done on a bike, the bikes became more specialized, and more cycling sub-cultures developed. Today, mountain bike options range from super lightweight rigid frames with or without a suspension fork to relatively lightweight full-suspension rigs to full-on downhill racing bikes that sport as many inches of suspension (also called "travel") as a motorcycle.

Cross-country Full Suspension

- Used for off-road riding of all kinds. Designed for rougher terrain.

- Has a front suspension fork and rear suspension built into the frame. Different frame designs vary the performance of the rear suspension.

- Rear suspension travel is typically measured by the amount that the rear wheel moves up and down (not by the amount of movement in the shock body itself).

- Uses 26-inch wheels with knobby tires and cantilever, V-Brakes, or disc brakes.

Downhill Mountain Bike

- Used for downhill racing and extreme downhill riding.

- Has an upright position, a longer wheelbase, and relaxed head tube and seat tube angles. Can weigh forty-plus pounds.

- Has more than five inches of travel on both the fork

- and rear suspension. Needs only one chainring.

- Uses 26-inch wheels with wide, knobby tires and disc brakes.

- Free-ride bikes, which are different from downhill bikes, are used for BMX-style riding, tricks, and jumps.

FIXED GEAR & SINGLESPEED
Some people prefer the simplicity of a bike with only one gear

The first bikes had a direct drive, meaning the crank was attached directly to the front wheel or a single gear connected to the crank via a chain. In other words, as long as the wheel was moving, so were the cranks and the rider's legs. The development of the freewheel, which allows coasting, was a huge improvement, making the bicycle safer and more accessible. This improvement also meant brakes were now needed, as one could not simply resist the forward pedaling motion to slow down or stop. The coaster brake was introduced in the American market at the beginning of the twentieth century, while rim brakes became popular in the British market. The freewheel also prompted the development and widespread use of the three-speed internal hubs.

Fixed gear bikes are most often associated with track racing,

Fixed Gear Bike

- Has a single fixed gear, meaning you cannot coast or stop pedaling while the wheels are moving. This also means you can pedal and move backward. Essentially the same as a track bike.

- Uses 700c wheels and may or may not have one or two brakes.

- Not optimal for commuting, especially in hilly areas. If you choose to use a fixed gear bike, you must be an experienced rider with developed skills in order to ride safely.

- Commonly used by bicycle messengers. Also called a "fixie."

Track Bike

- Singlespeed, fixed gear bike used for racing on the track or velodrome.

- Horizontal dropouts for the rear wheel allow chain tension adjustment.

- Track frames have steeper seat tube and head tube angles than a road bike for more responsive steering. A higher bottom bracket provides pedal clearance on steeply banked tracks.

- Uses 700c wheels and skinny, slick tires. Track bikes do not have brakes.

which uses an oval track with banked sides called a "velodrome." This form of racing was enjoyed by a large following in the 1890s. Bicycle track racing is thought to have inspired motorized bicycles and eventually auto racing. The bicycles used on the track today are essentially the same as those used in 1890, save for the more advanced frame materials and aerodynamic accessories.

BMX racing began in the 1970s in southern California. The term "BMX" derives from "bicycle motocross." Drawing inspiration from motocross, BMX racing uses dirt tracks with berms and jumps. The Schwinn Stingray was the early bike of choice due to its small wheels, low center of gravity, and handling performance. By the late 1970s, specially designed BMX bikes were offered nationwide. BMX racing gained full medal status at the 2008 Olympics in Beijing, China. Freestyle BMX also started in southern California when kids took their BMX bikes to skate parks and began to develop bike-specific tricks.

BMX Bike

- Used for BMX racing, freestyle, tricks, and jumps.

- Usually has a single speed but not necessarily a fixed gear.

- Large-diameter front and rear axles are designed to withstand the abuse of jumping.

- Most commonly uses 20-inch wheels. Uses high spoke count (thirty-six or forty-eight) for durability.

- Trials bikes were developed from BMX bikes. The trials discipline involves negotiating obstacles without a foot touching the ground.

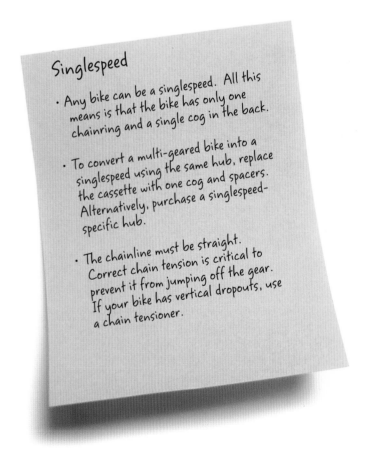

Singlespeed

- Any bike can be a singlespeed. All this means is that the bike has only one chainring and a single cog in the back.

- To convert a multi-geared bike into a singlespeed using the same hub, replace the cassette with one cog and spacers. Alternatively, purchase a singlespeed-specific hub.

- The chainline must be straight. Correct chain tension is critical to prevent it from jumping off the gear. If your bike has vertical dropouts, use a chain tensioner.

SPECIALTY BIKES

From handcycles and tandems to recumbent bikes, there is a mode of cycling for everyone

Cycling often transcends being merely a sport or a means of transportation and becomes a form of individual expression, lifestyle, and philosophy. Select bikes cater to individuals who are looking for something less ordinary or need alternatives beyond a traditional two-wheel bike. Whether you choose to ride a recumbent for personal reasons or a handcycle due to physical limitations, specialty bikes allow you to be part of the cycling community.

People who have back or neck concerns or who dislike the traditional bike seat will find the laidback position of a recumbent to suit their needs. Chances are, you've seen the stationary version of a recumbent bike at your local gym.

Tandem

- A bicycle ridden by more than one (usually two) person sitting inline. There are road, mountain bike, and hybrid-style tandems.

- The front rider, also known as the "captain" or "pilot," steers. The rear rider, or "stoker," only pedals.

- Tandems are often faster than a single bike due to a higher power-to-weight ratio yet similar wind resistance. Climbing faster on a tandem depends upon matching strength and coordination between the riders.

- Great for building trust and confidence in a relationship.

Handcycle

- A three-wheeled cycle powered by the arms rather than the legs.

- The Freedom Ryder performance handcycle has a low center of gravity, a means to support the rider's legs, cambered rear wheels, side-by-side crank position, a triangulation of the crank assembly, and patented body lean steering design.

- Performance bikes have disc brakes and frames that are sleek and simple and have no extra tubing yet provide strength and rigidity.

- Handcycles are available in off-road versions.

Handcycles allow those with lower-body disabilities to engage in cycling, racing, and touring. Steve Ackerman, pictured below, rode his handcycle around the world in 1995, covering 13,000 miles through sixteen countries. He is proof that it can be done.

Tandems are used in the Paralympics with a blind stoker and a fully sighted captain. Tandems also provide a simple way for two people of differing fitness abilities to enjoy cycling together.

ZOOM

Unicycles commonly use a direct drive setup with the cranks attached to the hub of the single wheel. There are different types of unicycles, including freestyle, trial, off-road, giraffe, and long-distance unicycles. Unicycles are most often associated with the circus, street performers, or other forms of entertainment. However, unicycling has its own competitive outlets and recreational followings.

Folding Bike

- Folding bikes have hinges that allow the bikes to be broken down or folded into a compact size.

- Great for traveling, mixed-mode commuting, and efficient storage. Some public transportation systems allow only folding bikes to be taken aboard. Some folding bikes fold small enough to fit into an airline overhead bin.

- Folding bikes may have maximum rider height and weight limitations, so be sure to check this.

Recumbent

- A recumbent bicycle uses a seated position where the legs are in front of the body.

- Recumbents are comfortable due to a backrest and a larger seating surface area than a traditional saddle.

- Lower position means you are even more likely to be overlooked by cars, so use a flag for increased visibility.

- The fastest speed for a human-powered vehicle is 82.33 mph (132.5 kph), set on September 18, 2008, by Sam Whittingham on a fairing-covered, tear-drop-shaped recumbent.

FRAME MATERIALS

Frames of old were cast iron and wood; today they are made of exotic materials

Frame material affects the cost, weight, stiffness, and strength of the bike. Today's choices include such space-age materials as titanium and carbon fiber. Which is "best" depends on personal preference (and the heft of your wallet).

Stiffness is defined as how much a material will flex when a set amount of force is applied. This is also called "elastic modulus." Most flex felt in a bike will more likely come from the seatpost, saddle, and tires rather than from the frame. Lateral stiffness has to do with the frame's ability to withstand the lateral force of pedaling without flexing. A bike that has too much lateral flex may cause the brakes to rub.

Strength relates to the durability of the material. This is also

Steel

- Steel alloys, especially chromoly, are most commonly used.

- Steel tubing is joined by fitting and brazing the tubes into lugs. Steel frames may also be aligned and welded together. Fillet frame tubes have notches or miters and are then brazed with brass at the joint.

- Advantages: Excellent stiffness and strength. Long-lasting. Usually less expensive.

- Disadvantages: Heavy and rust prone. Not optimal for large, light frames.

Aluminum

- Aluminum alloys have a lower strength than steel but a better strength-to-weight ratio. Oversized tubing is used to increase strength and to create a stiffer frame.

- Most aluminum frames are TIG welded. Some frames will combine carbon fiber parts that are glued to the aluminum.

- Advantages: Stiff, lightweight, relatively inexpensive, doesn't rust.

- Disadvantages: Not as strong as steel or titanium, can break. Not easily repaired or straightened.

called "yield strength" and is measured by the point at which the material yields to a force such that its shape changes permanently (that is, it breaks or bends).

Other variables besides the material itself include the shape of the tubing and how it is joined. The diameter of the tubing affects stiffness and strength. As a result, less-strong materials will use larger-diameter tubing. Wall thickness of the tubing also affects strength. Butted tubing is thicker on the ends or joints and thinner in the center, enabling a lighter tube overall without sacrificing strength where it counts.

Titanium

- Similar strength as steel but not as stiff, so thicker-walled tubing is needed. Lighter than steel.

- Most titanium frames are TIG welded. Difficult machining causes higher cost of construction.

- Advantages: As strong as steel, won't rust, can make a light frame for a large rider.

- Disadvantages: Expensive, can feel flexy if thin tubing is used.

Carbon Fiber

- Carbon fiber frames can be made of tubing that is lugged, or made from a single piece, called "mono-coque" construction."

- Advantages: Can be molded into different shapes and fine-tuned to be strong where it counts and provide some flex in other areas for comfort. Corrosion resistant.

- Disadvantages: Expensive. Poor design and manufacturing can mean it is too stiff or too flexible. Can crack from large rock hits, so may need protection for down tube of mountain bike frames.

TERMINOLOGY

Knowing the proper vernacular is the first step to understanding your bike

At best, your bike is an extension of your body, not simply a thing you ride. The better you understand your bike, the better it will perform for you. Even if you are not much of a do-it-yourselfer in terms of bike maintenance, a basic knowledge of how your bike works will go a long way should you have a problem on the road or trail. This knowledge also helps

when buying a bike as you will have a better idea of what to look for.

The starting point of this basic knowledge is knowing what the various components of your bike are called and what they do. At minimum, this knowledge will make communicating with a dealer or mechanic much more efficient (and

Bike Parts

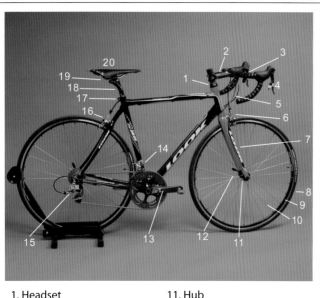

1. Headset
2. Stem
3. Handlebars
4. Shifters/Brake Levers
5. Cables and Housing
6. Front Brake
7. Fork
8. Tire
9. Rim
10. Spokes
11. Hub
12. Skewer
13. Crankarm
14. Front Derailleur
15. Rear Derailleur
16. Rear Brake
17. Seat Collar
18. Seatpost
19. Rails (part of the saddle)
20. Saddle

Frame

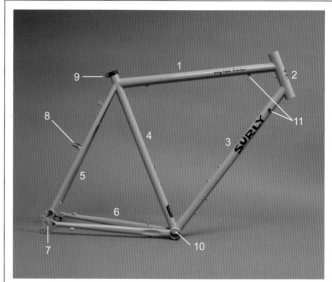

1. Top Tube
2. Head Tube
3. Down Tube
4. Seat Tube
5. Seat Stays
6. Chain Stays
7. Rear Dropout
8. Brake Bosses or Posts—for mounting rim brakes to the frame
9. Seat Collar—holds seat-post in the frame
10. This is where the Bottom Bracket goes.
11. Cable Guides—small fittings built into the frame that hold and guide the cable and housing for the brakes and derailleurs

perhaps a less expensive experience). After all, it may take a lot less time to find the problem if you come into a shop saying, "There's something wrong with my rear derailleur" instead of "There's something wrong with the thingamajig."

We're not asking you to become a bike expert or to memorize how each part functions. In truth, we firmly believe that you should trust the experts. Nevertheless, a little effort and homework on your part will elicit respect from others and instill confidence in yourself.

MAKE IT EASY

The diagrams below cover the names of most of the bike parts and a more detailed description of frame parts and the drivetrain. Test your knowledge by covering the list of parts in the bullets below each photo and seeing how many of the numbered parts you can name on your own!

Drivetrain

1. Pedal
2. Crankarm
3. Chainrings
4. Bottom Bracket
5. Chain
6. Front Derailleur
7. Rear Derailleur
8. Derailleur Pulleys
9. Barrel Adjuster
10. Cassette—made up of individual cogs

- "Drivetrain" is the umbrella term for the parts that are directly involved with transferring your pedal power to forward motion.

- In the United Kingdom and Ireland, the derailleurs are referred to as the "front and rear mechanisms," or "mech" for short.

Frame Sizing

- Frame size is determined by the length of the seat tube. Unfortunately, how this is measured is not consistent among frame manufacturers.

- Frame builders measure from the center of the bottom bracket to either the (1) center of the top tube, (2) top of the top tube, or (3) top of the seat collar.

- Road and cyclocross frames are measured in centimeters. Mountain bikes and some hybrids are measured in inches.

13

HANDLEBARS

Conventional handlebars include a drop and an upright style; each influences body position

Handlebars come in many creative shapes and sizes. The position of the handlebars affects how the bike handles and your body position. All handlebars should have an end cap or plug at the end for safety reasons. Handlebars have some kind of grip or tape where your hands will grab the bar. This ensures a better grasp and provides a cushion for your paws.

Flat bars and riser bars use grips, which are hollow rubber sleeves that slide onto the ends of the bar. A tip for installing grips is to spray the interior with hairspray to slide them into place. The hairspray will then dry, helping to prevent the grips from rotating. When removing the grips, slide a flathead screwdriver underneath and pour some soapy water in

KNACK CYCLING FOR EVERYONE

Road Handlebars

on the hoods

on the bars

in the drops

- Found on road, touring, and cyclocross bikes. Provide multiple hand positions.

- The most commonly used position is *on the hoods,* where you have quick access to the brakes.

- While climbing or cruising with no immediate need

to use the brakes, put your hands *on the bars*. This upright position will be the most comfortable when climbing as it allows you to fully expand your chest.

- Corner, descend, and sprint *in the drops*. This position gives you the most control over your bike.

Aero Clip-ons

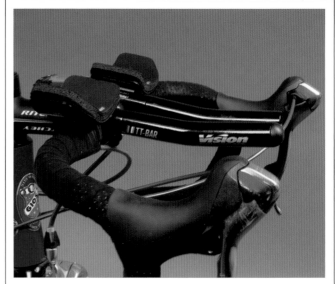

- Although a dedicated time trial bike has special aerodynamic handlebars, these aero clip-on bars can turn any road bike into a time trial machine.

- It is optimal to lower the handlebars or stem when using clip-ons for a more aerodynamic position.

- Practice using these before the big event. Remember that you cannot steer safely in this position, so grab the drops when you come to a turn or need to slow down.

14

between the grip and bar for easier removal.

Roadbars, also called dropbars, use bar tape wrapped from the end toward the stem, covering most of the bar. The hood is the rubber bit that covers the clamping part of the shifter and tapers over the bar to create a smooth transition. Bar tape is also used on handlebars that have multiple hand positions and require a larger area of coverage for your hands.

Flat Bars

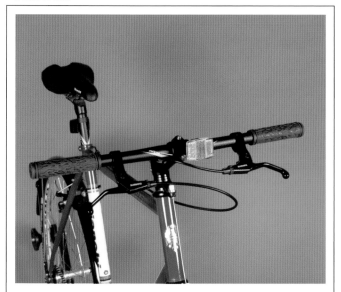

- Flat bars are most often found on mountain bikes and some hybrids.

- Flat bars have sweep—the amount of bend back toward the bike—and thus have a single correct position for installation.

- Bar ends are short extensions that attach to the ends of flat bars. These are used when climbing for a more upright and open-chest position.

- Oval-shaped grips provide a bit more of a platform on which to lean the heel of your hand.

Riser Bars

- Riser bars are most often found on mountain bikes and hybrid bikes. Riser bars also have sweep, so make sure they are installed the right way.

- As their name implies, they provide a more upright position. This can be helpful, especially when your stem is already raised as much as possible.

- If you are mountain biking, don't use bar ends on riser bars. There is no logical reason for this; it is simply considered uncool and will garner heckling.

STEMS & HEADSETS

To attach and detach handlebars, you must learn to properly adjust the headset

The headset is the bearing assembly that allows the bike to steer. If you lift the front wheel and swing the handlebars back and forth, the movement should be easy and smooth. A loose headset will mean excess movement in the front end of the bike and make it feel squirrelly. A headset that is too tight will create friction and make it hard to steer. A headset

that is worn or pitted will cause a sticking point and make the bike track in one direction.

The more recent development of threadless headsets has made adjusting your headset relatively easy. A threadless headset uses a binder bolt to adjust tightness. The binder bolt screws into a star-fangled nut that has been inserted

Fixed Stem

- Fixed stems have a set length and rise.

- Length is measured in centimeters or millimeters. Rise is measured by the number of degrees above horizontal.

- This stem is shown with a threadless headset. Some

- adjustment in height is possible by moving spacers above or below the stem itself.

- When building a new bike or installing a new fork, it is recommended to use several spacers to allow for some adjustability.

Adjustable Stem

- Some hybrid or comfort bikes come with an adjustable stem. This type of stem has a hinge and bolt that allows the rise to be adjusted.

- Remember that increasing the rise while keeping the stem length constant shortens the reach to the

- handlebars and vice versa. Changing the reach can alter how your weight is distributed and how the bike steers.

- Make changes in small increments, and if a big change is needed, perhaps a new stem is a better option.

inside the fork steer tube. The stem then clamps onto the steer tube of the fork, holding it all together. Therefore, a threadless headset must be paired with a fixed, clamping-style stem. This system is the most prevalent.

The stem is also an element of bike fit. Proper stem length and height are critical components to the comfort and handling of your bike.

If you need to remove or install a headset, we recommend bringing your bike to your local shop and having a trained mechanic do this for you. Removing and installing a headset require special tools. Incorrect installation can ruin the headset, the fork, or even the frame itself. If you have just purchased a new frame, it may need to be "faced," or have the headtube ends finished perfectly flat to ensure correct alignment of the headset bearings.

Threaded Headset

- Threaded headsets are still found on low-end bikes and bikes that were made before threadless headsets became prevalent in the late 1990s.

- Threaded headsets are used with threaded steer tubes. An adjustable race screws onto the steer tube with a locknut to secure it.

- The stems used with threaded headsets have a quill that extends inside the steer tube and expands to attach.

Threadless Headset

- The individual pieces of a threadless headset are shown here.

- Was also referred to as "Aheadset," a trademark by Dia Compe, which was the first to come out with the threadless headset design.

- The stack height of the stem is measured where the stem grips the steer tube. This measurement and any extra spacers that will be used determine where to cut the fork steer tube.

- Some new, high-end frames now have integrated headsets.

17

SHIFTERS

The shifting mechanism on a bike allows you to change gears on the go

Shifters are one of the most important components on your bike. Shifters allow you to change to an easier or harder gear as you climb or descend. Anyone who has had shifting problems will agree that a foul shifter can ruin any ride. Clean, crisp shifting is always the goal. This requires shifters in good working order, clean housing, unfrayed cables, and

properly adjusted derailleurs for the whole system to work together smoothly. "Ghost shifting" happens when the chain jumps from one cog to another on its own. Typically, this is an adjustment issue and can be fixed easily.

The quality of the shifter will affect the performance. There is a noticeable difference between a high-end shifter and

Road Integrated

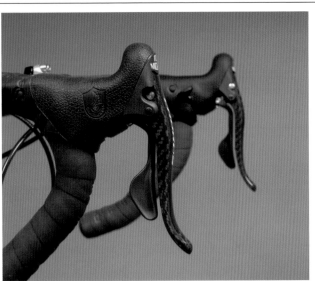

- The shifter is integrated with the brake lever. These shifters are referred to by the manufacturer's trademark.

- Shimano STI: Push the whole lever inward to shift to a larger cog. Push the inner shift blade inward for smaller cogs.

- Campagnolo Ergopower shifters work similarly but use a thumb button on the inside of the lever to shift to smaller cogs.

- SRAM DoubleTap: Push the inner shift lever once for larger cogs and twice for smaller cogs.

Shift Levers

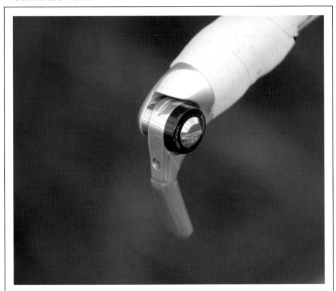

- Early road bikes used lever shifters mounted on the down tube. Later the levers were mounted to the ends of the handlebars for a more convenient reach.

- Time trial bikes have levers mounted on the bar ends, allowing the rider to shift while staying in an

aerodynamic position.

- Early mountain bikes used thumb shifters, which were a similar cable-actuated lever mounted to the handlebars next to the grip, such that you could change gears by moving the lever with your thumb.

the shifter on a low-end, department store bike. A high-end shifter will change gears flawlessly with the flick of a finger. For this reason, shifters are one of the most often upgraded components on a bike.

Almost all geared bikes will have two shifters—one that operates the rear derailleur and one that operates the front derailleur. Shifters change the derailleur position by means of a cable that is encased in housing. Derailleur cables and housing are different than those used for brakes.

Trigger Shifters

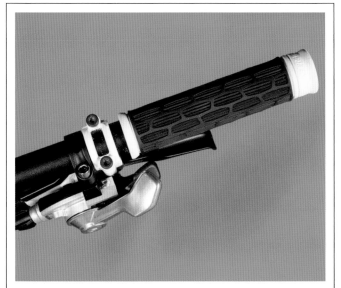

- You use your thumbs to shift by pushing and in some cases pulling on the lever under the handlebars.

- Used on mountain bikes and some hybrids.

- Shift by pushing with your thumb and pulling with your pointer finger on levers mounted below the handle-bar.

- Shimano's Dual Control Levers integrate the shifting with the brake lever, similar in concept to an integrated road shifter.

Twist Shifters

- In 1988, SRAM debuted Grip Shift, which used a twisting motion to change gears. Early versions were used on road and time trial bikes, but the real revolution occurred in the mountain bike industry.

- Twist shifters have fewer moving parts than inte-

grated shifters, which can make them easier to maintain. They are also more susceptible to decreased performance if dirt gets in the cables.

- Today, twist shifters are prevalent on low-end commuting hybrids, as well as on mountain bikes.

COGS & CHAINRINGS
The total number of teeth on your rear cog and chainring determines the gear

Chainrings, gear inches, cogs, sprockets, gear ratio, speeds, cassettes . . . the vocabulary for bicycle gears is a language unto itself. Luckily, it is not hard to demystify.

Two sets of gears make up a bicycle's drivetrain: front and rear. We will refer to the front gears as "chainrings." All bikes have one, two, or three chainrings. You might ask someone,

"Do you use a double or triple?" This is the same as asking if you have two or three chainrings.

We will refer to the gears in the back as "cogs." A set of cogs is called a "cassette." If someone asks you, "Are you running nine-speed still, or have you upgraded to ten-speed yet?" she means, "Do you have nine or ten cogs on your cassette?" In

Double Chainring

- Most road bikes come with two chainrings.

- A typical setup for flat terrain might have 42 and 52 tooth chainrings. If you live in a mountainous area, you might run a 39-53.

- Compact cranks have recently become popular. The name is deceiving because it is not the crank that is smaller, but rather the chainrings. A common compact setup will use 34 and 50 teeth chainrings.

Triple Chainring

- Mountain bikes come with three chainrings.

- A typical gear setup is 22-32-44. This used to be considered "compact" but has now become standard. Previously, the standard chainring setup was 24-36-46.

- Some road bikes and touring bikes have triple chainrings. These provide a lower climbing gear for riders who are less fit or who are touring with heavy weight. A typical setup is 30-42-53.

reality, the total number of gears is determined by multiplying the number of chainrings by cogs. But now "ten-speed" means ten cogs in the back instead of ten gears total.

Chainrings and cogs are measured by the number of teeth. Chainring sizing is referred to by listing the number of teeth on all chainrings. For example, "I use a 53-39 in the front." Cassettes are sold as a full set and referred to by the largest and smallest cogs, such as a "12-25."

ZOOM

Gear ratio or gear inches is a way to measure the combined gearing. Gear ratio equals the number of chainring teeth divided by the number of cog teeth multiplied by wheel diameter (in inches). Which is harder, a 52x14 or a 42x18?
$52/14 = 3.714 \times 27 = 100.3$
$42/18 = 2.333 \times 27 = 63$
so the 52x14 is the bigger (harder) gear.

Cassette

- Cassettes are sold as a cluster of cogs. Cassettes are referred to by the number of teeth on the largest and smallest cogs.

- Current road and cyclocross bikes will have nine, ten, or eleven cogs. Typical gear setups will have an eleven- or twelve-tooth cog for the hardest gear and a 21-, 23-, 25-, or 27-tooth cog for the easiest gear, depending on typical riding terrain.

- Current mountain bikes are nine-speed. Typical gear setups are 11-32, 11-34, or 12-34.

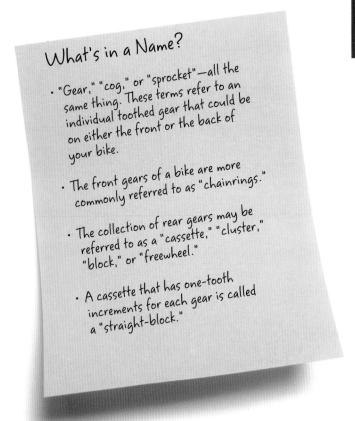

What's in a Name?

- "Gear," "cog," or "sprocket"—all the same thing. These terms refer to an individual toothed gear that could be on either the front or the back of your bike.

- The front gears of a bike are more commonly referred to as "chainrings."

- The collection of rear gears may be referred to as a "cassette," "cluster," "block," or "freewheel."

- A cassette that has one-tooth increments for each gear is called a "straight-block."

21

CRANKS & STANDARD PEDALS

Crank length determines the circumference of your pedal stroke— shorter means smaller, longer means larger

The cranks link your pedals to the chain to the rear wheel. In other words, the cranks turn your muscular effort into forward motion. Cranksets are an expensive component on your bike and generally a part that is upgraded only by people looking to shave weight off their machines.

You will find that most new bikes in a shop have flat pedals.

Usually these are a very basic plastic platform that allows the bike to be test-ridden. Some mid-range and high-end bikes may not come with pedals at all; it is assumed the buyer will have a personal preference for this piece of equipment. Flat pedals with more aggressive, sturdy, metal frames are used by some BMX and trials riders, as well as downhill racers. Prior

Crank

- The crankset is composed of the cranks, chainrings, and mechanism for attaching the crankset to the bottom bracket spindle.

- The spider is the multi-armed piece that connects the chainrings and arms. On most cranksets, the spider is an integrated piece, but some cranksets have a separate detachable spider.

- Special bolts and washers attach the chainrings to the spider.

- Cranks may be made of steel, aluminum, titanium, or carbon fiber.

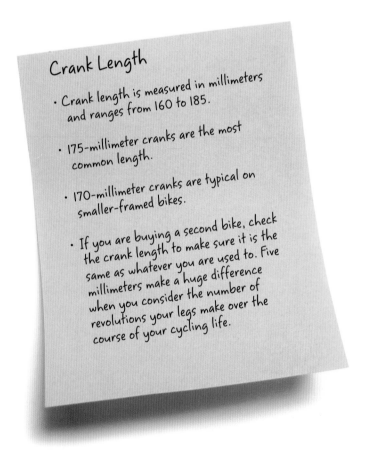

Crank Length

- Crank length is measured in millimeters and ranges from 160 to 185.

- 175-millimeter cranks are the most common length.

- 170-millimeter cranks are typical on smaller-framed bikes.

- If you are buying a second bike, check the crank length to make sure it is the same as whatever you are used to. Five millimeters make a huge difference when you consider the number of revolutions your legs make over the course of your cycling life.

to the development of clipless pedals, toe cages were combined with stiff-soled cycling shoes that gripped the pedals for optimal pedaling efficiency.

Less-experienced riders tend to favor flat pedals or loose toe cages. The perception is that you can remove your foot more accidentally than with clipless pedals. However, your feet can also more easily slip off flat pedals while riding. Toe cages, if tightened, are not necessarily easier to free your foot from.

MAKE IT EASY

Pedals are screwed into each crankarm via a threaded hole. The left crank is reverse threaded to avoid the pedal unscrewing itself while pedaling. The easiest way to remember this is to stand over the rear wheel of the bike. With your pedal wrench held parallel to the ground, you will push down on the wrench to remove the pedal from both sides and pull up to screw both onto the crank.

Flat Pedal

- Flat pedals are common on hybrids and other commuter bikes because they allow any shoe to be worn while riding.

- The advantages are that they are simple and safe for all ages if used on nontechnical terrain.

- The disadvantages are that your feet may slip or bounce off flat pedals, which can be dangerous. Riders will not be able to use their hamstring muscles to pull up on the pedal stroke, decreasing performance.

Toe Clip

- Toe clips or toe cages are meant to be tightened down over your shoe, allowing for more efficient pedal stroke and more secure attachment.

- Loose-fitting toe cages can provide a happy medium for commuting—more security because the cage gives your shoe something to push against without slipping but easy in and out.

CLIPLESS PEDALS

Having your foot attached to the pedal generates more power when riding

Clipless pedals have to be one of the most important developments in the cycling world. Clipless pedals generally use some kind of spring mechanism to attach directly to a cleat that is screwed to the bottom of the shoe. The use of clipless pedals requires the use of cycling-specific shoes that have ultra-stiff soles and specific threaded hole patterns for attaching the cleats.

The combination of a stiff-soled shoe and positive connection between the pedal and shoe means more direct power transfer to the pedal. Imagine now the contrast between this setup and a flat pedal with a slipper. Besides the obvious ability to pull up, across, and through the entire circular motion

Road Clipless

- Clipless pedals provide optimal power transmission to the pedal, by allowing a rider to pull up with each pedal stroke and manage cadence.

- A larger surface area, compared with mountain bike clipless systems, distributes pressure to the foot, helping with comfort on long rides.

- Look, Speedplay, and Shimano are the most popular road clipless pedals.

- Speedplay pedals have the lowest clearance for cornering and a double-sided entry.

Road Cleat

- The cleats for road clipless pedals attach to the bottom of your shoes with screws.

- Different cleats have different hole patterns, sometimes requiring a shim or conversion plate.

- When setting up the cleat for the first time, carry the proper tools with you on your first few rides so you can make small adjustments, as needed.

- Road shoes do not have a recessed sole where the cleat attaches, which makes them cumbersome to walk in and prone to slipping on smooth floors.

of the pedal stroke, you avoid loss of energy via the flexing of the shoe itself.

Nevertheless, clipless pedals remain one of the bigger hurdles for new riders to surmount. It is mostly mind over matter, and almost all become converts after they have gotten used to the clipless system. Some pedals have springs that can be loosened to make them easier to get into and out of. This is helpful while learning, although after you are accustomed to them you will want to make the setting more secure so that you avoid pulling out unexpectedly.

Mountain Clipless

- Shimano, Time, and Crank Brothers are the three most popular mountain bike clipless pedals. All mountain bike pedals are double-sided.

- The Crank Brothers Egg Beater is popular among cyclocross racers due to its mud-clearing design.

- Float, or small amounts of lateral movement built into the springs, adds comfort and makes setting up the cleats a less exact science.

Mountain Cleat

- The cleats for mountain bike clipless pedals use the same hole pattern.

- Two nuts set in slots in the bottom of the shoe allow for fore/aft adjustment of the cleats. Mountain bike shoes have a recessed sole and treads.

- Some cleats may require cutting away of the tread on the shoe to fit correctly.

- Mountain bike cleats and pedals are designed to resist cloggging due to dirt and mud better than road cleats and pedals.

RIM BRAKES

Knowing how long it takes your bike to stop will allow you to go faster

Rim brakes remain the simplest, most common, and lightest brake system for bicycles. Rim brakes work by applying friction pads against both sides of the rim via a cable-actuated brake lever mounted to the handlebars. Brake pads are generally made of a rubber compound and mounted in the brake mechanism called "shoes." Brake cables and housing are different than those used for the derailleurs.

The mechanics of how the pressure is applied to the rims varies depending on design. The main drawback of rim brakes is decreased effectiveness in wet conditions. After the rim gets wet, the amount of friction between the pad and the rim greatly decreases. If you are riding in wet conditions,

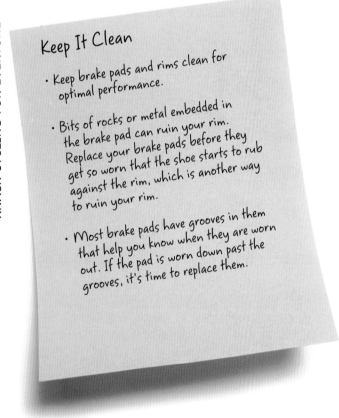

Keep It Clean

- Keep brake pads and rims clean for optimal performance.

- Bits of rocks or metal embedded in the brake pad can ruin your rim. Replace your brake pads before they get so worn that the shoe starts to rub against the rim, which is another way to ruin your rim.

- Most brake pads have grooves in them that help you know when they are worn out. If the pad is worn down past the grooves, it's time to replace them.

Caliper Brakes

- Caliper brakes attach to the bike at a single point above the wheel on the fork crown and seat stays.

- The most common dual-pivot, side-pull version has two arms that cross over the wheel, each holding a brake pad and attaching to the cable. One arm pivots at the center and the other at the side for better centering of the brake pull.

- They are ubiquitous on road bikes but not effective for wider wheels or bikes requiring more clearance for tread or mud, such as cyclocross bikes.

keep this in mind, lower your speed, and begin slowing down sooner than you might in dry conditions.

Rim brakes are also not a fan of mud. Wet mud can cause the same loss of effectiveness that water does. In addition, mud coating the rim increases its width, causing you to hear some rubbing of the brake pad as it scrapes against the dirt. Thick mud can accumulate around the brakes as the wheels turn. In extreme conditions this can add weight to the bike and eventually inhibit forward motion. Be sure to check your brake pads often if you ride in muddy conditions because all the extra friction from the water and dirt will wear the pads down much quicker than dry conditions.

"Riding the brakes" when descending can heat the rim. This causes brake "fade," or a decrease in effectiveness. Severe heat can increase tire pressure to such a degree that a blow-out may happen. This rim brake challenge can be eliminated by braking and then releasing repetitively when on a long descent to allow the rims to cool.

EQUIPMENT

Cantilever Brakes

- Cantilever brakes have two arms that mount on posts (also called "brake bosses") on the fork legs and seat stays. A centered cable pulls directly on the outwardly angled arms, squeezing them against the rim.

- Cantilever brakes are most commonly used on cyclo-cross bikes and were found on early mountain bikes until the development of V-Brakes.

- To prevent squealing the brake pads must be "toed in," or angled so the front of the pad hits the rim slightly before the back.

V-Brakes

- V-Brake is a Shimano trademark. You will rarely hear anyone refer to these style brakes by their generic names of "linear-pull" or "direct-pull" brakes.

- Used on mountain bikes and some hybrid and cyclo-cross bikes.

- Two arms attach to the brake posts. The cable runs through a "noodle" and attaches to the opposite arm. A stirrup on the other arm grabs the noodle at a notched point. The result is that the arms move the same distance as the cable.

DISC BRAKES
Disc brakes offer superior stopping power, modulation, and consistent performance

The mid-nineties saw the first mass-produced disc brakes. Early mountain bike disc brakes were heavy and mainly used in the downhill racing arena. Today, they are standard equipment on the majority of mid-range and high-end new mountain bikes and have even begun to bleed into the hybrid market.

There are two types of disc brakes: hydraulic and cable-actuated or mechanical. Cable-actuated disc brakes are less expensive, have less modulation, and are more susceptible to dirt and water getting into the cables. Hydraulic disc brakes use a closed fluid system to actuate the pistons in the disc caliper, which in turn actuate the brake pads.

Front Disc Brake

Rear Disc Brake

- The front disc caliper mounts to the left side of the fork.

- Rotors, which provide the braking surface, are attached to the hub. Different manufacturers have developed different mounting systems, but the industry standard (IS) is a six-bolt mount.

- Braking dynamics shift much of a rider's weight to the front wheel during braking. For this reason, some bikes will use a larger rotor on the front wheel or even a disc brake on the front wheel and rim brake on the rear.

- The rear disc caliper mounts to the left seat stay on the frame.

- The development of disc brakes meant frame manufacturers needed to beef up the seat stays at the mounting point, as well as the chain stays and rear drop-outs.

- Larger rotors are heavier but provide more braking surface and therefore greater stopping power, making them commonly used for downhill racing.

- An adapter may be needed to mount a touring rack and pannier bag, so they do not interfere with the caliper.

Disc brakes have several advantages over V-Brakes. Most obviously, disc brakes provide greater stopping power. If a disc brake wheel gets out of alignment, it doesn't change the braking capabilities or cause rubbing against the brakes. By far, the greatest advantage is the fact that disc brakes work equally well in wet or muddy conditions. As for the disadvantages, disc brakes are more expensive, heavier, less likely to be fixed on the trail if there is a problem, and prone to squealing. Rotors heat up. Don't touch the rotors after a long descent!

The push for better-performing equipment in the racing world drives technological developments for the whole sport. As an inverse example of this, the Union Cycliste Internationale (UCI) banned disc brakes on cyclocross bikes in 2003 despite the fact that their main advantage—working well in wet and muddy conditions—is hugely applicable in cyclocross racing. The reason for the ban ties to the goals of the governing body and stirs heated debate—beyond the scope of our concerns here. The practical result was research and development halted and disc brakes virtually disappeared from the cyclocross market.

Disc Brake Detail

The brake body is attached to the frame with two bolts

Brake Caliper

Brake pads (unseen) are held in the caliper body

Rotor

Other terms:

- "Bleeding" the brakes refers to the process of exchanging the brake fluid and removing any air from a hydraulic system.

- "Modulation" refers to the ability of the rider to control the amount of braking power without locking up the wheel.

- "Fade" is a loss of braking power, usually due to overheated brake pads.

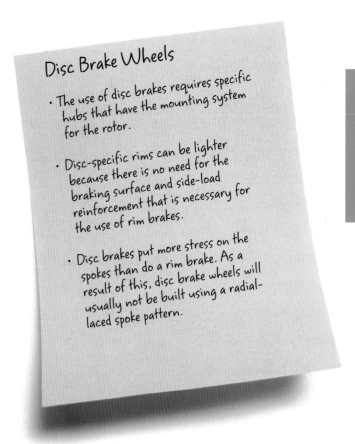

Disc Brake Wheels

- The use of disc brakes requires specific hubs that have the mounting system for the rotor.

- Disc-specific rims can be lighter because there is no need for the braking surface and side-load reinforcement that is necessary for the use of rim brakes.

- Disc brakes put more stress on the spokes than do a rim brake. As a result of this, disc brake wheels will usually not be built using a radial-laced spoke pattern.

WHEELS

Wheel size really has to do with what size tire fits on the rim

The wheels on your bike are made up of an axle, a hub, spokes, spoke nipples, and a rim. The front and rear hubs are different because the rear hub must also hold the cassette. The axle is what attaches the wheel to the frame or fork. A quick release skewer, the most common form of an axle, uses a lever for easy installation and removal of the wheel. Spokes thread through holes in the flange of the hub. The spoke nipples

hold the spoke in the rim. If your wheel is unaligned—called "out of true"—tightening some spoke nipples and loosening others will pull it back into alignment.

Rims come in different diameters and widths. The width of the rim will determine the width of the tires you can use on that wheel. Rims may also vary in depth, which is referred to as "dish." Deep-dish rims are more aerodynamic but can be

700c Wheel Size

- Used on all forms of road bikes, cyclocross bikes, and many hybrids.

- A new trend in the mountain bike world is 29-inch wheels. These are the same size as 700c wheels, only with a wider rim and tire for mountain biking.

- Larger wheels require more initial force to get moving, but carry momentum better. Larger wheels even out and better absorb uneven terrain due to the larger circumference.

26-inch Wheel Size

- Used on most mountain bikes.

- Some small-frame road bikes and time trial bikes use a 650c wheel, which is essentially the same size

as a 26-inch mountain bike wheel but uses a narrower rim.

- Smaller wheels accelerate more easily.

unstable in crosswinds.

Spokes even have their variations. Spokes may be straight, butted, or bladed. The number of spokes in a wheel determines its weight and durability. The pattern in which spokes are laced onto a rim—radial, two-cross, or three-cross—affects durability and shock absorption of the wheel.

The numbers used to describe wheel size are really an inconsistent mess. These numbers derive from measuring the outside diameter of a tire, not the rim, yet do not account for different tread depth. For example, all mountain bike tires (and wheels) are referred to as "26 inch." To make matters worse, some wheels and tires use inches—and some use millimeters. Our best advice is to simply accept this madness as one of the many eccentricities of our beloved sport.

20-inch Wheel Size

- Used on BMX bikes, some children's bikes, and foldable bikes.

- The small wheels accelerate quickly and are more durable.

- Smaller wheels do not handle rough terrain as smoothly as larger wheels, as they can get caught in potholes or other depressions more easily.

Mixed Wheel Size

- More bikes than you might think have been built with different wheel size. The early high-wheelers are perhaps the original and most dramatic example of this.

- The most recent manifestation of this concept is the Trek 69er, which has a 29-inch front wheel and a 26-inch rear wheel. The theory is that the larger front wheel provides greater momentum, whereas the standard-sized rear wheel provides maneuverability and handling.

TIRES

Where the rubber meets the road is the most important point of contact on your bike

Tire choice is another area of rich pontification in the cycling world. Some folks are quite adamant about a particular tread pattern. Others have a strong opinion on the tubular versus clincher debate. For most of us, it's enough to choose the right tire for the terrain and keep the rubber side down.

The issue of what kind of tread is mostly reserved for off-road riding because road tires have very little tread. More tread means more rolling resistance on smooth pavement, but also means more gripping action on dirt, rocks, and other surfaces. Some tread patterns are designed for loose, dry conditions, whereas others lend themselves to wet, slippery mud. How the knobs are shaped on the edges of the tire

Road Tires

- The average road tire width is referred to as "23c," but road tires come slightly narrower and wider. Width is limited by frame and brake clearance, which is why you cannot run cyclocross tires on a road bike.

- Most tires are clinchers. This means they have two hard beads (steel or Kevlar) on the edges that seat into the rim. A tube filled with air gives the tire shape. Flat tires occur when a sharp object punctures the tire and tube, allowing air to leak out of the tube.

Cyclocross Tires

- Commonly used cyclocross tire widths are 32c and 35c, a bit wider than road tires. Again, frame and brake clearance determine the maximum tire width.

- Cyclocross racers often use tubular tires for the advantages of better handling and cornering. Tubular tires can also be run at lower tire pressure for better traction and shock absorption.

will determine how the tire corners. The best way to find the right tire is to get recommendations from a trusted source and then try it out. After you find a tread pattern that works for your riding style and terrain, stick with it.

Air pressure is also a big factor in tire performance. When riding off-road, low tire pressure means greater traction, but also a greater risk of pinch flatting. Pressure that is too high will mean a harsh, bumpy ride. The rider's weight also comes into play; heavier riders will need higher pressure to avoid pinch-flats.

The rubber compound of the tire will also influence the stickiness of the tire on the pavement or dirt. Soft rubber tends to grip better but consequently wears out faster.

As well as pinch flats, low pressure on the road can result in rolling the tire off the rim during a high-speed corner (which will then cause a very bad crash). High pressure on the road is a good thing because it means low rolling resistance and a faster ride. Regardless of rider weight, road tires should be pumped up to no less than 100 psi (pounds per square inch).

Mountain Bike Tires

- The range of tire width that can be used on standard mountain bike rims is about 1.5–2.5 inches. Different tire manufacturers measure width slightly differently, so use the numbers as a guide.

- Skinny mountain bike tires are used for commuting or other situations that war-rant low rolling resistance and no need for traction.

- A hard hit can pinch the tire against the rim, resulting in a pinch flat. The pattern of two small holes in the tube from the rim edges is referred to as a "snake bite."

Tubular and Tubeless

- Tubular tires are used on road, track, and cyclocross bikes. They are tubular in shape, incorporating the tread and tube in one form. They are glued onto special rims. Most experienced cyclists consider tubular tires to have a superior feel and rolling resistance compared with clinchers.

- Tubeless tires, used on mountain bikes, have a bead that seals against the rim. The lack of a tube allows the use of lower tire pressure (and greater traction) without the risk of pinch flatting. A self-sealing liquid in the tire seals small punctures.

33

SADDLES

Contrary to popular belief, wide saddles are not necessarily the most comfortable for riding

There has been a lot of hype in recent years about male-and-female-specific saddles, and all kinds of funky shapes and sizes have come into the market. Never mind the marketing or allegedly gender-specific saddles; the right saddle for you is the one that is comfortable for your particular body and that supports your weight in the correct places.

A saddle should support your weight via your sit bones and pubic bone and avoid putting undue pressure on the perineum region. All the padding in the world won't make a saddle comfortable on a long ride if your weight is not supported in the right spots.

Although new cyclists will need some time to adjust to

Slim Saddles

Split Saddles

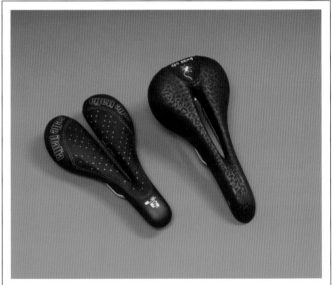

- Slim saddles boast light weight and more efficient pedaling. A slim profile means less rubbing with each pedal stroke.

- On a mountain bike, a narrow saddle is advantageous because it allows you to get your weight behind the bike more easily without getting caught on the saddle.

- Don't be fooled by appearances. Much research has gone into the design of some of these saddles, and they are often more comfortable than they appear because your weight is supported correctly.

- A few years back research showed that male cyclists have an increased rate of erectile dysfunction. This condition was blamed on the pressure that bike seats place on the perineal region. The cycling industry reacted quickly with a slew of new saddle designs to address this concern.

- Again, whether one of these saddles works for you or not is entirely personal preference. Don't be hedged in by what gender the manufacturer claims the saddle is designed for. In practice, this claim is not always accurate.

a bicycle saddle, common sense should prevail. If you are going numb or finding yourself very uncomfortable after an hour or so every ride, something needs to be changed—either a new saddle or position adjustment or both.

A shell and rails comprise saddles. The shell creates the shape of the saddle and may be made from plastic, leather, carbon fiber, or some combination of materials. Some saddles have a cover of foam, gel, or leather padding. The rails run underneath the saddle and are what the seatpost clamps to. Rails may be made of steel, titanium, magnesium, or carbon fiber.

······················· GREEN ● LIGHT ··················

The best time to try a new saddle is immediately after a ride when you are already sore. Keeping your bike clothes on, wheel on over to your local bike shop. Most shops will allow you to put a saddle on your bike and ride around the parking lot. If you've just finished a ride on your torturous old saddle, anything that feels okay now will probably be the way to go.

Wide Saddle

- Wider saddles are often found on hybrid and other commuting-oriented bikes.

- Some wide saddles even have springs to help absorb the bumps in the road.

- Wider saddles with more cushion may be preferable for riding short distances in street clothes. For longer distances, however, the width can cause chafing and will interfere with the full range of leg motion.

Listen to Your Body

- Most saddle-induced problems can be easily avoided by an ounce of precaution and common sense.

- As discussed earlier, find a saddle that properly supports your weight.

- Make sure your saddle is set up properly. This setup includes seat height and angle. Your saddle should be about level.

- Stand up or change your position from time to time on long rides. If your nether region goes numb, alleviate this numbness immediately and consider this a sign that one of the above factors needs to be changed.

EQUIPMENT

35

BUYING YOUR BIKE

Buying your bike should be fun and exciting, not stressful

Bike shops are the preferred locale for a first-time purchase. Even in the smallest of communities, there is usually a bike shop nearby. Typically, the owners and employees are cyclists and are passionate about bikes. Tell the staff what your desires are and let them help you with recommendations. It is likely that you will be able to test ride the bike, which is vital to ensuring that the bike fits prior to making your final decision.

Most bike shops have a repair department for follow-up maintenance.

Bike shops carry brands based on territory. This means you will generally find particular brands in one shop and different brands in another. If the shop belongs to the National Bicycle Dealers Association (NBDA), it is reputable and will have quality products.

Bike Shop

- Exercise patience when purchasing. Avoid buying the first bike you like. Test ride as many as possible and ask lots of questions.

- Ask yourself what you want from your bike first. Then determine a price range. Be realistic. You can't expect to buy a carbon fiber, light-weight machine for steel frame prices.

- Do your homework. Some time spent gathering knowledge will make your interaction with bike shop staff more advantageous and lead to a more informed decision.

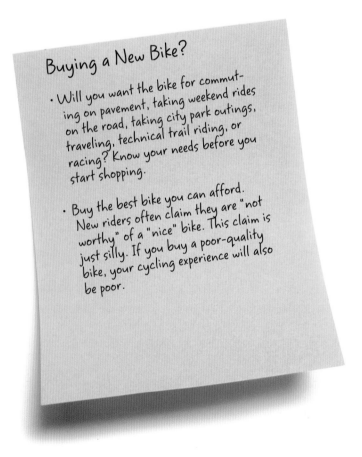

Buying a New Bike?

- Will you want the bike for commuting on pavement, taking weekend rides on the road, taking city park outings, traveling, technical trail riding, or racing? Know your needs before you start shopping.

- Buy the best bike you can afford. New riders often claim they are "not worthy" of a "nice" bike. This claim is just silly. If you buy a poor-quality bike, your cycling experience will also be poor.

Buying through the Internet or through a mail-order catalog works well if you know your size, geometry, and needs, or if you are looking for a particular product. Reserve this choice if you are a seasoned shopper and know specifically what you want.

Buying used can offer more bang for your buck. High-end frames and components are long-lasting and can make the purchase of a quality bike more affordable. However, the possibility of worn-out parts and a poorly tended bicycle is always a reality to consider.

Second-hand

- Use the Internet, classified ads, bulletin boards in bike shops, and word-of-mouth to start your search.

- Don't buy without seeing the product. Ensure that the frame has no cracks and has not been crashed. Ride the bike, checking the shifting and braking.

- If you aren't confident in your bike knowledge, bring a more experienced friend or ask the staff at your local shop if they will check over the bike before you buy it.

Buying a Used Bike?

- Put the word out that you are looking for a used bike. Buying from a friend or a friend-of-a-friend can be more trust-inducing. Sellers who are upgrading to a more current model are good referrals.

- Get a second opinion. If possible, take the bike to a bike shop and ask to have it inspected.

- Sometimes the price range is too good to pass up, but the bike really isn't right for you.

- Please don't buy stolen bikes. If you discover a shady seller, report him or her to the police.

BIKE QUALITY

Riding a high-end bike feels as delicious as driving a performance sports car

No one will fault you if you choose a bike because you like the color. Just make sure that you look under the hood, so to speak, before you make the purchase. Make your money go as far as you can. Quality counts with bikes. No doubt you will have to prioritize.

High-end bikes can run you $5,000 to $10,000. For that you'll get a lightweight frame and top-of-the-line, lightweight, sexy components. The more expensive the bike, the better it will climb, shift, handle, and feel. High-end is best suited for deep-pocket buyers who like the best and for racers who truly care about the winning edge.

Mid-range, quality bicycles will set you back between

High-end Components

- Having high-end equipment will spoil you. It will feel, look, and perform so beautifully that you will wonder how you ever survived without it.

- Quality counts. The expensive stuff truly works better, lasts longer, and is lighter.

- Top component manufacturers include Shimano, Campagnolo, and SRAM. Typically, the companies that have the best high-end products do exceptionally well on the low-end models as well.

Prioritizing Components

- If your budget requires making some compromises, start with a great frame and fork. Then choose a quality drivetrain, particularly shifters and derailleurs.

- Prioritize brakes and wheels next. Remember that you can always swap out pedals, handlebars, tires, the stem, and the saddle later.

- If money is your main concern, choose components that work well synergistically. Your bike shop service person should be able to help you determine how to best spend your limited dollars.

$2,000 to $3,000 and are suited for all levels. For this amount, you can find a bike that will perform well, last a long time, and have numerous above-average features.

Low-end bikes can be purchased for next to nothing through second-hand and discount shops. Low-end bikes provide a means to get started. Expect the bike to weigh more than high-end bikes and to potentially have problems with the components. Be prepared to pay the equal amount to fix the problem.

The Bike Frame

- The frame is a key part of the decision process and will affect the total weight of the bike.

- The frame is essentially your bike. No one refers to her bike by the brand of wheels or handlebars. Who makes it, what is it made of, and what does it look like?

- Major name brands have market penetration, but don't overlook the regional manufacturers and independent frame builders when making your decision.

Frame Quality

- Aluminum, steel, carbon fiber, and titanium comprise today's bike frame materials.

- How a frame is put together (that is, welded or weaved, for example) affects the quality.

- Bike builders take pride in welding aluminum and steel frames with precision beads and clean lines.

- The bottom line is that if the bike frame is not built well, it can break.

GETTING STARTED

BIKE FIT

Incorrect bike fit may cause back, neck, and knee pain and give you a sore bottom

"Bike fit" is a term that refers to how your bike is adjusted according to your body measurements. A correct bike fit is critical to staying injury-free and having a positive riding experience.

Bike fits are performed by professionals, as well as bike shop employees. If you are having pain while riding, a physical therapist who also does bike fits can help solve the problem by using her combined knowledge to look at the problem holistically. Shop employee bike fits are a great option for those shopping for a new bike. Either way, this is a worthwhile investment.

There are also simple steps you can take on your own to determine bike fit. Start by stepping over the frame and

Saddle Height

- Set up your bike on a trainer. Make sure the bike is level by placing a book or prop under the front wheel as needed.

- Wear your bike shorts and cycling shoes.

- Sit on the saddle, place your heels on the pedals (not cycling cleats), and rotate backward.

- With your heel on the pedal, your knee should be straight while your hips remain even.

- Use your multi-tool to adjust the saddle height as needed.

Fore/Aft Saddle Position

- Fore/aft position is the adjustment of your bike saddle in relation to the handlebars.

- With your bike set up on a trainer and level, pedal backward with feet in riding position and stop when cranks and feet are parallel to the floor.

- Have someone drop a plumb line from the top of the knee straight down. The anchor should fall directly above the ball of your foot or slightly behind. If the anchor falls over your toes, your saddle is too far forward.

standing flat-footed. The frame is too big if you have to tip-toe to reach over. While standing next to the bike, place your elbow on the front tip of the saddle. If your fingertips reach the stem, you're in the right range. Check and adjust seat height by pedaling backward with your heels on the pedal. Without rocking your hips, there should be no knee bend at the bottom of the pedal stroke. With proper saddle height, you will have a slight knee bend in your knees.

Handlebar height (in relationship to saddle height) can depend on riding type, flexibility, and personal preference.

For example, experienced road racers will often have handlebars lower or level with the saddle height. Cross-country mountain bike riders prefer the handlebars to be level or higher than the saddle height. Downhill racers and commuting cyclists will use a more upright position. Regardless of what kind of bike you are riding, you want to end up with 40 percent of your weight on the front wheel and 60 percent on the rear wheel while in a neutral riding position. This weight distribution will help with your comfort level and bike handling.

Upright Position

- Bike type has a lot to do with your body position. City bikes, hybrids, and many mountain bikes use a more upright position.

- For many, this position accommodates inflexibility and is less stressful (initially) on the lower back.

- Being upright allows you to look around more easily. It is also more comfortable for carrying backpacks.

- Ensure that your weight distribution remains 40 percent and 60 percent front and back, or else you may experience discomfort and compromised bike handling.

Aggressive Position

- An aggressive position is more aerodynamic and provides greater stability when descending and cornering at speed.

- This position requires some strength and flexibility in the lower back.

- Power improves as you use more muscles in the glutes (buttocks) and hamstrings, especially when climbing.

- To ensure that your neck does not become strained, relax and retract your shoulders and avoid excessive chin tilt up.

PRERIDE BIKE CHECK

Don't assume that your bike, old or new, is safe until you perform a mini-inspection

Too often we jump onto a bike to go for a ride and assume that all the nuts and bolts are tight and that everything is ready to go. This is not always the case. Get into the habit of giving your bike a quick once-over before every ride. An ounce of prevention is worth a pound of teeth and bones.

Check the tires to make sure they are in good shape, are

pumped up, and hold air. Most tires have a recommended pressure range written on the outside of the tire. Fatter tires need lower pressure, and narrower tires need higher pressure. Regardless of tire width, if you can squeeze the tire easily with your hand or if you sit on the bike and the tires squish under your weight, you need more air.

Tire Check

- Replace a tire when the tread is thin or damaged, lumpy, or bulging. Dry rot develops when the tire has been in the sun for too long or is simply old.

- Slashes in the tire that don't go through the casing can worsen and increase the chance of flats.

- Underinflated tires have more rolling resistance making the ride more laborious and slower. They also may pinch flat or come off the rim when cornering.

- Too much air causes a bike to bounce and makes for a rough ride.

Checking Brakes

- Always check to make sure the brakes are engaged and in the closed position prior to riding. Reconnect any cables that may be unattached from loading the bike in and out of your vehicle. Check the wear and positioning of rim brake pads.

- Never descend on your bike without feeling confident that the brakes are in proper working order.

- To test the brakes, lift the wheel off the ground and squeeze the brake lever. Also check that the brake is not rubbing on the rim or frame.

Ensure that the quick release skewers are tight and that the lever is positioned back. If your bike has a bolt in lieu of a skewer, check that it's secure with a wrench.

Are the brakes engaged? Squeeze each brake lever and roll the bike back and forth to see if it grabs. This will also provide an indication of whether the headset is tight. Finally, check the handlebars and stem.

Skewer Check

- The quick release skewer comprises the axle and the clamping system that attaches the wheel to the bike.

- The lever uses a cam design such that it can be tightened and loosened by hand.

- If the skewer is not tight, the wheel can shimmy or fall off the bike.

- "Lawyer tabs" are safety flanges on the front fork dropouts that prevent the wheel from coming off completely if the quick release comes undone.

Headset, Stem, and Handlebars

- To check the headset, turn the handlebars so that the wheel is perpendicular to the frame. Engage the front brake and place the other hand on the headset. Push forward, rocking the bike back and forth.

- There will be no movement in a properly adjusted head-set. If you feel movement at the headset, it needs to be tightened.

- Check the handlebars and make sure they don't rotate up or down. To avoid stressing the handlebars, always tighten bolts in a cross pattern.

GETTING STARTED

43

ESSENTIAL ITEMS

Be prepared for the inevitable; tires will puncture, and bikes will falter at some point

Carrying a few essential flat-tire changing and repair items for every ride is worth the effort. Even if you don't know how to change a flat tire, carry the tools necessary anyway. You may find someone on the road or trail to help you. Or, under pressure, you might just figure it out yourself. If you fail to bring these items along, you may have a long walk home or need to rely on the goodwill and generosity of others.

Similarly, you may encounter someone else who needs help. Always pay it forward; don't be stingy with your extra tube or time. The good gesture will come back around to you someday.

Tire irons will help you unseat the tire from the rim. On road

Flat-changing Items

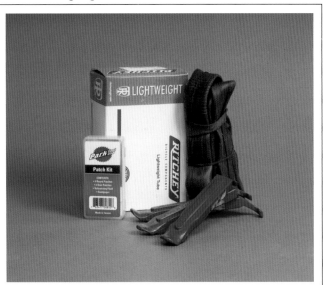

- Tire irons are small levers made of plastic or aluminum used for unseating the tire from the wheel. One end is scooped, and the other has a hook to attach to the spoke to hold the iron in place.

- A trick to packing the tube is to fold it up tightly and secure it with a rubber band. Keeping the tube inside a plastic baggie with baby powder will keep it from sticking to the tire later.

- Patch kits contain a patch, a small sandpaper square, and glue for repairing small holes.

Pumps and CO_2

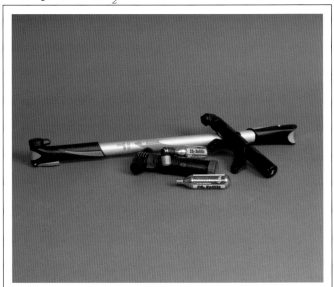

- Mini pumps are lightweight and designed to be carried on the frame, in your jersey pocket, or in a hydration pack.

- Typically, pumps have a valve adaptor that can be used with both Schrader and Presta valves by unscrewing the pump end and reversing the inside pieces.

- CO_2 cartridges are convenient for their small size and quick tube-filling ability but can be used only once, cost more, and create unnecessary waste. Note that CO_2 cartridges cannot be carried on airplanes.

tires, this is a necessity. Some mountain bike tires can be unseated by hand, but it takes skill to learn this technique of lifting and rolling the tire off the rim.

A pump or CO_2 cartridge will be needed to put air back into the new or repaired tube. CO_2 cartridges are mini canisters of pressurized air that use an adapter to inflate the tire very quickly. CO_2 cartridges are great for their speed and small size, but are only good for one fill and create waste. If you want reliable reassurance that air will always be available, carry a pump.

Multi-tool

- A variety of manufacturers make small, relatively lightweight multi-tools. These clever little clusters incorporate commonly used hex wrench sizes, a chain tool, spoke wrenches, and screwdrivers into one compact bundle.

- Some multi-tools even include tire irons and a bottle opener.

- At minimum, a mini set of hex wrenches will enable you to tighten or adjust most bolts on your bike.

.... YELLOW ● LIGHT ....

Don't forget your sunscreen. Excessive sun exposure can cause sunburn, premature skin aging, and brown spots. It also places you at a higher risk of basal cell carcinoma, or malignant melanoma cancers. When you are riding a bike, the breeze often makes the intensity of the rays seem less severe. Don't be fooled. Sunscreens with UVA, UVB, and UVC will protect you from dangerous rays.

Good Things to Carry

- Take your cell phone on bike rides when possible. Even if you go out of range, it may provide information in case of an emergency.

- Wear a Road I.D. It's a sports wristband with laser-engraved, vital information for first responders.

- Carry your business card and cash and a list of emergency contacts, medical conditions, and allergies in an air-tight plastic baggie.

- Consider having your name decaled on the bike top tube. If you are unconscious, it's an easy, visible way for someone to identify you.

GETTING STARTED

45

LOCKS

Protect your bike from theft, but realize that no lock is foolproof

Thieves are clever. Those who have made a profession of stealing bikes will always be one step ahead of the latest locking systems. Follow preventive measures to ensure you are not a bike theft statistic. Where you live will dictate the degree of security that should be employed. However, you can never be too safe.

Always lock your bike. Many bike thefts are a product of

opportunity rather than a high-tech, organized operation. An unlocked bike is an irresistible temptation to the lazy but opportunistic thief. When you are popping into the grocery store, even for a couple of minutes, lock your bike.

The safest method is to make sure the lock runs through the frame and both wheels. Big city cyclists may use a monster chain and pad-lock to secure their bikes. College students,

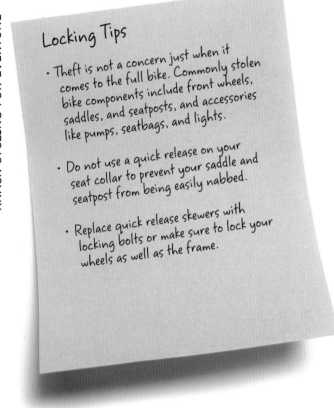

Locking Tips

• Theft is not a concern just when it comes to the full bike. Commonly stolen bike components include front wheels, saddles, and seatposts, and accessories like pumps, seatbags, and lights.

• Do not use a quick release on your seat collar to prevent your saddle and seatpost from being easily nabbed.

• Replace quick release skewers with locking bolts or make sure to lock your wheels as well as the frame.

Cable Lock

• If your cable lock is long enough, you can thread it through both wheels and the rear triangle of the frame.

• Alternatively, by removing the front wheel, a shorter cable or even a U-lock

can get everything locked together.

• Make sure the post you are locking your bike to will not allow a thief to simply slide the bike and lock off the top.

commuters, and vacationers may find that hauling a heavy chain is impractical. Therefore, Kryptonite locks, or a combination cable, may be a better choice.

If you have no lock and must leave your bike unattended, put your bike in the hardest gear possible and loosen the skewers and seatpost. Doing this may thwart a getaway because the thief will discover that he or she cannot roll away easily (or will crash while doing so).

U-lock

- U-locks are heavier and more restrictive than cable locks but provide a greater level of protection.

- Buy a U-lock that is long enough to lock both the front wheel and the frame. A full-length U-lock may allow you to lock both

  wheels by removing the front wheel.

- Two locks are better than one: Use the U-lock on your frame and a cable lock for the wheels. The longer it will take a thief to break the lock(s), the less likely your bike will be targeted.

Incorrect Lock

- Some bike racks are designed to hold the bike by the handlebars. This setup makes it easy to run the cable through the front wheel only without locking the frame.

- Roughly 480,000 bikes were stolen in the United Kingdom in 2006–2007.

  Over 200,000 were reported stolen in the United States in the same year.

- Some cities have bike registry systems to help prevent theft or to recover stolen bikes. Check your municipality to see what options are available.

BIKE ACCESSORIES

LIGHTS

Lights enhance visibility, and serve as a safety precaution

Riding at night can range from being a harrowing experience to a soulful adventure with the right lights. Practically speaking, commuting in the dark hours requires lights for visibility—your own and so that others will see you.

As with a car, use a white light in front and a red light in the rear. The rear red light can be steady or flashing. Reflectors on moving parts—specifically on the side of the bike and

on your pedals—are great for increasing your visibility. Clip-on lights, or those with elastic ties, fit securely on a variety of surfaces. New to the arsenal of products are aftermarket spoke lights (not reflectors) that allow for better side visibility. For extra protection, use a reflective safety vest or a safety triangle attached to your pack. Local laws will determine what you must have, and you can get a ticket for noncompliance,

Handlebar Light

- A handlebar light is a great inexpensive option for short-distance commuting.

- A mounting system that allows you to easily remove the light will help prevent theft and battery drain from leaving the light on the bike in the cold.

- In a pinch, use a camping headlamp or a flashlight attached to the handlebars with tape.

- LED lights are brighter and last longer on the same battery than conventional bulbs.

Helmet Light

- For long commutes or night riding, a high-powered helmet lamp is a great option.

- These systems have a rechargeable battery that mounts to the back of the helmet or can be put in your backpack.

- Having the light source

on your helmet means the light follows your head movement instead of where the handlebars are pointed. This is crucial for night trail riding and can increase safety while commuting. You can turn your head to shine the light at a driver who may not otherwise be able to see you.

but this is usually a minimal requirement. To make sure you are seen, don't do just the bare minimum.

Beyond commuting, recreational night trail riding can be an incredible experience. High-powered lights will be needed to illuminate your entire path of travel. In this scenario, turn off the flashy red tail light because it can be very distracting to your riding partners behind you.

Right Light for the Ride

- Bike lights span a wide price range, from inexpensive, battery-operated lights to expensive, rechargeable, long-lasting lights as bright as a car's headlights.

- The latter is used for rides that last for a few hours and may go through locations with no ambient light. Ultra-endurance events and twenty-four-hour races have resulted in a demand for lighter and longer-lasting batteries and brighter bulbs. For optimal lighting, use both handlebar- and helmet-mounted lights together.

Rear Light

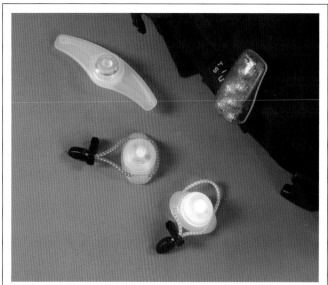

- Use a red light on your hindside so other vehicles can spot you from the back.

- Blinking lights clipped onto your body or bag at eye level are more easily seen than a light mounted on the seatpost.

- Reflectors on the wheels, pedals, and your ankle strap will help ensure that you are seen from the side.

BIKE ACCESSORIES

PROTECTIVE ACCESSORIES

Protective accessories are handy whether you encounter cars, road grit, or other riders

Cars have horns. Bicycles do not. Get yourself a bell if you plan to share the road with pedestrians or ride multi-use paths. It's not just a good idea; in many areas it's the law. If you are coming around a blind corner, a bell will signal your presence to others. It takes just one bicycle collision to remind you how vulnerable you are. Plus, bell design has come a long way.

With the plethora of stylish bells on the market, you can signal your approach and make a fashion statement.

Protect yourself from road grit with fenders or mudguards. There is nothing worse than the wet or muddy stripe up your backside resulting from spray off your rear wheel, affectionately called "buffalo butt" by some. Not only will the dirty

KNACK CYCLING FOR EVERYONE

Reflective Ankle Strap

- Ankle straps are a great tool for keeping your pants out of your chainrings. The visibility afforded by reflective versions gives ankle straps a dual purpose.

- Ankle straps are primarily used on the right leg

because that leg is on the drive side, but your pants leg can get caught on the corner of the non drive-side crank as well, so using them on both legs is advisable.

Bells

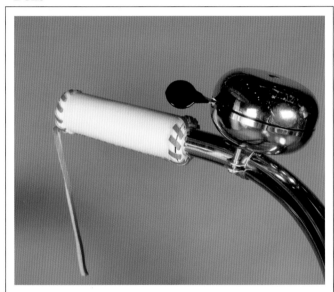

- Bells warn others of your presence on bike paths, under narrow bridges, or on blind corners.

- Bike bells come in all shapes and sizes, from low-profile dingers to decorated mechanical ringers to air horns.

- Bells are required equipment in some jurisdictions, so check your local laws to make sure you are in compliance.

streak on your behind be embarrassing, but it is a sure-fire way to ruin your pants.

If you are commuting or riding with long pants, an ankle strap is a must. This keeps your pants from getting caught in the chainrings, dirty, or ripped. If you don't have an ankle strap, you can roll up your cuff or tuck it into your socks. With regard to items getting caught in your chainrings, watch the shoelaces when commuting in regular shoes.

Full-length Fenders

- Also called "mudguards."

- If you commute in a rainy location, these are the way to go. A front fender will prevent water from spraying up onto your shoes and lower legs. The rear fender will keep your bottom and back dry.

- Some bikes come with full fenders already installed. For your road, hybrid, or cyclocross bike, you can get aftermarket fenders.

- Full-length fenders are not optimal for muddy conditions because there is not much clearance between the fender and the tire.

Quick Release Rear Fender

- This style of rear fender is a great option for muddy or wet off-road rides. Because it mounts on the seatpost, it provides plenty of tire and mud clearance and can be used on any bike.

- Not only will your butt stay clean, but also your friends riding behind you will appreciate the rooster-tail-arresting property of this fender.

- The easy on-off mounting system means you can snap the fender off when conditions dry out.

BIKE ACCESSORIES

SMALL CARRYING ITEMS

When you don't want to carry anything extra on your person, specific bike bags provide storage

Because you already know that carrying a few tools on your bike is essential to every ride, the question then becomes where to put them. A small seat bag is the most popular option for your multi-tool and flat-changing items. Seat bags can be compact or quite large with an expandable compartment. However, a small seat bag, just big enough to carry the essential items and no more, is best. Larger seat bags can rub against your leg with each pedal stroke and cause rattling if there is extra room for stuff to bounce around inside.

Top tube boxes are perfect for easy access to your food, gels, and energy bars. As you ride, you will need to keep your caloric intake consistent with your energy expenditure.

Seat Bag

- Good for carrying your spare tube, tire irons, CO_2 cartridges, multi-tool, and some money.

- Best to have a seat bag on every bike you ride with the pertinent items already loaded. This way, you'll have one less thing to remember for each ride and never get caught out with a flat tire and no way to change it.

Handlebar Bag

- Great for secure storage and provides easy access to key items.

- Plastic map insert is helpful for route finding, even in inclement weather.

- May use straps to attach directly to the handlebars or have its own mounting system.

- Avoid heavy loads because this will negatively affect the steering of the bike.

Therefore, having an option to eat while on the go is advantageous, especially on long rides..

The handlebar bag will accommodate larger loads. Many have a plastic sleeve for easy map reference while riding. Remember to keep the weight fairly light here (tools are not recommended) because more weight on the bars negatively affects the way your bike handles.

And then there's the basket. It should conjure up visions of French bread, flowers, and relaxed trips to the market. A wicker basket on a high-end bike would look silly, so reserve it for a bike with personality. If you have a cruiser, a townie, or an urban machine, consider a basket for around-town errands. If you are carrying a lot of weight (that is, books), use caution because a wicker basket may not be designed for such loads. Again, from the perspective of bike-handling, the handlebars are not the optimal place for heavy parcels.

Top Tube Box

- Great option for grabbing gels, bars, and small items on the go.

- Popular option for triathletes and ultra-endurance athletes who need to refuel often and conveniently over a long ride.

- Velcro straps provide easy mounting to any bike without getting in your way.

Basket

- Not just for the Wicked Witch of the West. Great for carrying light, irregular-shaped loads, taking quick trips to the coffee shop, or picking up flowers for that special someone.

- Old-fashioned wicker or metal baskets are still available, as are new-fangled plastic weaves in bright colors.

- Attaches easily to wide or flat handlebars.

- Avoid heavy loads because they will impair steering of the bike.

53

PANNIERS & TRAILERS

Equipping your bike to carry cargo will ease the load on your body

For long rides, touring, or commuting, a backpack or messenger bag may not be large enough to accommodate your cargo. Carrying heavy weight on your person can cause back pain, strain your neck, and be uncomfortable where the straps cross your collarbone(s). By mounting your cargo on the bike or towing it, you'll lower the center of gravity and transfer the strain from your skeletal frame to your cardiovascular system.

As important as what you use to carry things on your bike is how you distribute the weight so that your bike does not become a wheelie-popping, out-of-control fun-sucker. Keep handlebar-mounted loads to a minimum; otherwise, steering is compromised. Make sure that weight is evenly distributed in side-mounted bags. Overall, aim to have 40 percent of the total weight on the front and 60 percent on the back.

Bike Rack for Panniers

- The bike rack is the frame to which panniers attach. Carriers can attach to the top surface and both sides of the rack.

- The frame and wheel size of your bike will determine the size of the bike rack.

- If your bike has mounting eyelets on the seat stays, get a rack that attaches this way. If you bike does not have eyelets, bike racks with a universal mount are also available.

Panniers

- Panniers attach to the sides of the bike rack and come in many styles.

- Dry bags—closable waterproof bags—are great for serious touring or foul weather conditions.

- Open-topped bags with or without framing are great

for commuting or taking trips to the grocery store.

- Compression straps are a nice feature to prevent flapping when empty.

- Pack extra bungee cords to tie down loads.

Also keep in mind that not all bike frames are designed for carrying heavy loads in places other than the saddle. If you are loading up for a long haul, check that your frame can withstand the weight.

Cargo trailers are the best option for pedaling with high volume or weight. Towing your cargo avoids compromising the way your bike handles. Single-wheel trailers have the advantage of maintaining your bike's narrow profile. Off-road versions are available, expanding your touring options even further.

Quick Release Beam Rack

- An easy quick release mounting system clamps to the seatpost of any bike. No need for eyelets or special racks.

- May be rated up to a certain weight, so make sure your cargo is within the specifications.

- Great for light touring, also referred to as "credit card touring," or when you don't want to use a backpack.

- Remove the whole thing for cargo-less riding, once you've reached your destination.

Cargo Trailer

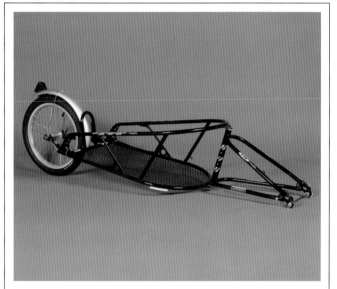

- Can carry up to 70 pounds. Not made for transporting kids or animals.

- Available with knobby tire and suspension for off-road touring.

- Regardless of how you carry your cargo, remember that more weight means more effort. You will want to have easier gears and powerful brakes to ensure you can get up the hills and stop at the bottom of them.

MESSENGER BAGS & BACKPACKS
Designed for transporting your wares, bags also make a personal statement

Positive marketing has done wonders for the popularity of messenger bags. Considered more hip than backpacks, they are the top pick for style. Messenger bags are worn across your chest. This allows easy access to the bag contents by simply swinging it around to your front side without having to remove it from your body.

If using a messenger bag on a bike, make sure that it has a chest strap to stabilize the bag. This front strap, combined with an ergonomically designed shoulder strap, will keep the bag from slipping and swinging. Messenger bags allow air to circulate between the bag's material and your body, such that you'll experience less sweat concentration in the back area.

Messenger Bag

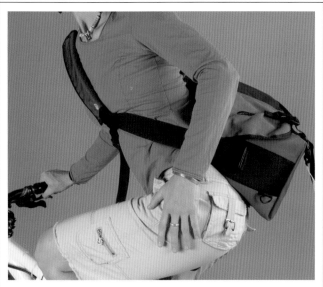

Wild Swinging Bag

- Easy access and use due to one shoulder strap, chest-crossing design. Good for carrying clothes or variable-shaped items.

- Not recommended for heavy books or laptops due to asymmetrical weight

- distribution and capacity to swing when loaded down.

- Large overlapping flap is a better design for keeping your cargo dry. Choose a bag that has a durable, waterproof exterior.

- Purses are not optimal for cycling. They will swing and easily slide off your shoulder, making for a dangerous distraction.

- Messenger bags that are poorly designed or lack a cross strap tend to swing to the front after you start rid-

- ing. Stick with the messenger bag brands that actual bike messengers use.

- Do not hang a bag off your handlebars. Doing so will affect your steering. The bag can also swing and hit your knee.

The main drawback of a messenger bag is asymmetrical weight distribution. Besides straining one shoulder disproportionately, this also means a medium or large bag can stick out on one side, which is not ideal in tight quarters.

Backpacks distribute the load evenly across both shoulders and are better equipped to stay put in the center of your back. The heavier the load, the more you will want both shoulders sharing the burden, rather than concentrated on one shoulder as with a messenger bag. The best way to wear a backpack is firmly positioned high on the back, but not impinging on the shoulders and neck. Chest and waste straps provide further support and stability.

Lumbar packs keep the weight off your shoulders altogether. Cinching around the waist, these bags typically have one main compartment and a couple of smaller pockets. Lumbar packs provide an anti-theft alternative to a seat bag for carrying your trailside essentials.

Backpack	*Lumbar Pack*

• Backpacks are preferable for heavier loads, such as books or a laptop, because the weight is distributed evenly over both shoulders. Backpacks are less likely to swing, but more difficult to access mid-ride.	• Choose a backpack that has a chest or waist strap or both, which helps keep the shoulder straps in place. Waist straps also provide another point of support for weight distribution. • For wet conditions, some backpacks include their own waterproof cover.

• Straps around your waist for carrying light loads. • Allows quick and convenient access by sliding it to the front.	• Wide straps and padding along the back will help it stay in place and not swing around unexpectedly. • Good for carrying essential tools, wallet, keys, map, and first aid kit.

TRACKING YOUR RIDE

Quantitative accounts of your trip are more accurate with a map, GPS, or bike computer

The technological advancements of the digital age have infiltrated the cycling world. The options for tracking your ride can create enough analytical data to keep you busy 24/7.

Bike computers can tell you exactly how far you've ridden, how long it took, how fast you've gone, and your maximum and average speed. Having this quantitative information

may provide motivation by allowing you to compare your performance on a set route and track your improvement. Fancier computers may also include cadence, an altimeter, and a heart rate monitor for a more complete picture of your effort. Some of these systems have accompanying software for downloading your data to your computer and creating

Cycling Journal

- A cycling journal is a great way to record your progress. Specially made books have a place to log your mileage, time, route, and notes about the ride. Training-oriented journals will also remind you to keep track of sleep, diet, resting heart rate, and perceived effort.

- If you are not much for writing, make your own spreadsheet to track the hours in the saddle.

- It's nice to look back and see how far you've gone.

Computers

- Basic bike computers have three components: the computer itself and its handlebar mounting hardware; a sensor that mounts on your fork; and a magnet that attaches to a spoke.

- Read the instructions for proper setup—the com-

puter needs to know tire and wheel size to accurately calculate distance.

- Most computers will log total time and ride time, allowing you to know just how much those traffic lights can add up.

charts and graphs of all the variables.

A Global Positioning System (GPS) determines your location and direction using microwave transmitting satellites. The GPS was developed by the U.S. Department of Defense and has expanded to applications in cars, planes, boats, mobile phones, and beyond. Along with similar features of a regular bike computer, now you can see where you are and get directions as you pedal. You will never get lost again! (Is that a good thing?) Oh, and don't forget about good, old-fashioned maps; they still do the job, too.

GPS System

- GPS-enabled bike computers can be loaded with area street maps and have small screens that show your exact location at all times.

- This information can be downloaded and interfaced with Google Earth to map your ride when you get home.

- For tech weenies, this is the ultimate toy—it's possible to have one system that combines bike computer, GPS, heart rate, cadence, and altimeter all in one. Now, if it could just predict the weather . . .

Maps

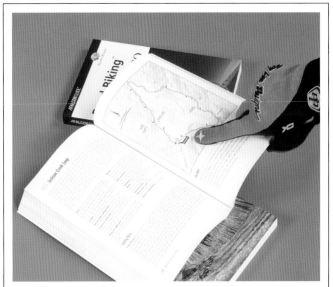

- Maps are a great way to get to know the general area and plot your route before you ride.

- Relief maps will give you an idea of where the steep climbs are and what kind of terrain is involved.

- Many transportation departments make cycling-specific maps that show where bike paths, lanes, and cyclist-friendly routes are located.

- For off-road riding in remote areas, a good map is essential equipment.

HELMETS

After you use a helmet, being without one will leave you feeling vulnerable and naked

Is it that you don't want to mess up your hair or that you like the wind in your hair? Perhaps you think that a short ride isn't really worth putting one on your head? Are you just not willing to plunk down the dough to buy a new helmet? We've heard all the excuses, and excuses are all that they are!

The alternative to not wearing a helmet is injury and possibly death. Helmet laws also exist in various jurisdictions, resulting in fines for noncompliance. So, strap one onto your head every time you go out on your bike. No excuses.

As for design, helmets have come a long way. They are lighter, have more vents, and come in a variety of styles and colors. Regardless of how they look, helmets are made

Poor Helmet Fit

- Your helmet is not a bonnet!

- It should rest horizontally on your head just above your eyebrows.

- A poorly fitted helmet may be too small, crowning the head, or too big, which means it will flop around and come off easily in a crash.

- Not only does wearing your helmet back on your head expose your forehead and prevent the helmet from protecting you, but you also look ridiculous.

Correct Helmet Fit

- Your helmet should fit snugly. Keep your field of vision clear. Tighten the chin strap securely with no more than space for a finger's width between the strap and your skin.

- The side straps should fall in front and behind your ear, coming together just under your earlobe and then fitting appropriately under your chin. Uneven or loose side straps will compromise the fit of the helmet.

- Likewise, a loose chinstrap will not keep your helmet on your head in the event of a crash.

to protect the brain and skull during an impact. They must pass testing procedures. Approved organizations include the American National Standards Institute (ANSI), Snell Memorial Foundation, the American Society for Testing and Materials (ASTM), and the U.S. Consumer Product Safety Commission (CPSC). The labs determine the performance and ability standards in different environmental conditions, like heat, cold, and wind. The helmets must also pass tests for impact, stability, dynamic retention, chin bar, penetration, and flame resistance.

Helmet with Visor

- Visors are most common on mountain bike helmets. Although, some people wear them wherever.

- When you are in an aerodynamic or aggressive riding position, a visor will impede your vision and force you to lift your head, potentially causing neck and shoulder ache.

- Most visors can be removed from the helmet.

- For a stylish alternative, Yakkay (not shown) makes commuting helmets and groovy fitted covers that look like regular caps or fashion hats.

Downhill Full-face Helmet

- Full-face helmets offer the highest level of protection.

- Primarily used for BMX, free-riding, slalom, four-cross, or downhill racing.

- The outer shell is made of high-impact construction, and typical designs have a liner that can be removed for washing.

- Cheek pads inside the helmet are needed for proper fit. When positioned, they should touch your face with no pressure points. The pads will compress over time.

EYEWEAR & HEADWEAR

Quality sunglasses protect your eyes from the elements and reduce irritation from road debris

A good pair of shatter-resistant, lightweight, durable sunglasses is key. Cycling eyewear is fashion-forward and functional. Most popular cycling brands can be custom ordered with prescription lenses, if needed.

Lenses and styles are available for various weather and lighting. Look for a pair with UVA/UVB/UVC protection, ideally polarized. Studies show a 98 percent reduction in road glare with polarized lenses. Glare is particularly bad off horizontal surfaces, like asphalt during a bike ride. The polarized lens will increase depth perception and have a soft effect on the eye.

Tapered Lens Technology (TLT Optics), available with Smith Optics models, corrects visual distortion that can occur when

Sunglasses and Lenses

- Interchangeable lenses are the most cost-effective sunglasses for cycling.

- Choose a lightweight frame and avoid wire rims. Make sure that the coverage is adequate over your eyes, but that the glasses are not so big as to slip off the nose or float on top of the nose.

- Wash your nose pieces with soap and water occasionally to avoid skin irritations.

- If you experience excessive fogging of your lenses, try wiping them with Rain-X.

Eyewear and Helmet Fit

- The arms of your glasses should go over your helmet strap and behind your ears. If your glasses don't fit right, however, you can use the helmet strap to keep them positioned on your face.

- Cycling-specific glasses, such as Oakley, Giro, Specialized, Bollé, Smith, Zeal, Rudy Project, and Tifosi, are popular brands because they fit well with a helmet.

light waves hit an overly curved lens. This means that you will have more optical clarity.

If sweat is pouring into your eyes on a ride, chances are that no eyewear will help you see well. Thus, a good cycling cap, sweatband, or skull cap is needed. A traditional cycling cap is made of thin cotton. Not only does this cap keep hair tucked away, but also it provides protection from the sun. The bill, turned up, acts as a gutter for rain. Worn backward, it provides more shade for your neck.

Headwear

- To keep the sweat out of your eyes, wear a headband, skull cap, or traditional cycling cap.

- Headwear may also help keep your helmet from slipping.

- In cold conditions, it is important to keep your head warm. Eighty percent of body heat is lost through the head.

- If wearing a winter cap, make sure your helmet still fits properly. Helmet padding can be removed to make room for a warmer layer.

Music in Your Ears?

- It is quite common to see cyclists wearing headphones and listening to music. Music can help pass the time and add a unique dimension to a solo ride.

- However, listening to music is not recommended for safety reasons. Whether it's an approaching car, the sound your bike makes, or communication by other cyclists, your sense of hearing provides important information and warns you of dangers.

- Check your local jurisdictions because headphones may be illegal.

SHOES

Don't go dancing in ski boots or use your cycling shoes for long-distance running

Cycling shoes are designed to provide performance benefits during a bike ride. They have stiffer soles that offer stability and greater power transfer. Your floppy tennis shoes will not work well for cycling.

Sneakers are disadvantageous and can be dangerous. Yet, most casual bike riders opt for this footwear. Shoe laces can get caught in the chain and chainrings, putting a halt to your pedal stroke and potentially damaging your knees or causing a crash. Tuck those laces in or tie them short enough to not get caught. If you are using a flat pedal or cage system, any shoe with a smooth sole can easily slip off the pedal. There's no way to secure it into place. If wearing regular shoes while

Road Shoes

- Road shoes are designed for optimum performance and are used with a cleat system on a road bike.

- Typical shoes will have hook-and-loop closures and no shoestrings. The soles are stiff, and there is no tread. Road shoes are not designed for walking.

- All types of riders will benefit from using cycling-specific road shoes

- The power transfer creates a more efficient pedal stroke and thus less energy expenditure over the long run.

Mountain Bike Shoes

- Mountain bike shoes are made for performance on and off the bike. Designed with a stiff sole (for more transmission of power), they also have a tread for when you have to get off the bike.

- Clipless systems will give you the best combina- tion for off-road, technical riding.

- Shoes should fit snugly but not too tight. Make sure the shoes fit securely at the heel cup so that there is no heel slip when you are hiking uphill.

riding, use a stiff shoe with a grippy sole.

Cycling shoes, set up with a clipless system, are the ultimate in riding pleasure. A clipless system has a specific pedal that attaches to a cleat, which is, in turn, attached to the shoe. The two fit together much like a ski boot and binding. To get into the pedal, place the ball of your foot over the pedal and gently step down. To get out, simply twist your heel outward 45 degrees, and the cleat comes unclipped. On the first couple of tries, this process can be frustrating. With time, you will find that it's quite easy and convenient. Always practice

getting into and out of clipless pedals on a grassy area. Also, if possible, loosen the spring tension so that you can enter and exit the pedal easily while learning. As you become more skilled, tighter tension will ensure that you don't come off your pedals inadvertently.

Sandals

- Sandals, and especially flip-flops, are not recommended for cycling unless you are merely taking a quick trip to the market and are not in a hurry. Slick bottoms and exposed feet can be a bad combination.

- The great news is that clipless system-compatible sandals are available. Enjoy the benefits of the positive power transfer of a stiff sole while feeling the wind between your toes.

- If wearing sandals, don't forget to put sunscreen on your feet!

BMX Shoes

- BMX shoes are used with flat pedals by BMX riders and some downhill racers. A sticky rubber sole provides grip against the pedal while allowing the rider to easily put a foot out for stability while riding or performing tricks.

- These shoes may be made of leather or high-tech material and come with or without eyelets.

- The midsoles are stiffer than a sneaker, but not as stiff as a mountain biking shoe. Added protection can be found in the toe and heel portion.

CYCLING SHORTS & JERSEYS

Use the full cycling kit if you want maximum comfort, performance, and motivation

Historically, cycling shorts and jerseys were made of wool. Shorts were only black, and jerseys were one solid color with sewn-on sponsor names. Today, both are manufactured with high-tech fabric for cool, dry comfort in every color imaginable.

Shorts have multiple-panel construction. The panel design provides compression and helps with muscular fatigue. It also increases aerodynamic efficiency. Look for shorts with flat seams, so you'll get the best chafe-free fit and a hem with a gripper to keep the shorts from riding up your legs.

A typical length for cycling shorts is mid-thigh. Measured by the inseam, they run about 8 inches, or 20.32 centimeters.

Cycling Shorts

- Cycling shorts come with a regular waistband or with a suspender-like upper, referred to as "bibs."

- Cycling shorts are made from stretchy fabric to allow freedom of movement without getting caught on the saddle or catching wind.

- News flash! Do not wear your underwear under cycling shorts. You will chafe, seams will rub you in the wrong places, and your privates will not breathe. Plus, those panty lines scream "rookie."

Chamois

- The purpose of the chamois, which is seamlessly sewn into cycling shorts, is to provide comfort when sitting on a saddle.

- Chamois are designed to be worn against the skin.

- To reduce the incidence of saddle sores (a sore, skin irritation, or hot spot "down there"), consider using a chamois cream. The cream should be applied to your skin, not the chamois, and is designed to reduce friction and fungal and bacterial infections. Petroleum-based products are not recommended for this purpose.

Although shorter shorts are becoming more prevalent, they won't protect your inner thigh from the repetitive friction caused by pedaling.

Cycling jerseys are comfortable and convenient. After you wear a jersey, you'll abandon your cotton T-shirt for riding. The fabric is designed to wick away moisture, and the cut is ideal for the forward position on a bike. The back of the jersey is slightly longer than the front, so that your lower back is protected and covered. Deep pockets can hold extra jackets, gloves, knee and arm warmers, food, and personal items.

Cycling Jersey

- Front zippers allow ventilation, while a narrow fit prevents flapping. A longer back conforms to the bent-over position on the bike.

- If you are wearing bib shorts, a full zipper is a bonus because you can remove the jersey easily for bathroom breaks.

- Team jerseys with sponsor logos are often for sale and acceptable to be worn by anyone. Support your favorite team.

- World champion cyclists have custom jerseys with rainbow stripes. In this case, if you didn't earn it, don't wear it.

Jersey Pockets

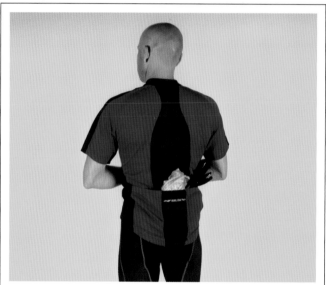

- Rear pockets are the best part about a cycling jersey, providing easy access to essential items.

- Traditional cycling jerseys have three pockets. They are fairly narrow and deep.

- Distribute your cargo evenly in the pockets, with larger or weightier items in the center pocket to avoid pulling the jersey to one side.

- Tying a jacket around your waist is not recommended and is dangerous because hanging sleeves can get caught in your rear wheel.

KEY CYCLING APPAREL

Layering clothing allows you to add or subtract articles to accommodate temperature changes

Prior to heading out on your bike, you must assess the weather to determine what to wear. Because we've already built a strong case for traditional cycling shorts and a cycling jersey, let's assume those items constitute your base layer. A good pair of socks fits into this equation, too. With all due respect, riding without socks is about as socially acceptable

as spitting on the sidewalk. Save yourself and others from the inevitable foot odor and invest in a pair of sport socks.

If the weather is brisk, you will want to add layers. A pair of arm warmers and leg or knee warmers will help cut the chill tremendously. Because knees have a tendency to get stiff in damp and cold conditions, protect this vital joint in

Wind Jacket and Vest

- Wind jackets and vests are designed to block the wind, reducing the wind chill.

- Your vest or jacket should fit well, without extra room in the torso. Otherwise, it will become a wind-catching sail, defeating its purpose.

- Some designs have mesh or ventilation under the arms or on the back.

- Water-resistant fabrics provide limited protection from rain and will eventually become saturated. Waterproof fabrics have sealed seams and will repel water in harsh conditions.

Arm and Knee Warmers

- Arm warmers look like long, tight sleeves. They have a gripper on the top band and a tapered wrist.

- Knee warmers and full-length leg warmers are worn over the bottom part of the leg and knee and tucked under the legs of the cycling shorts. An

elastic gripper holds them in place on the thigh.

- Arm, knee, and leg warmers are a handy and efficient clothing accessory, providing versatility and easy adaptation to changing weather. Lightweight and cold-weather options are available.

temperatures below 65°F. Getting into and out of arm and leg/knee warmers is quick and easy. Start off on a ride with both, and when you warm up, simply pull over, take them off, and store them in your jersey pocket.

A wind vest and jacket will be your best buy when it comes to cycling clothing. Covering your chest with a wind-proof layer prevents evaporative cooling and maintains your core temperature, making you more efficient.

As a side note, if you don't have a wind vest or jacket and find that you are cold during a ride, use a newspaper. Fold the front page of the paper in half and place it under your jersey to help reduce wind chill. European racers use this trick a lot. Then again, European racers have also been known to rub their bodies with goose fat to keep warm, too. Luckily some of the old-school solutions to cold-weather riding are not needed now that modern fabrics and cycling clothing are available.

Gloves

- Cycling gloves make holding the handlebars safer and more comfortable.

- They protect the hands in the event of a crash and from the sun.

- Long-fingered gloves are most common for mountain biking because of the elements and increased chance of spills.

- And here's the best part: You can use your gloves to wipe your nose! Seriously, a little plush piece of material on the outside of the thumb or pointer finger is just for this purpose.

Socks

- Thin socks or thick socks? High or low? Black or white? Personal preference will dictate.

- Wool, as well as cotton blends, are popular for cycling because of their stretch and durability. Make sure socks fit well and don't bunch up in your cycling shoes, which can cause hot spots or pinching.

- Wigwam makes performance socks that will not slip off the heel and have patented dry-release and moisture-control technology.

ALTERNATIVE CLOTHING

If tight Lycra-Spandex blends are not your style, get yourself some clothing with attitude

Today, options abound for cycling clothing. The days of black shorts and white socks-only and solid-colored wool jerseys are long gone. The advancement of technical fabrics and design has resulted in cycling apparel that looks more like street clothes while retaining functionality.

Each subculture of cycling has developed its own style.

Road riders tend to be buttoned up and tidy in their colorful, matching team kits. Commuters have taken advantage of street-wise style and riding comfort. X-Gamers prefer baggie tops and long shorts. That being said, there are no rules, and you can create your own style.

Regardless of the style you choose, consider comfort and

Cycling Skirt

- Skirts designed for riding come with a built-in chamois and shorts, or matching shorts. Built-in shorts may fit better but also mean you are limited to the chamois they come with.

- Nice for a feminine option or for someone who is self-conscious in just Lycra.

- A disadvantage is that the skirt can get caught on the saddle. This leads to challenges with bike handling.

Baggie Shorts

- Baggie shorts are comfortable and functional, whether you are walking or riding. They provide the benefits of traditional cycling shorts while looking like street clothes.

- Lightweight cycling shorts often come with a chamois or a custom liner sewn in.

- Different from everyday shorts, cycling baggies may be cut higher in the back, have pocket closures, an adjustable waistband, and be made of rip-resistant and quick-drying material.

- Beware: loose fabric is prone to getting caught on the saddle.

practicality. Looser-fitting clothes may look cooler but can also get caught on your bike or shift around uncomfortably during dynamic riding such as mountain biking. Make sure that the fabric that hits your thighs is a four-way stretch so that your legs don't feel constricted.

Downhillers, and those inexperienced riders who want the extra protection, should consider body armor. Not only will you feel like a superhero, but also you'll have a buffer when crashing. And, for the record, you will crash your bike at some point in your riding career.

Freestyle Jerseys

- Freestyle jerseys are loose fitting and shaped more like a T-shirt made from wicking fabric. These are a favorite among the trials, downhill, BMX, and mountain biking free-ride crowd.

- This style of jersey often lacks pockets due to the loose fit or has only one small zippered pocket for an ID, money, or keys.

- For this reason, freestyle jerseys pair well with a hydration pack, where you can store your necessary items for a ride.

Body Armor

- Used by all-mountain, free-ride, and downhillers for extra protection against the inevitable crash.

- Built-in pads have hard-plastic exterior armor.

- An integrated upper-body garment absorbs impact and provides protection for shoulders, elbows, forearms, chest, and spine.

- Wear and tear are inevitable, but quality products are worth the extra investment. Mesh liners will eventually rip, and Velcro straps may lose holding power with discount body armor.

WINTER CLOTHING
It is possible to live in a frigid climate and ride your bike year-round

With the right clothing, cycling can be an all-season sport. Even in the coldest mountain towns, it is not unusual to see folks getting around on bikes, sometimes with skis, to get to the hill. The warmth generated by your body and the proper breathable clothing let you stay warm without overheating.

If you are heading out for a fitness ride, you may want to stick to flatter terrain. One of the biggest challenges of cold-weather riding is dealing with the wind chill factor. Long climbs and descents are especially tough because one tends to overheat on the way up and then freeze on the way down. It is very difficult to carry enough clothes on the way up to be well-insulated for a long downhill. By staying on flatter terrain, you can better modulate your temperature by maintaining a more steady effort.

Cycling Tights

- Winter cycling tights are lined with a thermal-fleece material and may have wind-stop on the front.

- Tights may have a built-in chamois, or not, and can be worn over regular cycling shorts.

- Flatlocked seams and multi-stretch fabric are comfortable for riding.

- Bibs are preferred because they have less constriction at the waist and continuous fabric at the midsection where heat loss occurs. The drawback is that they are challenging when it comes time for bathroom breaks.

Winter Jacket and Vest

- A high-quality, thermal cycling jacket or vest can last for years of cold-weather riding. These items usually have a fuzzy, brushed interior and wind-proof exterior for protection from the cold.

- Favorite features include ventilation, pockets, high collars, full-length zippers, and a soft flap at the top of the zipper so that your chin won't chafe.

- A winter thermal vest can be the most versatile cold-weather item, providing a plethora of layering possibilities to cover a range of temperatures.

Besides having the right clothing, there are other cold-weather considerations. If the temperature is close to or below freezing, your water will freeze. Even if your water doesn't freeze, it is hard to motivate yourself to drink cold beverages when riding in an icebox. You might want to carry a Thermos of hot tea instead. In winter climates, studded mountain bike tires are an option for superior traction on snow-packed and icy roads.

Keeping Warm on the Bike

- Purchase good gloves. Lobster gloves or mittens with wind-stopper material are warmest.

- Frozen fingers? Make a fist inside the palm area of your glove. Start quick squeeze/release movements. Or try resting your fingers on top of the handlebars and lightly tapping them to increase circulation.

- Toes freezing? Get off the bike and run or walk quickly while pushing the bike for a bit.

- Keep tea in a Thermos. Wear a thermal skull cap that fits under your helmet or cover your head and face with a balaclava (ski mask-style headgear) to help guard against windburn.

······ RED ● LIGHT ······

Wind chill can make a 40°F (4.5°C) ride at 15 mph feel like 23°F (-5°C). At 0°F (-17°C), you risk difficulty performing, frostbite, and hypothermia. Your clothing, age, health, and body characteristics determine the degree to which wind chill and cold temperatures affect you. The best advice is to ride in extreme cold conditions for only short durations to see how your body reacts. Think comfort and safety.

Toe Warmers and Shoe Covers

- Keeping your feet warm is a challenge when cycling. Your feet need protection from the wind and moisture, yet they need breathability to avoid getting clammy.

- Booties slide completely over your cycling shoes, with an opening on the bottom for cleats. Toe warmers are perfect when full booties are overkill.

- Thin socks that let you wriggle your toes during the ride are often warmer than thick socks that can restrict circulation.

73

HYDRATION & RECOVERY DRINKS

During an hour ride, you lose up to two quarts of fluid through evaporative losses

Dehydration is defined as more than 1 percent loss of body weight as a result of fluid loss. During a bike ride, your body loses fluids through perspiration and respiration. Dehydration affects heat regulation, muscle cell contraction times, and overall performance. Specifically, fluid losses result in a decrease in circulating blood volume and lack of water content in the muscle cells.

Hydration is as important as calorie replacement. For rides lasting less than two hours, plain water is adequate to keep you feeling strong. Drink every fifteen minutes and aim for one to two small cycling water bottles per hour. Other factors, such as heat, humidity, and altitude, play a part in the

Water

- One to two cycling bottles of plain water should be consumed every hour during a bike ride.

- On rides lasting more than two hours, your body depletes glycogen stores. In this case, drink liquids containing calories and carbohydrates.

- Adding salt to your pre-ride meal—ideally the day before a hot bike ride—may help prevent muscle cramping so long as you are adequately hydrated.

Performance Mix

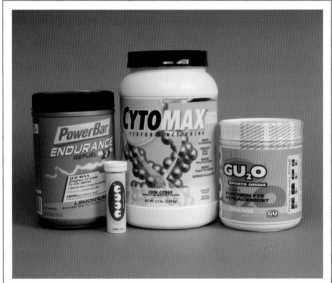

- When your exercise duration lasts longer than two hours, sports drinks help keep you hydrated and replenish the depleted glycogen stores.

- Liquids that contain glucose deliver calories to the muscles in as little as ten minutes, much faster

than solid foods, which are absorbed more slowly.

- In high heat or humidity, a performance drink containing electrolytes will replenish sodium, potassium, and chloride, which are lost through sweat.

amount of fluids you should consume. If you're in vacation mode, and you've had a few cocktails the night before, you should add one cup of fluid for every two drinks consumed.

Regular coffee drinkers shouldn't have to make adjustments in fluid intake to compensate for the diuretic effect because the body will be adapted to consistent use. But if you are not accustomed to caffeine, then it will indeed cause diuretic symptoms, which may hinder performance.

Recovery Drinks

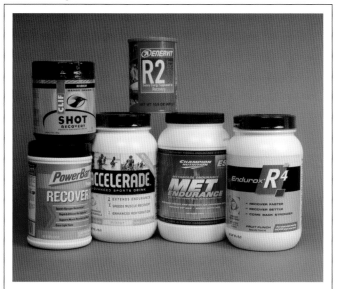

- Recovery drinks are designed to help your body repair and prepare. Typical recovery drinks contain protein, carbohydrates, amino acids, and glutamine.

- The first half-hour after a ride is the most important for taking in calories and water.

- After hard efforts, it is normal to feel apathetic about eating. Drinks are simple to consume and easily digested.

- Cold drinks are refreshing but may result in electrolytes, water, and glucose taking longer to filter into your system.

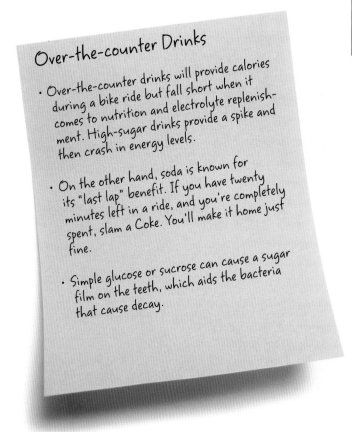

Over-the-counter Drinks

- Over-the-counter drinks will provide calories during a bike ride but fall short when it comes to nutrition and electrolyte replenishment. High-sugar drinks provide a spike and then crash in energy levels.

- On the other hand, soda is known for its "last lap" benefit. If you have twenty minutes left in a ride, and you're completely spent, slam a Coke. You'll make it home just fine.

- Simple glucose or sucrose can cause a sugar film on the teeth, which aids the bacteria that cause decay.

WATER BOTTLES & CARE

Refillable, eco-friendly, BPA-free cycling water bottles are best for you and for the environment

A health concern centers around clear polycarbonate plastics containing Bisphenol-A (BPA). Upon reviewing seven hundred BPA studies, scientists issued a warning that people using this type of plastic bottle were at an elevated risk of uterine fibroids, endometriosis, breast cancer, decreased sperm count, and prostate cancer. When placed in the hot sun, microwave ovens, or dishwashers, the BPA in plastics can leach out, becoming especially problematic.

To determine whether your cycling bottle contains BPA, look for the triangle at the bottom. Numbers 3, 6, or 7 have chemicals that should be avoided. Plastics that are considered safer include #2 HDPE (high-density polyethylene), #4

Cycling Water Bottles

- Cycling bottles are currently manufactured using eco-friendly, FDA-approved materials and are BPA-free.

- They come in sizes ranging from 20 to 30 ounces.

- They are designed to fit snugly into a standard cycling water bottle cage.

- Designs include wide mouth and snap top.

- Better than single-use bottles because they are refillable, and you won't have to stop pedaling and unscrew the top to drink.

Stainless Steel Bottles

- Stainless steel is more durable than aluminum, BPA-free, and environmentally friendlier.

- It does not leave an aftertaste as plastic does.

- Stainless steel cycling bottles have pop-up spouts for easy drinking.

- Look for bottles designed for bicycles. Some stainless steel models look like they will fit into a bike water bottle cage, but they don't.

- Most stainless steel bottles will rattle during a ride, which can be distracting.

LDPE (low-density polyethylene), or #5 PP (polypropylene).

Grocery store water bottles are typically #1 and tend to leach toxins, if heated. Avoid the temptation to refill and reuse these, especially on your bike ride. Furthermore, these bottles are not designed to fit well into the bike cage and tend to bounce out unexpectedly.

Furthermore, these plastic bottles do not break down in landfills and when burned, they release toxic fumes. Invest in good water bottles that you can wash and reuse.

ZOOM

On average, one person uses 166 disposable plastic water bottles each year. If everyone in New York City were to use a reusable water bottle for one week, for one month, or for one year it would make a significant difference in reducing waste. One week equals 24 million bottles saved; one month equals 112 million bottles saved; one year equals 1.3 billion bottles saved.

Water Bottle Cages

- Water bottle cages are most commonly mounted on the top of the down tube and front of the seat tube. They can also be mounted on the bottom of the down tube, front of the handlebars, and back of the saddle.

- A jersey pocket is another storage location.

- New bikes are rarely sold with water bottle cages.

- Cages can range in price from $5.99 for basic models up to $70 for aesthetic, aerodynamic, and lightweight models.

Cleaning Water Bottles

- Air-dry the bottle upside down on a drying rack. Avoid placing the water bottle upside down on a towel, which will not allow air to reach the inside.

- Older bottles may need a drop of bleach to eliminate stains and bacteria. Rinse well prior to reusing.

- When it is not in use, store the bottle with the lid off to stop mold from growing.

- Washing bottles in a dishwasher is questionable due to concerns of plastic leaching.

HYDRATION PACKS

Cyclists should carry—and consume—enough water to stay hydrated

A hydration pack is an alternative to water bottles. A narrow backpack is designed to hold a multi-liter-capacity plastic bladder, or reservoir, with a long drinking tube so that you can sip frequently during exercise. The drinking tube runs through a hole in the pack and connects to the straps on the outside of your pack. This prevents the tube from dangling and getting in your way during exercise. A lockout mechanism is built into the nipple at the end of the drinking tube, so that water does not drip out.

Hydration packs are a must-have for long, remote rides, especially on a mountain bike. The advantages of a well-designed pack include a compartment in which to store

Hydration Pack—Back View

- The sleekest packs have little to no cargo space and a reservoir that holds 1–1.5 liters. These are ideal for rides lasting less than one hour. Remember to carry repair tools elsewhere on your bike if not in your pack.

- Medium packs have enough cargo space to hold neces-sary tools, personal items, and a jacket. The reservoir holds 1.5–2 liters. This option is best suited for rides lasting one to two hours.

- Large packs have monster-size carrying capacity and hold a reservoir up to 3 liters. Use these for rides over two hours.

Hydration Pack—Front View

- Hydration packs come in a variety of sizes. Women-specific models have shorter pack lengths and repositioned waist and shoulder straps.

- Packs can be washed in a washing machine. To do so, remove the bladder and all stowed items.

- Consider purchasing a spare reservoir in a different size if you are a frequent rider. This helps with clean-ing and gives you fluid capacity-carrying options.

food, extra clothing, repair tools, and personal items. Packs that have bungee cords on the exterior are perfect for quick storage of outer gear.

Small bicycle frames and full-suspension mountain bikes often have space for only one water bottle cage, which is not enough for longer rides. Mountain biking tends to be bumpy and rough at times, making drinking out of a bottle challenging. For this reason, hands-free drinking on the bike is much easier and makes hydration more convenient and consistent, which, in turn, improves performance.

Road cycling and hydration packs are gererally a fashion faux pas. To avoid being teased by fellow road-riding snobs, plan to refill your water bottle on a road ride or carry extra bottles in your jersey pockets. Hydration packs during road racing are also frowned upon and usually unnecessary due to race-support via feed zones. In addition, the added weight and sweaty back impedes performance. The exception to this is time trialists, who sometimes use a thin, aerodynamic bladder under their skinsuit with the tube tucked under the helmet for easy hydrating without changing their position.

Bladder

- The bladder, or reservoir, which holds the water in a hydration pack, can be a breeding ground for micro-organisms and other bacteria if not cleaned and maintained properly.

- Sugary drinks inside the bladder are not recom- mended because they promote bacteria growth.

- Mountain bikers who ride on muddy trails where dirt containing bacteria can splash onto the mouth- piece should wipe the mouthpiece off to be safe.

Clean Your Bladder after Every Ride

- Use dish soap, warm water, and a clean sponge or brush.

- Remove the mouthpiece from the tube. Run a tiny, cylinder-shaped brush connected to a long wire through the hose. Camelbak makes an accessory for this chore.

- Use a sterilizing tablet/solution every so often.

- Dry the bladder hanging upside down so all the liquid drains from the bag and tube. To do so, insert a clean wire coat hanger into the blad- der to hold it open.

- Any droplet left inside is an invitation for bacteria.

PERFORMANCE FOOD
Liquids, gels, and energy bars are convenient and easily digestible fuel sources

Any ride lasting more than two hours will tap into your energy reserves. If you don't consume additional carbohydrates, you will surely hit the wall. American cyclist call this "bonking." This occurs when your glycogen stores are depleted.

If your legs are shaking, your head is spinning, and you can't muster the energy to keep pedaling, eat! Glucose or carbohydrates are your body's preferred energy source for maximum performance and aerobic activity. A number of energy bars on the market provide instant calories and energy. They are extremely convenient and designed to be ingested with little discomfort to the system. Gels and bite-size nuggets can be eaten while pedaling, providing an even

Energy Bars

- Bars are an excellent source of energy for the body.

- Because they are sealed and wrapped, energy bars stay fresh, even on long rides.

- They have nutritional value, often with added essential vitamins and minerals. Varieties include protein,

carbohydrate, organic, vegan, kosher, raw, and a combination of the above.

- Even if you don't think you'll need an energy bar on a ride, take one anyway. You never know when a potential mechanical problem will keep you out longer than expected.

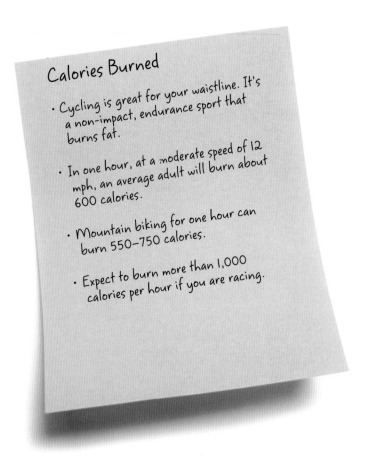

Calories Burned

- Cycling is great for your waistline. It's a non-impact, endurance sport that burns fat.

- In one hour, at a moderate speed of 12 mph, an average adult will burn about 600 calories.

- Mountain biking for one hour can burn 550–750 calories.

- Expect to burn more than 1,000 calories per hour if you are racing.

more convenient source of energy. If you're caught with no energy bars, bite-size nuggets, or gels, eat a candy bar or a sugary snack, or drink a Coke. Okay, so you'll lose some nutritional benefits, and your dentist will scold you, but the truth is that when you're out of gas, anything goes.

Products that contain caffeine and guarana, a Brazilian seed that is highly caffeinated, are excellent stimulants. If you are racing, check with the banned substance list from the governing body. High doses of legal stimulants can get you in trouble.

Caffeine has been shown to benefit the performance of athletes. An average cup of coffee contains 100–150 milligrams of caffeine, enough to increase blood-free fatty acids. Caffeine has a positive effect on muscle fibers and is a central nervous system stimulant. Use caution if you are new to caffeine. The diuretic effect on those not accustomed to ingesting it may cause dehydration and headaches, off-setting any performance gains.

Gels

- Gels are a preferred fuel sources for racers because they are easily digested, quick to assimilate into the body, and convenient to consume.

- Just tear off the top and squeeze into your mouth. Store the wrapper in your pocket (not on the side of the trail or road).

- Most gels are made of a combination of simple sugars and complex carbohydrates.

- A variety of flavors, fat-free options, and performance-boosting ingredients, is available.

Bite-size Nuggets

- When you need an entire energy bar, or a gel just doesn't appeal to you, bite-size fuel is available.

- Clif Bloks come in flavor-filled chewable cubes. Three pieces deliver 90 calories, replacing carbohydrates and electrolytes during activity.

- Resealable packaging on some brands keeps the product fresh and easy to access.

- Read the ingredients prior to use to ensure that bite-size nuggets are appropriate for your dietary needs and goals.

81

PREPARED FOOD

There comes a time when you crave nonprocessed, natural food that's homemade

"What should I eat before, during, and after exercise?" This is one of the most common questions for athletes. The answer depends on the type of cycling, your training level, intensity, duration, and other factors. Do yourself a favor, though, and don't assume that because you are cycling, it's an open invitation to pile on the calories.

Generally speaking, every athlete should eat a balanced diet. Consume a variety of nutrient-dense, organic foods and drinks along with the basic food groups. Choose foods that are nonprocessed and restrict your intake of saturated and trans fats, cholesterol, added sugars, salt, and alcohol.

Carbohydrates, proteins, and fats are classified as macro-

Preride Meal

- Eat a small meal high in complex carbohydrates and moderate proteins approximately three hours before your workout. Doing this allows your body to properly digest the food.

- Aim for a meal totaling 500–600 calories. Overeating can make you sluggish.

- Extra calories, not burned by the body, will turn to fat.

- If you don't have dietary restrictions, eat healthy fats with your meal. But keep fat intake to less than 25 percent of your total calories. Fat helps prolong delivery of energy into your system.

Postride Meal

- After a ride, consume a light meal or meal replacement, complete with some carbohydrates and protein.

- Your body is the most receptive to replenishing depleted stores thirty minutes after exercise. You'll notice more muscle tissue repair and increased recovery by following this guideline.

- Approximately two hours after the workout, eat a healthy, well-balanced meal.

- Remember to continue drinking water or an electrolyte replacement drink after the ride, too.

nutrients. Cycling diets advocate 60–70 percent of calories from carbohydrates. The remaining calories come from protein and fat sources. Each plays a role in your performance.

Carbohydrates (carbs) are compounds made up of sugars. They are important for replacing glycogen and maintaining blood glucose levels. Carbohydrates are the primary source of Adenosine-5'-triphosphate (ATP), used for high-intensity exercise.

Fats consist of a glycerin molecule with three fatty acids attached. They are needed to keep cell membranes functioning properly, to insulate body organs, to keep body temperature stable, and to maintain healthy hair and skin. Fat is the primary source of stored energy for low-intensity exercise and provides vitamins and essential fatty acids.

Proteins are organic compounds that consist of amino acids joined by peptide bonds. Protein is a minor source of energy for cyclists but is essential for growth and development of muscle. Because the body cannot manufacturer some amino-acids (called "essential amino acids"), you need to get these through your diet.

Prepared during-the-ride Food

Calories and Hydration during a Ride

- Eat and drink before you are hungry and thirsty.

- Take in 30–60 grams of carbohydrates per hour when cycling.

- Carbohydrates in the form of a liquid or gel are more easily absorbed in your body.

- Drink water every fifteen minutes and aim to have the equivalent of one to two small cycling water bottles per hour.

- Consume an electrolyte mix that includes potassium and sodium to replenish nutrients lost during heat exposure and activity.

- Prepare your own cycling snacks for a ride.

- Good options include jelly on a pita or bread. Use peanut butter if your intensity is low and you can wash it down and digest it.

- A sandwich is appropriate if your ride is leisurely.

- Foil is easier to open and seems to protect the food better than plastic wrap.

- If you plan to eat a banana, do so early on the ride before it gets squished.

- Please do not litter.

WORKSHOP & STORAGE

Store your bike in a place that is secure, yet convenient

We can't lie to you: Bikes do require some work. But we promise it will take a lot less energy than raising children or tending to animals. And the rewards far outweigh the effort.

A well-maintained bike will ride better, last longer, and give you less headaches and dents to your wallet in the long run. Although you can certainly employ your local bike shop for repairs and the periodic tune-up, some basic knowledge

can go a long way to make you more self-sufficient and save you money.

Ideally you might have a garage or work area with a bike stand, all the necessary tools for minor repairs, a hose, and some rags. This is the ideal, not what is absolutely necessary for keeping your bike running smoothly.

If you are setting up a workshop, invest in the essential

Bike Work Stand

- A good bike stand will be sturdy and have an easy-to-use clamping system that grabs the seatpost.

- Do not clamp the top tube or other part of the frame because some frames use

very thin-walled tubing and are not designed to withstand pressure in this way.

- Many bike stands built for home use are also foldable, making them easy to store or travel with, as needed.

Makeshift Work Stand

- If you don't have a bike stand, you can always balance the bike upside down on its saddle and handlebars to work on it.

- You might want to do this in a grassy area to avoid scratching the saddle and

handlebars, or scuffing the bartape.

- Turning the bike upside down enables you to work on the drivetrain because the rear wheel is off the ground.

84

tools. These key items will cover most of the do-it-yourself home repairs you are likely to want to tackle. You should have the following: a full set of Allen wrenches; a pedal wrench; medium- and small-size flat-head and Phillips screwdrivers. You may also want to invest in bike-specific cable cutters and a third-hand tool for adjusting brake cables. Don't forget to have grease and chain lube on hand as well.

YELLOW ● LIGHT

Balconies are popular places to store a bicycle. They are also common places for the theft of bicycles, even on upper-level floors. Make sure your balcony or deck is truly secure, and if there is any question, run a cable visibly through the frame and both wheels of your bike. Also, consider the weather; a good tarp to protect your bike from rain and snow is recommended.

Bike Storage

- Make sure to have a place to store your bike that is out of the way and secure.

- Rubber-coated hooks are an inexpensive way to organize your garage and prevent your bike from scratching your vehicle (or vice versa).

- If you are storing your bike in your home, special bike racks are available and are attractive and efficient, turning your bike into "art" when you are not riding.

Floor Pumps

- A good floor pump is a mandatory item. Air pressure tends to leak out of your tires over time, especially in cold temperatures. You will need to pump up your tires frequently and should do so before riding.

- Choose a pump with sturdy construction. A wide handle and base are easier to use.

- A pressure gauge is an important feature for getting to know what tire pressure you prefer.

CLEANING YOUR BIKE

Have you noticed that your car drives better clean? The same concept applies to a bike

That's right: Your bike needs a bath, just like you do. Keeping your bike clean will keep it running smoothly and looking good. A clean drivetrain, rims, and brake pads (if you use rim brakes) are especially important for proper shifting and braking.

A scrub brush and some citrus degreaser, or a little Simple Green, will remove all that gunky grease that likes to cling to your chain and chainrings. You may notice that a brand new chain comes with a thick coating of sticky grease. Although this makes the chain run smoothly and quietly, it also attracts dirt like flies to garbage. You may want to wipe down a new chain with some degreaser to avoid the eventual clean-up job.

Cleaning Utensils and Products

- A bucket, scrub brush, old toothbrush, and some degreaser are the key ingredients for a make-your-own bike-washing kit.

- Pedros makes an all-in-one bike-washing kit that includes several nifty brushes that get the hard-to-reach places.

- Special chain-cleaning tools are also available, but not necessary.

- A bike-specific bio-degradable degreaser, or Simple Green, works great to remove gunk from the chain, chainrings, and cassette.

Washing a Bike

- Rinse the bike with plain water first to remove dust and large dirt deposits.

- Use minimal water pressure and avoid spraying hubs, headset, bottom bracket, suspension fork legs, and linkage points directly.

- Scrub the frame, drivetrain, and rims with a scrub brush and some degreaser.

- Rinse with water and wipe the bike dry with an old towel or T-shirt.

- Tip the bike upside down to drain any water accumulation inside the frame.

The combination of rim brakes and wet conditions causes a black residue to coat your rims and brake pads. Make sure to vigorously scrub down the rims after a wet or muddy ride to remove this film. Check the brake pads for embedded bits of rock or other material.

Use a mild, nonabrasive soap (dish soap works great) and a nonabrasive sponge and/or brush for the frame and other painted parts. If you really want to get after it, finish the job with some bike polish for a sparkling machine.

Lubing the Chain

- Apply lube to the dry chain. Put lube on both sides of the chain while turning the crank slowly backward to get each link. Wipe excess off with a rag.

- Lubes are made for different kinds of riding conditions. Dry, waxy lubes are good for dusty areas.

- Do not use WD-40! This is a solvent, not a lubricant. Stick to bike-specific chain lubes.

- A dirty chain or a chain with too much lube (or both) will result in "rookie marks" or a "chain tattoo"—a chain grease imprint running down the back of your calf.

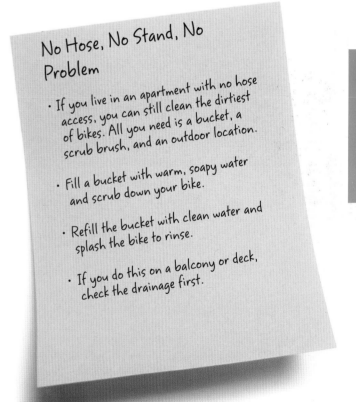

No Hose, No Stand, No Problem

- If you live in an apartment with no hose access, you can still clean the dirtiest of bikes. All you need is a bucket, a scrub brush, and an outdoor location.

- Fill a bucket with warm, soapy water and scrub down your bike.

- Refill the bucket with clean water and splash the bike to rinse.

- If you do this on a balcony or deck, check the drainage first.

BASIC MAINTENANCE

CHANGING FLATS—PART 1

Flat tires are an inevitable part of riding; know what to do for peace of mind

First and foremost, you should feel comfortable with fixing a flat tire because this is the most common problem you will encounter while riding. You should always carry the necessary tools to change at least one flat. Many people also carry a patch kit in case they get a second flat.

With the ubiquity of mobile phones, some people think they don't need to know how to change a flat and will just call for a ride if such bad luck befalls them. Think for a minute about the practicality of this. If your friend or significant other happens to be home when you call, is he or she really going to want to run out of the house and come pick you up just because you can't change a flat tire?

Remove the Wheel

- With a front wheel flat, disengage the brakes and release the skewer to remove the wheel.

- With a rear wheel flat, shift the bike into the smallest cog in the back. Disengage the brake and release the skewer to remove the wheel.

- You may have to push the derailleur out of the way with your hand as the wheel slides out of the dropouts.

- Lay the bike down on its nondrive side.

Unseat the Tire

- Let any remaining air out of the tube by pressing on the valve.

- A tire iron helps release the tire off one side of the rim.

- Push the tire off the rim away from you.

- If the tire is tight on the rim, use a closed fist when pushing hard to avoid ramming your fingers against the spokes.

- There is no need to take the tire completely off the rim.

We have included a step-by-step guide to changing a flat tire over the next two spreads. If you have never changed a flat before, we highly recommend that you practice this once in the safety and shelter of your garage or backyard. Don't rule out the possibility of getting a flat tire on a cold day or during a rainstorm. To practice, you don't have to actually have a flat tire. Just let all the air out of a good one and pretend.

Remove the Tube

- Remove the tube, beginning at the stem.

- Check the outside of the tire for obvious punctures.

- If you find an object, remove it from the outside (the way it went in) so it does not break off in the tire.

- Run your fingers along the inside of the tire. Sometimes a piece of glass or a thorn will lodge itself in the tire, causing another flat as soon as you pump up your tire.

Replace the Tube

- If you have a spare tube, get that ready by unrolling it and adding a bit of air to give it shape.

- If you use Presta valve tubes, you can slightly inflate the tube by blowing on the open valve with your mouth.

- Insert the new tube, beginning at the stem, and work your way around the rim so that it is resting on the rim and within the tire.

CHANGING FLATS—PART 2
Even if you have no spare tube, most flats can be patched

The directions for using a patch kit are usually included with the packaging, but you may also want to familiarize yourself with those before you are in a situation where you have to use them. Standard patch kits have a sheet of sandpaper, a tube of glue, and patches of varying sizes. We show and describe this process below.

Some glueless patches work surprisingly well. When you use these patches, the area around the hole may still need to be roughened up for optimal adhesion. After that is done, you merely need to stick the patch on, and you are done.

Whether you use a spare tube or patch a flat tire, be very careful not to pinch the tube when reseating the tire on the rim. It is very easy for a bit of the underinflated tube to get caught between the tire bead and the rim. Sometimes,

Patch a Tube

- To patch a flat, fill the tube with some air to determine where the hole is.

- You may need to add extra air to give the tube shape while patching it.

- Roughen the area around the hole with sandpaper.

- Apply the glue to the area and let it dry a bit.

- Apply the patch, rubbing it with the end of your finger to make sure it is adhering to the glue.

- Gently remove the plastic cover from the patch.

Reseat the Tire

- Reseat the bead on the rim using your hands first. Use the tire irons, if necessary.

- Tuck the partially inflated tube completely inside the tire. Be sure not to pinch the tube between the rim and the bead while doing this.

- After the tire is reseated, use your hands to feel along the rim to make sure that it is seated evenly and that the tube is not protruding.

you cannot see that this has happened. As you add air, the pressure builds, squeezing the tube until it bursts. There is no danger involved, but the loud pop will clue you into the problem abruptly and mean you must start over again.

To keep from pinching the tube, add air slowly. Periodically pinch the tire near the rim. You should see a clear space between the two.

Inflate the Tire

- Inflate the tire to full pressure.

- Minimum of 100 psi for road tires.

- Use 35–50 psi for mountain bike tires and 35-60 psi for cyclocross or similar tires (depending on rider's weight).

- If you are using a CO_2 cartridge (or a pump with no gauge), you will need to keep checking the tire pressure by feel with your hand. You want enough tire pressure that the tire will not easily give way to the rim.

Replace the Wheel

- Remount the wheel to the bike, secure the quick release, and reengage the brake.

- If you are replacing the rear wheel, line up the chain with the bottom cog as you pull the wheel into the dropouts.

- Make sure that the wheel is aligned in the center of the brakes and that nothing is rubbing or crooked.

- Take everything with you and get riding again.

DRIVETRAIN MAINTENANCE

The reward for keeping your bike parts clean is how well the bike functions

Even if you keep your bike spotless and your chain well lubed, your bike will need some regular maintenance. Mostly this will revolve around the drivetrain because that is the area of your bike with the most moving parts.

It is important to replace your chain before it wears considerably. A chain that has been used for too long will also wear the chainrings and cogs, resulting in the need to replace all at the same time. This is much more expensive than replacing just the chain. There is no set timeframe or mileage for how often to replace your chain. Wear will be determined by a combination of mileage and riding conditions.

Old chains are said to "stretch." What really happens is that

Chain and Cogs

- Keep the cassette free from dirt, road grime, or grease build-up in between the cogs because this will cause the chain to skip.

- To clean between cogs, you can use a rag pulled tight and wipe between the spaces. The teeth, however, may tear the rag. Special brushes and tools can make the job easier.

- Check your most commonly used gears for obvious wear, uneven wear, and missing teeth as a sign they need to be replaced.

Breaking the Chain

- "Breaking" the chain simply means releasing a link so the chain is no longer continuous. This is the only way to remove an old chain or put on a new one.

- Change gears so the chain is in a small cog and small chainring. Using a chain tool, push one of the pins out just far enough to release the links next to it with your hands.

- Some brands require a special pin for reassembly.

the pins wear down, decreasing in diameter ever so slightly so that the chain appears to have gotten longer. Chain stretch of more than one-sixteenth inch per foot of chain length means it's time to replace the chain. Bicycle chain links are exactly a half-inch from the center of one pin to another or one inch per full link. Stretch can be measured using a foot-long ruler or tape. If a chain pin is more than one-sixteenth inch past the end of the ruler, it's time for a new chain.

Rear Derailleur

Barrel Adjuster

Pulleys

VROOMEN.WH

- Hold the end of a flat-head screwdriver against each pulley while turning the crank to clean off the caked-on dirt and grease.

- Many rear derailleurs have barrel adjusters, where the housing goes into the mechanism.

- If your shifting is slow shifting into an easier gear, turn the barrel adjuster counter-clockwise or toward the wheel.

- If the shifting is slow to go into a harder gear, turn the barrel adjuster clockwise or away from the wheel.

Derailleur Hanger

- Many bikes have a separate piece called a "derailleur hanger" that attaches to the frame.

- The hanger is often made of a material that is less stiff than the frame so that if the bike takes a hit around the rear derailleur, the hanger gets bent, instead of bend-ing the frame. This piece is easier and less expensive to replace than having the frame straightened or replacing the whole frame.

- A bent derailleur hanger will cause irregular shifting.

BRAKE ADJUSTMENT

When left unattended, brakes can seize, pads can become brittle, and stopping power can falter

Brake adjustment can be tricky business. If your brakes need some help, it may be best to consult a mechanic. Nonetheless, understanding a few basic concepts and skills will prevent you from getting into a bind and help you to diagnose the problem.

Proper brake pad alignment is easy to achieve and maintain with newer-style rim brakes. Caliper and V-Brakes rarely squeal and hold their alignment when pads are replaced. Generally, after you replace the pad and adjust the cable, you are good to go. Be careful not to misplace or drop the small part—usually a small screw or pin—that holds the brake pad in place. When sliding a new pad into the shoe, don't push

Correct Brake Alignment

- Align brake pads squarely on the rim. The pad should not hang below the edge of the rim because this will cause uneven wear and sticky braking.

- A brake pad that is set too high can rub against the tire. This arrangement will eventually rub a hole through the sidewall and cause a flat (as well as ruin your tire).

- Loosening the brake pad screw allows you to adjust the brake pad position.

Worn Brake Pads

- Most brake pads have grooves in them that help displace water on the rim and allow you to know when the brake pads need to be replaced.

- Check the brake pad wear if the brake lever pulls all the way to the bar.

- Brake pad surfaces may get polished from wear, which reduces effectiveness. File the surface lightly to roughen it up a bit, restoring the brake pad's grip.

too hard. Doing so may break the pad in half.

Squealing brakes are aggravating to you and to others. This is a problem most often associated with cantilever brakes. To avoid this squealing, the brake pads should be "toed in." This means the brake pad is aligned in the shoe so that the front end of the pad hits the rim first. An easy way to toe in the pad is to place a slim piece of plastic, such as the end of a zip tie, between the rim and the brake pad when tightening the shoe bolt.

Brake housing and cables come in a standard length. Prebuilt bikes will have the same length housing regardless of the bike size. Housing that is too long will make the brake lever action less crisp. Ask your mechanic to trim the housing down. Housing should be long enough to allow for full range of motion of the handlebars and suspension fork, but no longer.

Disc Brake Concerns

- Do not squeeze the brake levers when the wheels are removed. This can cause the brake pads to collapse together. If this happens, you will need to reset the pistons. Remove the brake pads and use the box end of a 10 millimeter wrench to reset the pistons.

- To avoid this problem, place a piece of thin plastic between the pads when the wheel is off the bike.

- Make sure to be careful not to drip lube or other chemicals on the rotors, calipers, and brake pads.

Brake Levers

Barrel Adjuster

- If a brake lever pulls all the way to the bar before activating the brake, most likely your brake pads have worn or cables have stretched.

- Some brake levers have a barrel adjuster at the lever that allows you to tighten or loosen the brake cable on the fly.

- After you get home, check your brake pads. If they do not need to be replaced, take up the slack by shortening the cable where it attaches to the brake body.

GETTING OUT OF JAMS

Out-of-the-ordinary problems can inspire your creativity and problem-solving capabilities

Let's face it: Unexpected mishaps are a part of life. Off-road riding lends itself to a broader range of potential dilemmas, yet road riding and commuting are not impervious. Pay attention to tips for temporary fixes as this arsenal of knowledge can prevent you from getting stranded.

Some mishaps will simply make your bike unrideable. For example, a broken chain will mean a long walk home (unless the walk happens to be all downhill). A broken spoke that throws the rim so out of true that the rim rubs against the frame can also make riding impossible. However, the right tool can rectify both of these situations. This is why carrying a good multi-tool is imperative. Even if you don't know

Sliced Tire

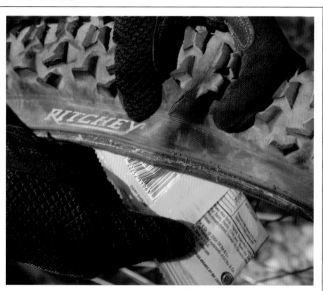

- If your tire is sliced through the casing, you will get repeated flats. "Boot" the tire for a temporary fix.

- Place an energy bar wrapper or dollar bill between the tube and tire. The pressure of the inflated tube will hold it in place and "patch" the slice.

- A tube patch or any thin material that has some amount of plasticity or strength will work for a boot. Regular paper will not work for this repair.

No Spare Tube

- Fill your tire with grass or brush if you have no spare tube. Try to put an even amount of debris along the whole tire to protect the rim.

- Put the tire back on the rim and ride slowly.

- This is an emergency fix only.

- Riding on the rim and an uninflated tire can ruin your rim and your tire, costing you money (besides being very uncomfortable).

how to use it, you may be able to flag down another cyclist who does. Alternatively, a tool plus time may equal newly acquired skills.

Other calamities simply require some perseverance. A broken saddle or seatpost means you'll have to reach your destination by riding standing up. A broken pedal or missing cleat means riding with one leg. Focusing on the solution and engaging your creativity can turn a bad situation into a good story at the pub.

If you break a spoke and have a spoke wrench, you can true your wheel on the spot. Keep the wheel mounted on the bike and use the brake pads as your "truing stand" to find the rubbing spot. Along this spot in the rim, loosen the spokes on the same side and tighten the spokes on the opposite side. The spoke side is determined by which side of the hub the spokes initiate from.

Broken Spoke

- If you break a spoke, twist the broken spoke around an adjacent spoke to get it out of the way.

- A broken spoke will cause your wheel to go out of true and wobble, and thus your brakes will rub. If you don't have a spoke wrench, open the brake pads to lessen the rubbing. This is not an issue (and an advantage) if you have disc brakes.

- Check to see that the wheel is not so out of true that it rubs your frame.

Broken Derailleur

- If your rear derailleur breaks, you can use a chain tool to break the chain, remove the derailleur, and turn your bike into a singlespeed.

- Doing this is tricky because the chain tension must be just right; otherwise the chain will skip or bounce off the gear.

- Choose a medium gear ratio. You may need to remove several links of the chain before deducing the right length.

BODY POSITION ON BIKE

Proper body position on the bike means safer riding, better balance, and more fun

What exactly does it mean when someone says, "It's just like riding a bike"? Usually it means the activity is easy, you need to learn it only once, and you'll never forget how to do it—or some combination thereof. But if you think of the first few moments spent balancing on two wheels, often with an intermittently proud and anxious parent hovering nearby,

it certainly didn't seem easy then. Learning to ride a bike is a major milestone in the lives of many children. Realistically, the level of aptitude with which we begin our initial foray into cycling is probably not the same level of aptitude with which we want to join the throes of rush-hour traffic or descend a rock-strewn mountainside. Perhaps it is the skill of balancing

Incorrect Lower-body Position

- Incorrect form on a bike includes a rounded back and a rolled pelvis.

- This position stresses the lower back and puts the body weight on the back of the sit bones and the back of the bike instead of dis-

  tributing the body weight evenly over the bike.

- Because the back is rounded, the arms stretch to reach the handlebars, which can result in less control over the front end of the bike.

Correct Lower-body Position

- Correct lower-body position on a bike allows you to more easily engage your glutes and hamstrings while pedaling. It alleviates pressure to the lower back.

- The body weight is supported by the sit bones and the pubic bone. The body

  should sit squarely on the saddle, enabling you to maintain steady hips while pedaling.

- A proper lower-body position, allows the arms to reach naturally to the handlebars.

on two wheels that we need to learn only once. Riding a bike safely, competently, and confidently is a much bigger task than the old saying implies.

This chapter covers the basic riding skills that apply to all kinds of cycling, from commuting to school or work to riding the most technical mountain biking terrain. This is the starting point for all forms of cycling.

Before we can begin to talk about skills on the bike, you must make sure your position on the bike is correct. After all, even the most skilled cyclist will be inept on a bike that doesn't fit correctly. Incorrect position on the bike can translate into compromised riding skills, discomfort, unsafe riding, and even injury. Different than bike fit, which has to do with changes to the bike's setup to best accommodate your body, bike position relates how you sit on the bike or your cycling posture.

Incorrect Upper-body Position

- Hunched shoulders will cause neck stiffness.

- Locked elbows are dangerous because this posture does not allow you to absorb bumps in the road and can cause swerving or a crash.

- Having locked elbows is hard on your joints and can cause pain over an extended period of time.

- Craning the neck forward will also cause stiffness and discomfort.

Correct Upper-body Position

- Elbows should be slightly bent, arms relaxed and ready to absorb bumps in the road.

- Keep a firm grip on the handlebars—no white knuckles!

- Shoulders should be relaxed.

- Depending on how low your position is on the bike, your neck will maintain a straight line with your spine. Use your eyes to look up instead of craning your whole head.

PEDALING
Strive for efficiency and energy with each crank revolution

Proper pedaling is all about efficiency. A telltale sign of an inexperienced rider is a choppy pedal stroke. In contrast, when you ride behind an experienced cyclist, you will notice how smooth and effortless his or her pedaling looks. This is always your goal. Multiple factors contribute to smooth pedaling: proper seat height, proper leg alignment, uniform pedal stroke pressure, and proper foot position.

Starting from the hips down, you need to have the right saddle height to maximize your pedaling efficiency. A saddle that is too low will mean you are not getting a full extension of the leg, robbing you of power. A saddle that is too high will cause your hips to rock in the saddle, resulting in friction, strain on the joints, and unnecessary movement.

Moving down the leg, you want to make sure you have the

Steady Hips

Hips should remain steady

- Your hips should not rock in the saddle but rather should remain even and still so that you could draw a horizontal line across them.

- If your hips do rock, this could mean that your saddle is too high or that you have some muscle tightness in your hips and legs.

- Stretching the quads, hamstrings, hips, and lower back can help maintain steady hips and efficient pedaling on the bike.

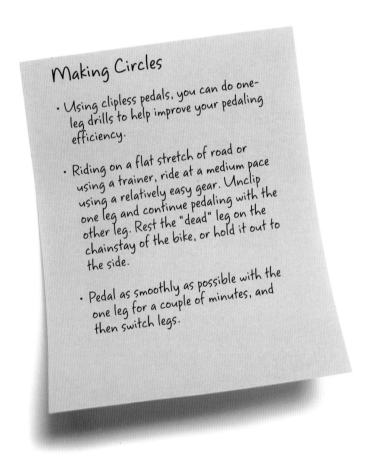

Making Circles

- Using clipless pedals, you can do one-leg drills to help improve your pedaling efficiency.

- Riding on a flat stretch of road or using a trainer, ride at a medium pace using a relatively easy gear. Unclip one leg and continue pedaling with the other leg. Rest the "dead" leg on the chainstay of the bike, or hold it out to the side.

- Pedal as smoothly as possible with the one leg for a couple of minutes, and then switch legs.

100

best alignment possible from your hip to your knee to your toes. If your knees bow out or in, your power to the pedal may be compromised.

Each pedal rotation completes a full circle, but that does not necessarily mean that you are applying even pressure to the pedal throughout that circle. There is a natural emphasis on the downstroke due to its having the greatest gravitational advantage and primary use of the large quadriceps (thigh) muscles. Try focusing on the other parts of the pedal stroke: pulling up, pushing across the top, and pulling back as if wiping mud off the bottom of your shoe. You will notice that you use different muscles in your legs for each part of the circle, thus taking some of the burden off of your thighs and increasing your stamina. This is easiest to do with clipless pedals or toe cages, but even with flat pedals, you can try to push across the top and pull back at the bottom by dropping your heel and toe.

Toe Position

- Your foot should line up parallel with the crank. Avoid turning your toes in or out.

- Center your foot on the pedal with the ball of your foot over the spindle.

- Keep your foot flat while pedaling. Avoid dipping your heel or pointing your toes.

- Visualize a piston. Go straight up and down. If you experience lateral movement or can't hold your toes straight, consider orthotics or a biomechanical adjustment.

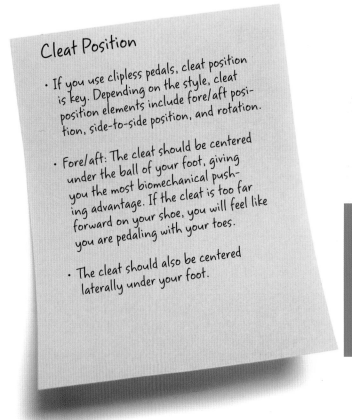

Cleat Position

- If you use clipless pedals, cleat position is key. Depending on the style, cleat position elements include fore/aft position, side-to-side position, and rotation.

- Fore/aft: The cleat should be centered under the ball of your foot, giving you the most biomechanical pushing advantage. If the cleat is too far forward on your shoe, you will feel like you are pedaling with your toes.

- The cleat should also be centered laterally under your foot.

101

BRAKING
Front brake, rear brake, both brakes—it makes a difference

Your brakes are one of the most important features on your bike. Yet, they are often the most taken for granted. It is not enough to simply know that squeezing your brakes will slow you down or cause you to come to a stop. Understanding how each brake works and why will help you ride safely.

Like motorcycles, bicycles have a front and a rear brake that operate separately. The front brake demands both respect and caution; it provides 75 percent of your braking power but can also cause you to go over the handlebars if used excessively. The rear brake provides more subtle braking power and provides some steering ability in advanced circumstances. Using both brakes simultaneously will bring you to a stop most quickly.

Body position assists when braking. Imagine you are riding

Rear Brake Lever

- The right brake lever activates the rear brake.

- In locations where drivers drive on the left side of the road, the rear brake is mounted on the left side.

- The harder you squeeze the brake lever, the more braking power you have.

- If you use too much rear brake, you will lock up the rear wheel and skid.

- This is why the best advice is to apply equal pressure to both brake levers.

Front Brake Lever

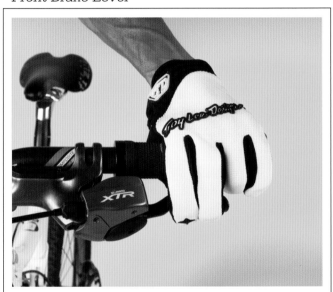

- The left brake lever activates the front brake.

- In locations where drivers drive on the left side of the road, the front brake is mounted on the right side, like a motorcycle.

- The vast majority of your braking power comes from the front brake.

- If you use too much front brake, you may go over the handlebars or wash out the front wheel (which can also result in your body leaving the bike).

along a street at 15 mph. This means both you and the bike are moving at the same speed. When you apply the brakes, your bike alone slows. Your body, if relaxed and unresponsive, will keep traveling at the same rate of speed. You must adjust your body position, using your arms and legs, to arrest the body's inertia. The more dramatic the speed reduction, the more you need to move your weight to the back.

Braking Skills Drill

• Find a flat stretch of pavement free of cars and practice stopping using only the rear brake, only the front brake, and then both.

• Ride in a straight line. Begin braking at the same point each time. Notice the distance it takes to come to a complete stop for each run.

• Next, apply the rear brake sharply enough to skid the rear wheel. Although skidding is not a desired result, it is good to understand how the bike handles in such a situation.

Emergency Braking

• If you need to come to an emergency stop, squeeze both brakes hard at the same time.

• Press on the pedals and shift your weight back, rounding your back and keeping low over the bike. This should stop your body from pitching forward.

• If your rear wheel skids or the bike drifts to the side, let off the brakes slightly to correct your direction. Use your inner thighs to grip the saddle and continue stopping.

BASIC RIDING SKILLS

SLOW TURNING & CORNERING

You can change directions by steering and leaning, depending on your speed and circumstances

There are actually two ways to turn or change direction on a bike. You can turn the handlebars and steer to change direction, or you can lean the bike into the turn. You probably already do a combination of tactics without even thinking about it every time you go around a corner.

Turning by steering or turning the handlebars is used for slow, sharp corners. These turns are also called "short-radius turns." Examples of when you might do a short-radius turn are when turning from a sidewalk onto the road or turning from a stop. Keep the bike upright at slow speeds. Make sure your head is up and resume pedaling as soon as possible for balance.

Slow Turn Start

- Look ahead to where you will end up after the turn.

- Steer the handlebars while maintaining some momentum.

- Small bike frames may have toe overlap. This means that when the front wheel is turned significantly, it will hit your toe at the front point of the pedal stroke.

- Timing your pedal stroke so that the outside foot is not at the front of the pedal stroke as you turn the wheel will alleviate this problem.

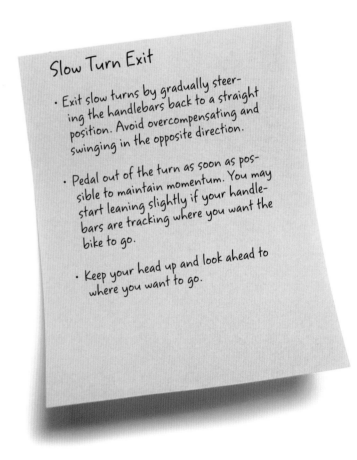

Slow Turn Exit

- Exit slow turns by gradually steering the handlebars back to a straight position. Avoid overcompensating and swinging in the opposite direction.

- Pedal out of the turn as soon as possible to maintain momentum. You may start leaning slightly if your handlebars are tracking where you want the bike to go.

- Keep your head up and look ahead to where you want to go.

Leaning is used for higher-speed turns. The faster the speed, the more you will need to lean the bike to make the corner. For basic riding purposes, you will most likely use a bit of both—steering and leaning—on most corners. Understand the difference, though, as a foundation for more advanced skills to come later.

Always look ahead when turning. Regardless of how fast or slow you are going, you should be looking through the turn and to where you will end up. More simply put, look where you want to go.

Cornering Start

- Finish braking before entering the turn. If you have room, swing wide before starting your turn so that you can carry your momentum.

- If in traffic, adjust your speed so that you maintain your position in your lane of traffic.

- Look ahead to the exit of the turn or where you will end up.

- Keep the outside leg down or straight, weighting the foot and driving pressure through the pedal.

Cornering Apex and Exit

- Lean the bike into the corner while keeping your outside pedal down and your inside pedal up.

- As you finish the turn, bring your bike back to an upright position to carry on in a straight line.

- If brakes are needed, feather them lightly and avoid squeezing hard.

- Pedal out of the turn as soon as possible to maintain momentum.

- Keep your head up and looking ahead to where you want to go.

CLIMBING & DESCENDING

Adjusting your weight distribution on the bike makes going up and down hills more trouble-free

Safe and comfortable climbing and descending depend upon proper body position. As the hill becomes steeper, you will need to adjust your weight distribution on the bike. If you stay in the same seated position on the bike, on a dramatic uphill, more of your weight will be on the rear wheel due to gravity. Similarly, on a steep downhill pitch, gravity will cause more of your body weight to be on the front wheel instead of evenly distributed over both. Standing, sliding along the saddle, and lowering your upper body are all techniques that allow you to adjust your weight forward or backward to compensate for the pull of gravity.

When climbing, whether steeply or gradually, you want to

Seated Climb

- Keep the upper body relaxed and quiet. Do not bob your upper body up and down; doing this wastes energy.

- Use all the muscles in your legs, including your glutes, for a smooth, efficient pedal stroke.

- Shift your weight forward on the saddle when the hill is steep for a more advantageous pedal stroke.

- Stay on the bike. It's easier to keep pedaling slowly and consistently than to get off the bike and walk.

Standing Climb

- Standing may be necessary on steep pitches to power over the top of the hill.

- As you stand, shift your weight forward slightly. Maintain a firm grip on the bars and a steady upper body.

- You will use your arms to counterbalance against each pedal stroke. Do not exaggerate this motion or bob your shoulders side to side.

- Use caution with flat pedals because your feet may slip off.

be as efficient as possible. Keep your upper body relaxed. Your shoulders should be loose and elbows slightly bent. Keep a light but firm grip on the bars in an upright position. Breathe from your diaphragm with your chest upright and open. Do not rock side to side because this is a waste of energy—after all, you want to go forward! If you have clipless pedals or toe cages, concentrate on pulling up and wrapping the pedal over the top of the stroke.

Seated Descent

- Stay seated on only the most gradual declines.

- Use your arms to brace against gravity while maintaining relaxed shoulders and slightly bent elbows to enable absorption.

- Use your abdominal

muscles to help provide stability.

- Staying seated on a steeper decline is dangerous because gravity will pull more of your body weight to the front of the bike, which can result in crashing more easily.

Standing Descent

- Stand with the pedals in flat or horizontal position and shift your weight back.

- The steeper the decline, the farther back you will want to shift your weight.

- Keep your arms and knees slightly bent and keep a

firm grip on the bars and pedals, ready to absorb any bumps in the road.

- If you are using flat pedals, make sure you have a good foothold. Shoes with grippy soles are recommended.

BASIC RIDING SKILLS

GEARS & SHIFTING

Shifting into a gear that is too small or too big will waste energy

Using the correct gear makes riding a bike more efficient. If you are in a gear that is too easy—undergeared—you will be pedaling madly but not going anywhere quickly. Conversely, if you are in a gear that is too hard—overgeared—you will have a hard time turning over the pedals. The best gear is the one that allows you to stay on top of the pedal stroke. This means you need to apply a fair amount of pressure to turn

the gear over but not so much that you are bogged down.

Looking ahead to anticipate upcoming terrain is helpful. If you see a steep hill coming, you will want to shift to an easier gear prior to reaching the steepest pitch. On the other hand, you don't want to shift down too early because doing that will cause you to lose all your momentum coming into the hill.

Easy (Granny) Gear

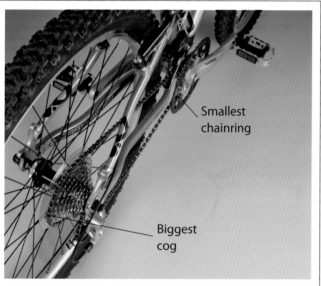

Smallest chainring

Biggest cog

- The easiest gear—biggest cog and smallest chainring—is often referred to as the "granny gear."

- The easiest gear is mostly reserved for steep hills. As the hills flatten or as

you crest a hill, shift into a harder gear to carry your momentum.

- Unless you are starting on a hill, you will want to be in a midrange gear to get moving.

Hard Gear

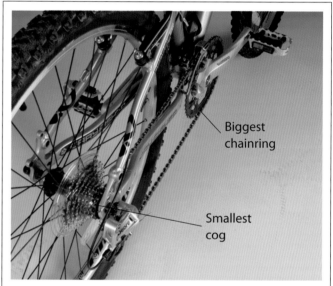

Biggest chainring

Smallest cog

- The hardest gear on any bike is the combination of the smallest cog and biggest chainring.

- You will use this gear when pedaling downhill, when sprinting along a straight road, or when riding with a brisk tailwind.

- On technical mountain biking descents that do not require pedaling, you may still use the large chainring. Doing this will stretch the chain against the rear derailleur and reduce chain slap against the chainstay.

Talking about gears can be difficult because it is tempting to use the word "big" when referring to a harder gear or the gear used when going fast on flat terrain or pedaling down a hill. But "big" is not a very helpful term because the biggest cog is actually the easiest gear in the back, yet the easiest chainring is the smallest one.

Incorrect Chain Crossover

Never shift into a big chainring and big cog

- When you use the biggest chainring and the biggest cog, the chain is said to be "crossed."

- Chain crossover is bad because it stretches the rear derailleur unnecessarily. If the chain is not quite long enough, crossing the chain can destroy the rear derailleur.

- To be safe, shift from the big chainring to a smaller one when you are halfway up the cassette in back.

What Gearing?

- When buying a new bike, discuss what kind of terrain you will be riding with an expert to make sure the bike you are buying has suitable gears.

- Take some time to become familiar with the gears on your bike and how to shift properly. Make sure you know which shifter operates which derailleur and in which direction to shift for an easier or harder gear. Later we discuss coaching and clinics, which will help with these factors.

HAND SIGNALS

Communication is key; hand signals let vehicles and other cyclists know your intentions

The bicycle is a great way to get from one place to another. In addition to basic transportation, you get a workout at the same time. In some urban centers, the bike can be your fastest option for getting around. Bicycles are also the most agile; you leave when you are ready instead of being beholden to a bus or train schedule, and there is no need to circle around

looking for a parking spot. Cycling instead of driving means less congestion and less air pollution. For this reason, some major international cities have developed progressive programs to encourage bicycle commuting and discourage driving in dense areas.

Although anyone with a bike can hop onto the roads and

Left Turn

- Extend your left arm straight out to the side, horizontal to the road, to signal a left turn.

- Signal prior to turning and hold your arm there for a couple of seconds so that other vehicles will have a chance to see you.

- Put both hands back onto the handlebars for the actual turn.

- To be safe, look back one last time prior to turning.

Right Turn

- In the United States and Canada, extend your left arm out to the side, with your upper arm up/vertical and palm facing forward.

- In all other locations, extend your right arm straight out to the side,

horizontal to the road. Signaling this way is easier for other vehicles turning right to see.

- The right arm signal is also recognized in most American states and in Canada.

get going, some basic knowledge will make your experience safe, responsible, and successful. Because bicycles have no turn signals or lights, you must learn the basic hand signals to communicate your intentions. The most common hand signals you will use are those to signal turning, but it is also helpful to signal when you are slowing and when there is debris in the road. These latter signals are helpful in relation to other cyclists.

Slowing/Braking

- In the United States and Canada, extend your left arm to the side, with your upper arm down/vertical and palm facing back. Most riders will recognize the signal if you use either arm.

- In the United Kingdom and Ireland, extend your left arm straight out to the side, palm down, and wave your arm up and down.

- In Australia and some European countries, extend your right arm vertically, palm facing forward.

Pointing at an Object

- Point to the object well in advance. Use the arm that is on the side where the object is located.

- The cyclist in front should ride around the object in a predictable and gradual manner.

- Try to avoid swerving at the last moment or other erratic movement because doing so can cause the person behind you to crash.

- Yelling out the type of obstacle is also helpful.

TRAFFIC FLOW

Bicycles are recognized as vehicles in almost all locations, so follow the rules of the road

In 1968, the United Nations Vienna Convention on Road Traffic recognized bicycles as vehicles. The goal of this international treaty was to increase safety and facilitate international road travel. You can safely assume that anywhere you travel, laws will require bicycles to follow the rules of the road and require some minimal safety equipment.

About one-quarter of the world drives on the left side of the road; the remainder drives on the right side. Because our photos were taken in America, you will see right-side situations. However, the principles of cycling in traffic remain the same regardless of which side of the road you are on.

On that note, always ride with traffic, not against it. Ride

Riding with Traffic

- Ride in the same direction as traffic. If there is no shoulder or bike lane, stay to the outside of the lane.

- Do not ride in the gutter. Ride out from the curb or edge of the road a few feet so you will be seen more easily.

- Maintain your position and move predictably. Practice signaling and looking behind you without turning the handlebars or wobbling.

Turning with Traffic

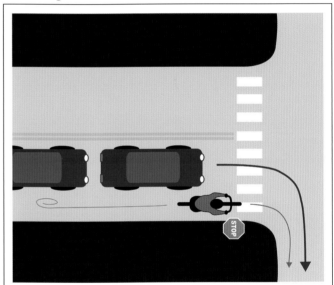

- When traffic is stopped, move to the front of the lane if possible where cars will see you. Some jurisdictions provide an advance stop area in front of the lane for just this purpose.

- Stay to the outside of other vehicles that may also be turning or going straight.

- Hold your hand signal while waiting at a light or stop sign so the vehicles behind you will know you are turning.

confidently and own your space on the road; be assertive of your presence without being aggressive. Stay alert and aware of everything going on around you. Assume that cars do not see you and try to gain eye contact with drivers turning onto your path. Be especially cautious of large trucks and buses that have significant blind spots and need a wide radius for turning. Stay well in front of these vehicles or well behind and pass them quickly on a straight section of road.

Turning across Traffic

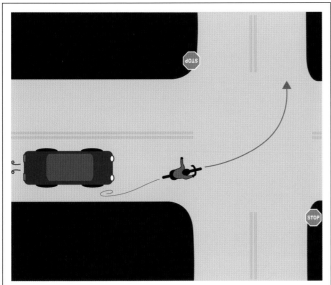

- When riding along a single-lane road, start thinking about moving to the center of the lane well before the intersection.

- Look back, signal, and merge over as you approach the intersection. It is easier to merge carry-ing some speed so that you are not moving drastically slower than traffic.

- If traffic is stopped, move to the front, signal, and position yourself slightly in front and to the outside of other vehicles turning with you.

Multi-lane across Traffic Turn

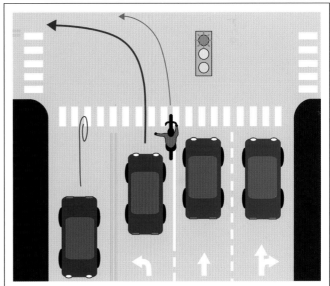

- Where there are multiple lanes at a traffic light, and you are turning across traffic, the principles of a single-lane scenario apply.

- Look back, signal, and merge into the turning lane.

- Position yourself to the outside of other turning vehicles so that you will end up at the outside of the road. Be ready for the light to change so you can complete your turn ahead of other turning traffic.

COMMUTING CONCERNS

HAZARDS
Urban commuting can be an exciting endeavor involving all kinds of challenges

In addition to inattentive drivers, commuting can present a slew of other hazards. Being aware of the most common ones and knowing how to deal with them will turn a hazard into an easily surmountable challenge.

Animals can pose an especially vexing situation. Dogs, in particular, may decide that your ankles look quite enticing

and are at a convenient nipping height as you pedal along. Know that if you are descending, you will quickly outdistance dogs. If you are not lucky enough to be on a downhill, try yelling "no" or "stay" in a stern voice. You may also try squirting the dog with your water bottle. As a last resort, you may need to take your foot off the pedal and kick in their direction,

Potholes

- Potholes are best avoided if at all possible. Hitting a pothole with force can cause you to pinch flat. Worse, if you are not paying attention, hitting a pothole can throw you off balance.

- Sometimes potholes just can't be avoided. In this

case, ride over them in a standing position with an energetic stance. Use your arms and legs to absorb the bike's movement.

- Be light on the bike; don't slam it into the pothole.

Pedestrians

- Watch for people stepping out from between parked cars because they may not be looking for you.

- Remember that while on your bike, you are considered a vehicle and must yield to pedestrians.

- Some cities have special

pedestrian crosswalks with particular signage or lighting. Make sure to familiarize yourself with these and note their locations.

- After you dismount your bike, you are usually considered a pedestrian and may cross an intersection at a crosswalk.

which will usually prevent a bite.

Friendly dogs that are unfamiliar with bikes have a tendency to run toward you, effectively running toward your front wheel. Slowing down and calling to them will enable you to avoid a collision and may encourage the dogs to move to the side. Other dogs may simply decide they want to join you on your journey. They often get tired, but yelling "stay" and "go home" in a commanding voice may remind them that you are not their owner.

Parked Cars

- Parallel parked cars are a pesky problem. When a door is opened right in front of you, you have little time to react.

- Glance in side mirrors to spot drivers who are still in their cars but may be about to exit.

- If you can move at the speed of traffic, or if there is no traffic, you may pull into the road away from the parked cars.

- With diagonal parking, watch for reverse lights. Assume that drivers don't see you.

Animals

- Animals, like daydreaming pedestrians, may end up in your path of movement.

- Pay attention to all that's going on around you. Scan the sides of the road with your peripheral vision. Always be prepared by keeping your hands hovering over the brakes.

- Keep an eye out in wooded or grassy areas for deer along the side of the road, especially during high-speed descents.

INCLEMENT WEATHER

In Colorado, we have a phrase: "Wait ten minutes, and the weather will change"

Commuting on your bike is an easy sell on sunny, warm days, but it seems like only the heartiest souls brave the elements year-round. The truth is that using your bike for transportation in all four seasons requires a bit more preparation and proper gear, and the weather-specific accessories and clothing discussed earlier become worth their weight in gold.

Riding in inclement weather can also involve some specific riding skills. Building upon the basic riding skills you already have, add these to your arsenal. Perhaps you'll need a sense of adventure, too.

In slippery conditions, reduce your speed and begin braking sooner than usual. When cornering, don't lean the bike

Rain

Snow

- Wet rims can compromise your stopping ability. In rain, keep your speed checked and begin slowing sooner than usual.

- Fenders and waterproof outerwear will keep you dry and clean.

- Use clear or amber lenses in your glasses for enhanced vision in low light conditions.

- Wear your cycling shoes and bring spare shoes and socks. Waterproof booties that cover your shoes are key. In a pinch, place a plastic bag over your sock and inside your shoe.

- Staying warm can be the biggest challenge in snowy climes. Use your ski clothing, particularly goggles, gloves, and toe/hand warmers, on especially frigid days.

- Lower tire pressure will help with traction. Be mindful that ice may be prevalent under snow, so ride cautiously. Mountain bikes are the bikes of choice for snowy riding.

- If the roads in your area stay snow-covered for much of the winter, studded tires may be a worthwhile investment.

as much; instead, keep the bike upright and lean your body to make the turn. Doing this will help keep the maximum amount of tire contact with the road through the turn. For icy patches, maintain momentum, ride in a straight line, and do not touch the brakes. Always maintain a "ready" body position on the bike: relaxed upper body, slightly bent elbows, and firm grip on the bars. Keep some weight on your feet so you are not sitting too squarely on the saddle. Maintain your momentum and look ahead.

············ YELLOW ● LIGHT ············

The stripes that make up crosswalks and other road markings become excessively slick when they are wet, so take care when cornering through an intersection in the rain. Try to keep the bike upright when passing over the zebra stripes to avoid ending up on the ground. Roads are slickest when rain just starts to fall due to oil on the road from cars. As the rain becomes heavier, this oil washes off.

Heat

- In extreme heat, adequate hydration is mandatory. Drink plenty of cold fluids to keep your core body temperature down.

- Try to avoid riding in the heat of the day. Remember that the heat off the pavement will make the air feel even hotter.

- Wear light-colored clothing that wicks moisture and don't forget the sunscreen.

- Know the signs of heat exhaustion: cool, moist skin; fast or weak pulse rate; and fast or shallow breathing. Seek medical attention immediately.

Wind

- High winds or gusts may make you want to stop pedaling or brake—resist this urge.

- The motion of your pedaling helps to keep you balanced and upright and moving forward.

- Lean into a side wind to counter the force.

- Keep your upper body relaxed, keep a firm grip on the bars, and be ready to compensate for sudden changes in wind speed or direction.

MULTI-USE PATH ETIQUETTE
Bike paths are great diversions from traffic but have their own particular traffic issues

Dedicated bike paths are becoming more common in many cities. Often these paths are multi-use paths and not restricted to bicycle traffic only. These paths have both advantages and disadvantages.

Not mingling with cars and bypassing traffic lights can make your commute faster and more peaceful. Some paths

run alongside waterways, providing a respite from the hustle and bustle of the rest of the world. On the other hand, the variety of users and a lack of the standardized expectations and rules associated with roads can sometimes make multi-use paths feel hectic. Lunchtime on a sunny day may seem to bring out running groups, headphoned inline skaters,

Passing

- When passing bike path users, stay to the same side as you would if driving, even if there is no center line on the path.

- Use eye contact so that there is an understanding that you both see each other.

- If you detect that the people you are passing are not paying attention, use your voice to snap them back to reality. A simple hello will do.

- A nod, smile, or warm gesture is always good.

Overtaking

- When overtaking slower traffic, call out "on your left" (or whichever side you will be passing on) before passing. Speak loudly and clearly and consider that the person you are overtaking may be wearing headphones.

- Bells are also helpful to let the person know you are coming. Some jurisdictions require you to have a bell on your bike.

- Proceed only when you can see clearly that there is no oncoming traffic.

packs of stroller-pushing parents, pairs of cyclists riding two abreast, dog walkers with clothesline-like leashes, and erratic children all at once.

Sometimes, multi-use paths are not easy to find. Keep in mind that city planners try to use paths to route cyclists away from main arteries, so it's worth the effort to find these gems. If you are in a new place or new to riding, take some time to learn where the paths are and plot your journey using a cyclist-friendly route. Contact the local transportation department for cyclist-oriented maps of the area that will indicate where paths and bike lanes are located.

If you apply the rules of the road to multi-use paths, you will help to provide some order. Keep in mind, though, that not everyone else will follow the same rules. In this case, verbal communication is helpful. Be friendly, but speak loud enough that you will be heard. Give yourself additional time to get to and from your destination so that you aren't racing along a mellow bike path, contributing to the problem.

Controlling Speed

- Some multi-use paths have legal speed limits that are enforced. Make sure to keep an eye out for these.

- Generally, maintain a controlled speed such that you can stop at any given moment if needed. The bike path is not the place to clock your record time for getting to the office.

- One person's abuse of privileges has negative consequences for others. Look ahead and around you at all times.

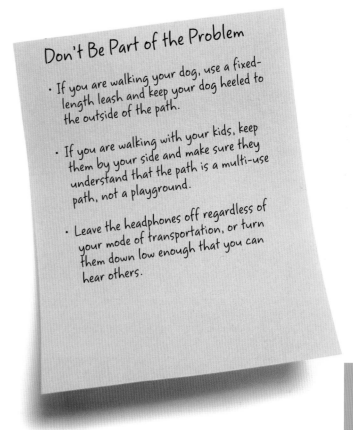

Don't Be Part of the Problem

- If you are walking your dog, use a fixed-length leash and keep your dog heeled to the outside of the path.

- If you are walking with your kids, keep them by your side and make sure they understand that the path is a multi-use path, not a playground.

- Leave the headphones off regardless of your mode of transportation, or turn them down low enough that you can hear others.

HOLDING YOUR LINE

The starting point for safe road riding is the ability to maintain a straight line

The beauty of riding in a group is the synergy of a collection of individuals moving along as a unit. But in order to enjoy this, some basic concepts and skills need to be understood and mastered. Riding close together requires a very keen awareness of where you are and where your co-riders are. Sudden movements in tight quarters can result in disaster. Therefore,

smoothness, grace, and predictability are the goals here.

Riding in a straight line is a primary skill that all cyclists need to begin with. That may sound silly, but riding in a straight line is harder than you might think. You must be able to ride consistently, regardless of the condition of the road, wind, weather, traffic stress, your fatigue level, and anything else.

Riding in a Straight Line

- Practice riding in a straight line on a road that is not busy, using the white line as a guide.

- Look ahead, relax your shoulders, and keep your elbows slightly bent.

- Aim to maintain a steady pace.

- Shift into different gears without wobbling or swerving at all.

- After you have mastered this, do the same out of the saddle or alternate sitting and standing positions.

Looking over the Shoulder

- After you are comfortable with holding a straight line, practice looking over your shoulder for traffic.

- Turn your head and use your peripheral vision. Try not to rotate your shoulders or take your hands off the bars.

- If you rotate your shoulders, you will inadvertently turn the handlebars also. Be aware of this and make sure your bike continues in a straight line while you look back.

Most commonly, turning your head to look for traffic or reaching for your water bottle can unknowingly cause your bike to swerve. But you must be able to do all of these things while maintaining a straight line and a steady pace. With time, this skill will become second nature, but a new cyclist or a cyclist new to group riding needs practice.

While you are alone, practice riding in a straight line. Use the line on the edge of the road as a guide. Remember to keep your head up, looking ahead several bike lengths. It's almost impossible to ride straight if you're looking down. Make sure to keep your elbows slightly bent and your shoulders relaxed. Get comfortable with simply looking ahead and riding along smoothly in a straight line at a consistent speed; practice drinking from your water bottle, looking over your shoulder for traffic, signaling with both hands, blowing your nose, and shifting. You should be able to do all of these things while maintaining a consistent speed and direction.

Riding with No Hands

- Find a flat, open area away from traffic.

- You need speed or a good pace to ride with no hands.

- Tuck the pelvis slightly and pull the belly button toward the spine. Doing this helps your balance.

- Lift your hands off the bars, sit up tall, and use your core for stability. Look ahead.

- Use small, controlled movements of your knees and body to maintain balance.

- Keep pedaling.

Drinking While Riding

- Drinking requires taking one hand off the bars to reach for the bottle and drink. Practice reaching for the bottle, drinking, and returning the bottle to its cage without swerving. Rehearse with right and left hands.

- Look ahead always, glancing down only to ensure that the bottle is secure.

- If the bottle drops, do not turn or stop the bike abruptly to retrieve it. Wait until you can safely go back to get it.

121

DRAFTING

Riding in the slipstream of another rider means an energy saving of 30 percent

Drafting is the art of riding close enough behind another rider to be in his or her "draft" or slipstream. The rider in front is said to be "in the wind," "pulling," or "working," and the rider in the draft is said to be "getting pulled."

Drafting behind another rider results in tremendous energy savings and, therefore, is a crucial skill for many situations.

Drafting allows you to keep up with a rider who may be stronger than you. By taking turns pulling, a group of cyclists can ride faster than if riding individually. Drafting can provide a recovery period after a hard effort. In racing, drafting is a given; this is where racing tactics begin.

Because of the close proximity involved in group riding, all

Basic Drafting

- Keep your front wheel approximately 12 inches or less behind the other rider's rear wheel. If you are farther back, you will not be in the draft.

- Do not stare at the rear wheel in front of you; doing this makes it harder to maintain a steady speed

and increases the risk of running into the front rider.

- Look ahead by finding a visual opening through the front rider and her bike. Keep your head up and be attentive, so that you are ready for any changes in speed or obstacles in the road.

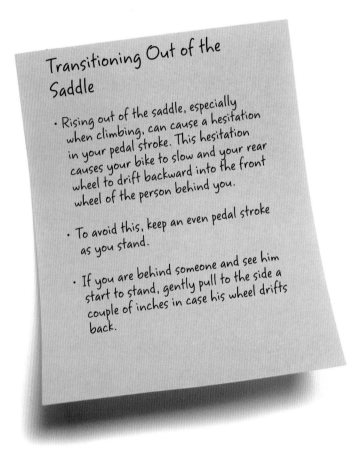

Transitioning Out of the Saddle

- Rising out of the saddle, especially when climbing, can cause a hesitation in your pedal stroke. This hesitation causes your bike to slow and your rear wheel to drift backward into the front wheel of the person behind you.

- To avoid this, keep an even pedal stroke as you stand.

- If you are behind someone and see him start to stand, gently pull to the side a couple of inches in case his wheel drifts back.

of your movements should be smooth, subtle, and predictable. For example, if someone is riding closely behind you, abruptly applying your brakes is not a good idea. If you need to slow down quickly, stop pedaling first and signal or verbalize your intention to stop. If you are the person behind, pay attention and keep your head up and looking ahead. You still have the responsibility to be aware of what's going on around you and what may be coming up ahead on the road.

One of the most common causes of crashing is overlapping wheels. If your front wheel touches the back wheel of the person in front of you, you will most likely be hitting the ground shortly thereafter. The rider in front is less likely to fall, because it is easier to recover from hits to the rear wheel.

Overlapping wheels is unsafe for novice riders. If you must ride thusly, do so with caution and be sure that both of you understand the repercussions. However, there are situations when overlapping wheels is acceptable among experienced riders. Regardless of your experience level, always "protect" your front wheel.

Drafting in a Group

- After you have mastered your drafting skills, get comfortable with riding close to your partner laterally, that is, with your handlebars 8–12 inches apart.

- By riding side by side and drafting, you create a compact group that can move more quickly and efficiently than if group members were riding individually.

- If there is a side wind, the leeward riders will be protected from the wind by the riders on the windward side of the group.

Drafting in the Wind

- Wind direction greatly affects where the optimal draft will be. In a side wind, the draft is slightly behind and to the leeward side of a rider.

- Rider formation in a side wind will resemble a diagonal, called an "echelon." This situation means there will be wheel overlap, which can be dangerous with inexperienced riders. In order to not take up the whole road, you may need to start a second echelon.

ROTATING PACELINE

Multiple cyclists working together can travel faster with less effort than an individual

A paceline is a more advanced form of drafting. A group of riders moves at a high speed, with each individual taking a turn setting the pace and then riding in the draft of the others. The most efficient paceline is one of constant rotation, which minimizes the time at the front or in the wind and maximizes the time in the draft. By doing this, a group

of cyclists can travel at a much higher rate of speed than an individual. This tactic is often seen in a race when a group is either trying to break away from or catch up to another group. Pacelines are most effective with four or more riders but can be done with fewer.

The easiest way to picture a paceline is like an oval. The

Rotating Paceline 1

DIRECTION OF TRAVEL

- The paceline shown here is rotating in a clockwise direction.

- Orange has just taken a pull and moved off to the right side as Red moves forward.

- At this point, Red will feel like the effort is harder because Red is exposed to the wind.

- Red must resist the temptation to surge at this point and continue riding at a steady pace.

Rotating Paceline 2

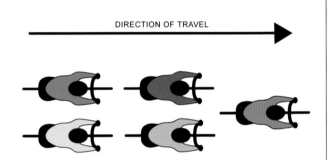

DIRECTION OF TRAVEL

- As soon as Red's rear wheel is even with Orange's front wheel, Red should start to pull to the right.

- Orange may yell "clear" at this point to help Red judge the timing. Ultimately, Red should be able to use peripheral vision.

- Red will move gradually, predictably, and subtly to the right. No swerving! This will give Orange time to adjust in case Red has sped up or slowed down too much while moving over.

leader is at the top of the oval and starts to drop back on one side as the other side pulls forward with a new leader. If all members are moving in synchronicity, the time at the front should be momentary before the next rider pulls around. The trickiest part of performing a paceline is timing.

A single paceline will use the formation below. Each person may take a longer pull at the front, such that the riders form a single line with one rider dropping back at a time. A double paceline is formed when members are riding two abreast, and the front riders peel off to each side, dropping to the back of the line they were just leading.

The most common mistake during a paceline is to "pull through" too hard, gapping the previous leader. If you pull over too soon, you risk hitting the front wheel of the previous leader and causing a crash. If you pull over at the right time but slow your speed drastically, you can cause the people behind you to brake, bunch up, and disrupt the pace. The ideal is to pull over gradually, while adjusting your speed slightly such that you create a draft for the former leader without his needing to adjust his speed or position.

Rotating Paceline 3

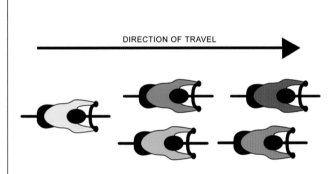

DIRECTION OF TRAVEL

- As Red moves into the "rest" column, Red soft pedals slightly while Blue moves forward. This change in speed should not change the overall speed of the group.

- If climbing, Red may need to continue to push to maintain the group's speed. If descending, riders in the draft may barely be applying pressure to the pedal, or even coasting due to the increase in draft.

Paceline in Action

- A successful paceline requires each rider to be comfortable with drafting and riding in close proximity to the other members.

- One wrong move, especially pulling over too soon, can take down the whole group.

- Master drafting skills and riding side-by-side before attempting a paceline.

- The best way to learn is to join a paceline of more experienced riders. In this way, you simply need to observe, follow, and do as they do.

ADVANCED CORNERING
A fast, properly executed corner is safe, smooth, and quite a thrill

To maintain a steady arc around a corner, keep your weight slightly back on the saddle, and your hands in the drops with one finger on each brake lever. You do not steer through a corner, but rather lean to turn the bike. The faster your speed or the tighter the turn, the more you will lean. Your outside leg should be down as you enter the apex of the turn. Drive your weight through the outside pedal while your inside hand pushes forward. Look ahead through the corner to where you want to go.

The fastest and best line in a corner is the straightest line to minimize your speed loss and need for braking. All of your braking should be done before you enter the turn. Heavy braking in a turn will cause the bike to track straight, missing the corner. Braking while the bike is leaned over can result in

KNACK CYCLING FOR EVERYONE

The Fastest Line

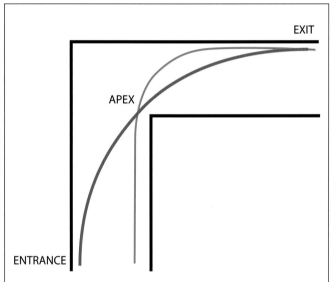

- Green: The fastest and safest line in a corner is the straightest line, thus minimizing your speed loss and need for braking.

- Swing wide for the entrance of the turn, cut in at the apex, and swing wide at the exit. Apply these principles within the lane width that you have.

- Red: If you approach the corner too tight, or start your turn too late, you will need to brake heavily to make the corner and avoid hitting the curb or blowing out of the turn on the exit.

Entrance

- Ride to the outside of the lane before approaching the corner.

- Finish braking before the entrance of the corner.

- Look to the exit of the corner as you set up your entrance. Begin to cut from the outside of the lane to the apex of the turn.

- Carry your speed into the corner and stop pedaling as you approach the apex.

your rear wheel skidding, or "fishtailing," or your front wheel washing out. If you have to brake, gently feather the brakes and apply both at the same time.

As soon as you pass the apex of the turn, resume pedaling to maintain your momentum. Generally, you do not want to pedal through the apex of a high-speed turn. Doing so can result in your inside pedal hitting the ground because the bike is leaned over.

Apex

- Look ahead and keep your shoulders relaxed and elbows bent in a ready, active position.

- Drive your outside leg down, weighting the outside pedal. Subtly push your inside hand on the handlebars through the turn.

- Develop a feel for this oppositional pressure. The more force you apply to your alternating hand/foot, the greater the control.

- The faster the turn or shorter the radius of the corner, the more you will lean the bike.

Exit

- Start pedaling after the apex of the turn when the bike returns to a more upright position.

- You can also safely shift your weight forward and sprint at this point. Acceleration out of a corner can mean the difference between getting dropped in a race and staying with the pack.

- Keep looking ahead and carry your momentum out of the turn.

- A well-executed corner will give the sensation of accelerating out of the corner.

SPRINTING

Successful sprinting is not merely a powerful burst of speed, but also an all-encompassing skill

When someone says "sprint," most people think of the sprint for the finish line. However, the explosive speed of a sprint is a useful tool in everyday riding, such as when you sprint to make a light or to get out of the way of a vehicle that doesn't see you.

A sprint is an all-out effort, focusing on maximum muscle recruitment and acceleration. Sprinting also teaches you to be comfortable with speed and riding in the drops. Even if you are not racing, throwing a few sprints into a long ride can be exhilarating and get the blood pumping. Sprinting requires 100 percent of your effort and lasts ten to thirty seconds. Later in this book, we will explain in more detail how to

Shifting to a Harder Gear

- Shift into a harder gear. This starting gear should be hard enough that you can get a good initial acceleration without needing to shift again right away.

- However, the gear should not be so hard that you can't turn over the pedals quickly enough to generate powerful acceleration.

Rising Out of the Saddle

- After you are in the right gear and ready to start your sprint, rise out of the saddle with your hands in the drops.

- Your weight should be evenly distributed when you come out of the saddle and begin your sprint. Otherwise, you may skip your

rear wheel if you lean too far forward while pulling/pushing explosively on the pedals.

- A balanced position will enable the most efficient and maximum muscle recruitment for a grand acceleration.

train for sprints (see page 159).

A well-executed sprint requires coordination and strength from your entire body. The explosive push/pull your legs exert on the pedals will in turn require stabilization by your arms by pulling in opposition on the handlebars. Doing this may cause the bike to rock back and forth. Although some upper-body movement is expected, it should not affect the direction in which you are traveling, nor waste energy by being exaggerated. For this reason, good upper-body strength and core strength are required for effective sprinting.

train for sprints (see page 159).

ZOOM

Sprint finishes in racing are common and very exciting. Timing and placement are critical. You'll need to learn to judge the appropriate distance to start your sprint and keep in mind how this distance will vary depending on the pitch of the road and the wind. Tactics also play a huge role here. Road teams often have a designated sprinter and a person to "lead out" the sprinter.

Correct Sprint Position

- Pull up with one leg while pushing down with every ounce of strength you own. Use all the muscles in your legs for consistent pressure and acceleration on the pedals.

- Use your arms to counter-balance against the force of your legs on the pedals.

- Grip the drops firmly and bend your arms at the elbows for a solid upper body.

- Keep your head up and look where you are going.

Incorrect Sprint Position

- Sprinting with your hands on the hoods is less effective. You will not be able to recruit as much power from this position and will not have as firm a grip on the bars.

- Rising out of the saddle without shifting your body

forward slightly will cause your weight to be disproportionately toward the back wheel.

- If your gear choice is too easy, you will not be able to generate an explosive acceleration.

LONG ASCENTS & DESCENTS

Big mountain riding provides beautiful vistas, a sense of accomplishment, and the thrill of the descent

Good climbing ability is all about efficiency. A high strength-to-weight ratio is always a good start for being able to climb like a mountain goat. Genetics aside, you should master many other subtle skills to make the most of going uphill.

First, think about where you want to expend your energy. Any upper-body movement or rocking side to side is not helping you go forward and up the mountain. Generally speaking, your upper body should be loose and relaxed, with all your energy focused on your legs and turning a smooth pedal stroke. Develop your climbing strength in the saddle, using out-of-the-saddle climbing to climb for only the really steep sections or to accelerate as you crest the hill.

Seated Climb

- Relax your arms and shoulders and maintain a slight bend in your elbows.

- Put your hands on the bars and keep your chest upright and open for easier breathing.

- On a very steep pitch, you may need to slide your weight forward on the saddle.

- Make sure to use all the muscles in your legs for a smooth, evenly pressured pedal stroke.

- Be in the moment and don't let the climb intimidate you.

Standing Climb

- Put your hands on the hoods when climbing out of the saddle. Doing this allows you to counterpull with each downstroke.

- Align your hips over the bottom bracket. Gravity will help drop your weight down into the pedals.

- Concentrate on smooth pedaling, pulling up and wrapping the pedal over the top of the rotation.

- Imagine you are running over 2-foot-high barriers; bring each leg up and around for the next step.

Descending on a road bike can be poetry in motion with a few key skills. When descending switchbacked mountain roads, all of your cornering skills apply in a linked series. Always descend with your hands in the drops because you have more control in this position. Remember to look ahead, weight the outside leg, and drive the inside arm through turns. Because you are descending, you'll want to also shift your weight back on the saddle.

While descending fast straightaways, getting low and aerodynamic is a valuable skill. By lifting off the saddle and shifting your butt back, you can flatten your back, making a more streamlined body position. Tuck your shoulders and elbows into your body to reduce air drag. If the road is straight, you may also move your hands close to the stem on the bar while keeping your elbows bent and upper body low. This position decreases the air surface of your upper body, but does not allow for steering or braking, so do this only on a safe, straight section.

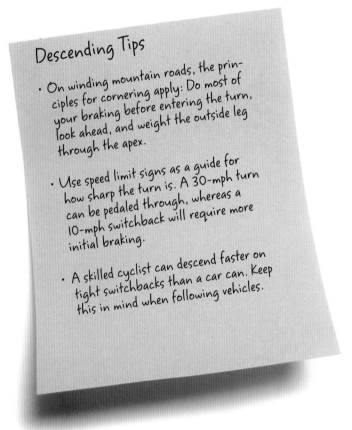

Descending Tips

• On winding mountain roads, the principles for cornering apply: Do most of your braking before entering the turn, look ahead, and weight the outside leg through the apex.

• Use speed limit signs as a guide for how sharp the turn is. A 30-mph turn can be pedaled through, whereas a 10-mph switchback will require more initial braking.

• A skilled cyclist can descend faster on tight switchbacks than a car can. Keep this in mind when following vehicles.

Descending a Mountain Pass

• A downhill tuck lets you slice through the wind. Think of your torso as a bag that catches air. You want to make the opening as small as possible.

• With the pedals in a horizontal position, scoot your butt back until your back is flat. Bring your belly low and your chin just above the stem.

• Having your knees up and lowering your upper body will direct air around you.

• Keep your head up and look down the road.

TRAILS & ETIQUETTE

We're in this together; let's commit to getting along and following the rules

Because mountain bikers are relative newcomers to the trails, trail access and user conflicts have become a hot topic. As a result, the International Mountain Bicycling Association (IMBA) was created in 1988 "to protect, create, and enhance quality trail experiences for mountain bikers worldwide." A small number of disrespectful riders can ruin the experience of many by causing trail closures. Know the rules of the trail, use common sense, and go out of your way to be courteous.

Consider your use of the trails and the opportunity to enjoy nature while riding your bike as a privilege. Respect your surroundings. Don't litter and leave no trace.

Trail etiquette includes respecting other cyclists. New riders

Share the Trail

- Bicycles must yield to all other trail users unless the trail is a bike-only trail.

- Horses are sometimes scared by bicycles. Getting off your bike and walking past them while talking helps.

- Although bikers are supposed to yield to hikers, many hikers will step off the trail to let you by. Be sure to thank them for this concession.

- Friendly communication with all trail users goes a long way in easing tensions.

Singletrack

- The term "singletrack" refers to a narrow trail, wide enough for a single rider.

- Downhill riders should yield to uphill riders.

- Anticipate other trail users around blind corners. Adjust your speed accordingly and call out or ring a bell.

- Muddy and wet trails are more vulnerable to damage. Riding in muddy conditions can leave long-term tracks in certain soil types, and bypassing the mud unnecessarily widens the trail. Consider alternatives in these conditions.

may feel less comfortable passing in close proximity while moving. On the other hand, you don't want to ride off-trail and widen the trail just to pass someone. In narrow situations, simply stop, move as far to the side of the trail as possible, and lean your bike out of the way instead of riding through the grass or brush.

The trails you ride will vary. Some are remnants of cattle/deer trails, and others were started by miners. Today, human-made trails are works of art. You, along with others, will covet these sweet spots. Take good care of them.

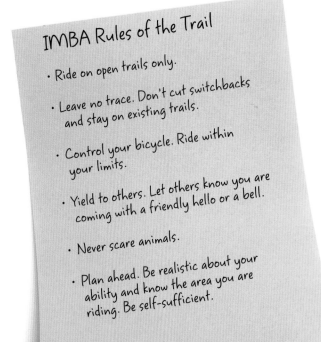

Dirt Path or Trail

- Paths popular for mountain biking include graded dirt roads, fire roads, Jeep roads, converted railways, canal towpaths, and doubletracks.

- Although some terms are used loosely and overlap in definition, they tell you something about the trails.

- Trails that run along old railroad routes have gentle grades. Jeep roads may be quite technical. Fire roads that run through forested areas are usually smooth and wide enough to ride side-by-side.

········· GREEN ● LIGHT ·········

When overtaking other trail users, it is helpful to let them know which side you are passing them on by calling out, "on your left" or "on your right" ahead of time. When you are passing others who are not in your group, communicate how many more people are with you. Call out, "There's three more coming" or "I'm the last rider" so that others will know what to expect.

IMBA Rules of the Trail

- Ride on open trails only.

- Leave no trace. Don't cut switchbacks and stay on existing trails.

- Control your bicycle. Ride within your limits.

- Yield to others. Let others know you are coming with a friendly hello or a bell.

- Never scare animals.

- Plan ahead. Be realistic about your ability and know the area you are riding. Be self-sufficient.

133

WEIGHT-SHIFTING & JUMPING

Take time to practice shifting your weight and learning how that shift affects your riding

Mountain bike riding skills can be boiled down to a few key elements. Most important is the ability to shift your weight on the bike. Doing this sounds rather simple, but it involves reading the terrain, having good timing, and having good balance.

The challenge and fun are in being able to negotiate over obstacles while staying on your bike, referred to as "cleaning"

a section of trail. Putting your foot down is called "dabbing." Although it's okay to do so, you'll realize that getting in and out of the pedals demands energy. On a long ride, that spent energy adds up. Also, adjusting where your body, and therefore your weight, is over the bike can make the difference between making it over a log and slamming your wheel into it.

Lifting the Front Wheel

- As you approach the obstacle, stop pedaling and press down into the bike (pedals and handlebars) to compress it. It's now spring-loaded.

- Shift your weight to the back wheel and quickly pull up on the handlebars. To

get the last bit of lift, bend your elbows more and suck up the front wheel.

- Practice a wheelie: Push down on one pedal, shift your weight back, and pull back and up on the handlebars. The saddle acts as a lever to help raise the front.

Lifting the Rear Wheel

- After your front wheel has cleared the obstacle, quickly shift your weight forward by pushing the handlebars away and rolling your wrists downward while sucking your legs up underneath you.

- Doing this unweights the rear wheel.

- If you are using clipless pedals or toe clips, pull up with your feet.

- Advanced maneuver: Pedaling forward on the front wheel only with the rear wheel lifted is called executing a "nose wheelie."

Broken down into bite-size pieces, being able to lift your front wheel, your back wheel, and both at the same time are crucial skills. The examples shown here are exaggerated for illustrative purposes. To skim over obstacles, merely unweighting and shifting your weight on the bike are often enough to navigate over many trailside challenges. "Unweighting" means lightening the load for a brief moment on your bike by shifting your body position or by lifting or pulling with your arms and legs, as needed.

············ GREEN ● LIGHT ··············

Skills drill: Practice lifting your front wheel and back wheel over an object on a flat surface. Beginners might start by simply practicing the movement on a flat surface and work up to using a 2x4 board, a low curb, or a railroad tie. Pick up your speed, practicing the timing of shifting your weight from back to front of the bike as your front wheel and then back wheel clear the obstacle.

Bunny Hop

- A bunny hop takes finesse, not brute strength. The front wheel comes up, arches forward, and leads the back wheel.

- Approach the obstacle with speed.

- Spring-load the bike and pop upward. Use your arms to push through the air and roll the wrists to lead the handlebars up and over the obstacle. Suck the bike upward with your legs.

- Try this on a flat surface first. Next, launch off a curb to land on both wheels.

When Do I Use These Skills?

- You might be wondering when you will use these skills in mountain biking. The most obvious application is getting up ledges and over logs and large rocks on the trail.

- But knowing how and when to shift your weight on the bike means you can pedal more quickly and more efficiently over rough terrain.

- As you get comfortable with shifting your weight, put this skill together with maintaining a constant and evenly pressured pedal stroke.

135

SWITCHBACKS

Many mountain trails incorporate tight switchbacks, requiring steady balance and concentration

A switchback is a hairpin turn. Think of it as a zigzag going up and down a steep mountain. The design is necessary to keep the pitch of the path reasonable enough for people to hike or ride it.

When climbing steep switchbacks on a mountain bike, apt balance, upper-body strength, and overall coordination are required to keep the pedals turning over, usually with hard effort. The slow speed involved tests your balance because you won't have momentum to help keep you upright. Arm strength and coordination come into play as you may need to pull up, push forward, and steer the handlebars simultaneously.

Uphill Switchback—Part 1

- Look ahead to where you want to go. Start your turn wide, using the outside of the trail.

- Do not lean your bike to turn. Stay upright and use the handlebars to turn the front wheel.

- Keep pedaling smoothly; stay high and to the outside of the turn.

- Drop your upper body and bend your elbows to lower your center of gravity. Scoot forward on the saddle, as needed, on steep pitches.

Uphill Switchback—Part 2

- Keep a firm grip on the bars as you steer around the corner.

- Use your outside hand as the guiding force when turning while also pushing the bike forward.

- Keep the bike upright and your body centered. At the apex of the turn, steer the front wheel toward the center of the trail.

- Increase your pedaling out of the turn to carry your momentum.

- Keep looking ahead to where you want to go.

When descending steep switchbacks, some of the same skills are called upon. Gravity can also work against you. A switchback, by nature, forces you to cut across the fall line of the slope. The fall line is the path of gravity; for example, the natural path that a rock or snowball would roll down the hill. After you start your turn, pointing your bike down the fall line, it is difficult to turn away from the pull of gravity. Completing the turn requires looking ahead, correcting body position, and shifting your weight back while maintaining control over the front wheel.

ZOOM

On a tight downhill switchback, locking up the rear wheel and sliding it around the turn area is one technique. However, this technique is not recommended because it also contributes to trail degradation. Similarly, braking late coming into a turn can create braking or stutter bumps in dry terrain. If you lack the skills to execute a safe turn, walk.

Downhill Switchback—Part 1

- As you approach the switchback, brake and slow down before the turn.

- Stand with your pedals horizontal and the inside leg back or press through the outside pedal and lift the inside.

- Look ahead at the line you want to take through the turn.

- Keep a firm grip on the handlebars with active arms to help steer and maintain control over the front end of the bike.

Downhill Switchback—Part 2

- Feather the brakes lightly as needed through the turn.

- If the surface is smooth, pedal forward so that your outside leg is weighted and down.

- If the surface has rocks or other obstacles in the apex of the turn, keep your pedals in a horizontal position and push your inside heel slightly toward the bike to help guide the bike around the turn.

TECHNICAL CLIMBING

Surmounting trail obstacles while climbing requires finesse and fitness

Technical climbing on the mountain bike has two crucial components: skill and fitness. Even someone with the best bike-handling skills will be unable to clear a technical climb if she lacks the fitness required to keep pedaling. Conversely, a super-fit athlete won't make it up a technical section if he lacks the skills to navigate the obstacles while climbing.

When faced with a steep pitch, beginner riders tend to automatically reach for the granny gear. However, your easiest gear may not always make for unproblematic climbing. On uneven surfaces, more torque is required to get over rocks, and so the easiest gear is not recommended.

Experiment with gearing on different climbs. As your skills

Seated Steep Climb

- On a flat, steep pitch, traction will be your biggest challenge. When riding on dirt, standing up is generally not an option because this position will move weight off the rear wheel and cause it to slip.

- Keep your head up and your body slightly over the stem. Drop your elbows while pulling down on the handlebars.

- Scoot forward on the saddle to keep the front wheel weighted. It may lift off the ground; this is okay. Keep pedaling.

Climbing Up Loose Rocks

- When climbing loose rocks, look far ahead. Choose the smoothest line.

- Maintain momentum and use a gear that you can spin efficiently, but not terribly fast. Soft pedal over the rocks; don't mash.

- Your body weight should be evenly distributed between front and rear wheels.

- If the bike veers offline, don't fight it. Let it move underneath you and keep your upper body relaxed. Readjust your line gradually to a smoother section of trail.

and fitness develop, so will your judgment for the correct gear. A good guideline is to pedal slowly and smoothly up and over technical sections as opposed to using an erratic, fast pedal stroke.

You can change gears in the midst of a climb, but doing this can put undo pressure on the chain. Shift up or down only one or two gears while the chain is under tension. It's best to be in the correct gear ahead of time. If you do shift, soft pedal for a moment, which helps make changing gears smoother.

········· GREEN ● LIGHT ·········

Many beginners ask how they can get better at climbing. They have the perception that for those who are fitter and faster, climbing is easy. In actuality, the effort level of a person with more fitness can feel much the same as that of a beginner. The difference lies in the speed with which the climb is completed. Increased fitness comes by challenging yourself and pushing beyond your comfort level.

Climbing Shelves—Part 1

- The skills used for climbing shelves, ledges, or large rocks are the same as those for weight shifting and bunny hopping.

- As you approach the ledge, unweight the front wheel, pull up on the handlebars, and apply a forceful downward pressure on the pedal with your dominant leg.

- You don't need to actually lift the front wheel up onto the rock. By unweighting the wheel and pulling up while pedaling forward, your tire will roll up and over.

Climbing Shelves—Part 2

- As soon as your front wheel has cleared the ledge, shift your body-weight forward to unweight the rear wheel.

- Keep pedaling while lifting up on the pedals a bit more as your move forward.

- If you have a hardtail mountain bike, this motion will need to be more exaggerated than if you have a full-suspension bike because the rear suspension will compress to help absorb the rock.

TECHNICAL DESCENDING

Mountain bikes are designed for rugged terrain; limitations come primarily from rider apprehension

Few things in life are more thrilling than completing a technical descent on a mountain bike. You'll experience equal parts fear, thrill, shock, and awe. It is an adrenaline rush, leaving you feeling proud and invigorated.

As we mentioned in earlier chapters, you must shift your weight back when descending. If you remained in a seated position while going down a steep hill, most of your weight would be on your front wheel, which can cause you to go over the handlebars. The importance of keeping your weight back cannot be stressed enough, especially on steep and bumpy pitches.

Braking also needs close consideration. Although you will

Steep Descent

- Stand on the pedals, cranks horizontal. Shift your weight back on the saddle (or behind it) so your weight is over the rear wheel.

- Squeeze the saddle with your inner thighs to help stabilize and steer the bike. Keep your arms bent

slightly to absorb bumps and maintain a firm grip on the bars. Keep your chin up, looking ahead, and engage your abdominals for stability.

- Control your speed with both brakes, using the front brake sparingly.

Descending Loose Rocks

- Carry your momentum. Limit braking on steeper pitches. A slow speed is harder. When in trouble, pedal!

- Look ahead and pick the smoothest line possible by envisioning how water flows.

- Stand on pedals with the cranks horizontal and shift your weight back to better allow the front wheel to roll over the rocks.

- Use your arms and legs to absorb the bumps as you let the bike move underneath you. Don't fight the bike.

want to control your speed on a downhill, you will also need to consider when and how to apply the brakes very carefully. Using too much front brake, or using the front brake at all in certain situations, can cause your front wheel to stick and result in an "endo" (going over the handlebars). However, not enough front brake and too much rear brake will cause the rear wheel to skid and will not slow you down.

Look ahead, scan the terrain, and choose your line accordingly. Keep your head up on steep drops. Your body tends to follow your gaze. If you stare at the large rock in the middle of the trail or cliff to the side, that's where you will end up. Repeat the mantra: "Look where you want to go," while riding technical terrain.

Finally, know your limits. Although challenging yourself leads to greater skills and confidence, getting in over your head can increase your fear and hesitancy, or even lead to injury. Push the envelope in incremental steps. If something is well beyond your capabilities, or if you are feeling a bit off on a particular day, make the smart choice and walk.

Dropoff—Part 1

- Slow down before the drop. Assess the landing ahead of time, if needed.

- The more vertical the drop, the more momentum you will need for the front wheel to roll through, so don't slow down too much.

- Stand on the pedals in a horizontal position and scoot your butt back over the rear wheel. Maintain a firm grip on the handlebars and keep your arms strong.

- Look up and ahead.

- Trust that the bike is designed for such a maneuver.

Dropoff—Part 2

- Do not touch the front brake during the drop!

- Let the bike drop down, absorbing the motion with your arms and legs.

- On a steep ledge, the saddle may slide between your legs as the bike drops, putting your body behind the saddle. This is okay.

- Use your arms to steady the bike laterally. Keep your chin up and look ahead.

- Reapply the brakes to control your speed after both wheels have landed.

141

TERRAIN TIPS—PART 1

Remind yourself that mountain bikes are designed to handle rough riding, so go for it

Mountain biking is an experiential sport. Part of its appeal is the fact that so many human senses are stimulated. The more you become adept at riding through varied terrain, the more heightened your experience.

The presence or absence of precipitation can greatly alter a trail surface, and therefore the riding experience. Trails that are muddy and slippery in the spring due to snow melt and spring showers may become loose, dry, and dusty by summer's end. The challenge of mountain biking is to acquire a quiver of skills that apply to any trail condition.

The International Mountain Bike Association rules of the trail recommend avoiding riding in muddy conditions. This

Sand

- Riding through sand requires you to be light on the bike while carrying your momentum.

- Get a little extra speed coming into the sand. Use a medium gear and keep pedaling.

- Do not brake in sand; doing so will cause the wheels to sink and stick.

- Keep your weight back a little and a light grip on the handlebars to allow the front wheel to surf through the sand instead of dive.

Mud

- Carry your momentum when riding through mud.

- The type of mud, depending on the clay and water content, will determine the rideability.

- Mud that sticks to your bike will lock up the wheels and

  mechanical parts. Use a stick to clean off the crud, or carry your "mud-heavy" bike.

- Avoid riding in high-clay content areas when they are wet. The tracks you leave will dry and harden, damaging the trail.

is because greater trail damage occurs when the trails are soft. This is especially true in arid climates where the soil has high clay content. In some locales, the trail may have a solid base beneath a layer of slop, making trail destruction less of an issue. When confronted with a puddle, it is better to ride through it than around it. Avoiding the puddle widens the trail. Ride responsibly by keeping the health of the trail, as well as your ride enjoyment, in mind. During a competition, race directors take into consideration mud and water conditions and may reroute the course.

Trail bridges come in all shapes and sizes. Some may be fully constructed practical affairs with a wide berth and handrails. Others may require keen balance to ride across. The North Shore of British Columbia inspired a whole new type of riding with human-made bridges and teeter-totters built into the trails for an added challenge. If you come across these kinds of obstacles, it is best to inspect the situation before riding. If you think you have the skills, go for it, but ride at your own risk!

Water Crossing

- Splashing through a water crossing can be fun. Look for a relatively smooth surface and carry your speed through to the other side. Murky water may hide deep holes or slick rocks.

- If the crossing is not rideable, consider carrying your bike across. Look for places with sure footing.

- In fast-moving water, carry your bike high enough to avoid it getting caught by the current.

- Clean and dry your bike after.

Bridges

- Bridges are either human-made or nature-made. Some may be a 2x4 plank of wood or a log over a stream.

- If a bridge is not rideable, carry your bike close to your body for better balance.

- If you feel unsure, hand your bike across to someone separately.

- Log crossings may be more easily navigated with bare feet versus stiff-soled mountain bike shoes, especially if the log is wet.

TERRAIN TIPS—PART 2
Full-suspension mountain bikes make technical riding plush and offer performance advantages

If you've been reading the previous pages on mountain biking skills, you may notice a trend. Distributing your weight and carrying your momentum figure greatly in many types of trail challenges. Those first skills meant to practice shifting your weight from one wheel to the other were not in vain.

We'd be deceiving you if we didn't tell you that your bike

makes a dramatic difference to how well you ride. Full-suspension bikes absorb the bumps and assist with traction, making terrain challenges more easily surmounted and reducing the margin of error. Full suspension offers you a "plush" ride compared to front suspension or a fully-rigid bike.

However, poorly set-up suspension can be worse than no

Dry Rock Gardens

- Sections of variable-sized loose rocks, euphemistically referred to as "rock gardens," present a challenge to be met with Zen-like balance and gusto.

- Keep your momentum by pedaling in a medium gear while shifting your weight

- as needed to let the bike move underneath you.

- Keep an eye out for larger rocks and time your pedal stroke so that you don't hit your pedal on the rocks.

- Riding aggressively is better than going slowly.

Slippery Roots

- Tree roots are slippery. Rubber tires just don't grab worn wood very well, especially when wet.

- If possible, approach roots perpendicularly and unweight each wheel while riding over them.

- If you must take roots at a more acute angle, lift each wheel over the roots.

- If your wheels do slide, don't fight the bike, but rather let it move beneath you, adjust your line as needed, and carry your momentum forward.

suspension at all. You'll know yours is set up incorrectly if it performs like a pogo stick or if the suspension rebounds too slowly. Similarly, a poorly fitting bike will greatly hinder your success in technical riding.

If you find yourself struggling, take some time to assess your bike fit and your suspension set-up. Read the owner's manual for your suspension fork and rear shock to best understand how they work and how to adjust the settings. Record this information and make incremental changes to determine your optimal settings.

ZOOM

Narrow trails cut into a steep hillside can be intimidating due to the steep drop-off to one side. When a trail slopes away from your desired direction, it is said to be "off-camber." The trick to staying upright is not to lean in to the hill (that makes the angle worse). When negotiating an off-camber turn, weight the outside leg to maintain traction.

Berms

- Berms are banked turns of varying heights that allow the rider to carry speed from entrance to exit.

- The fastest line is the lower part of the berm (shortest distance). The safest line is in the middle. The most fun is to hit the berm high at the apex and dive down through the exit.

- Use counterresistance by weighting the outside pedal and pushing on the inside bar. Use brakes subtly, if at all.

Carrying the Bike

- Unrideable sections of trail are referred to as "hike-a-bike sections," requiring you to dismount and carry your bike. If the hiking section is very steep, tight, or rocky, carry your bike up high so as not to get it caught on rocks or trees.

- Carry the bike on your right side, when possible, to avoid chain grease marks on your legs. Carrying the bike over the shoulder is most efficient for long hauls.

UPPER-BODY STRETCHES

Keep your shoulders, upper back, arms, and torso flexible by stretching before and after riding

Stretching is important no matter what activity you engage in. Stretching improves mobility, reduces aches and pains, and helps your coordination. It reduces muscle tension, improves blood flow and circulation, and increases your energy levels.

Failure to stretch may set you up for chronic problems.

Muscle tightness can create an imbalance, which leads to pain and potential injury. Cyclists are especially susceptible to upper- and lower-body tightness due to the repetitive motion of pedaling and using the muscles in a limited motion.

Cycling is a linear activity. All motion occurs in a single plane with no lateral movement. The limited range of motion of

Seated Twist

- Sit with a tall spine and legs extended to the front of your body. Cross the right foot over the left leg.

- Plant the right hand behind your body. Lift your chest and rotate your torso, bringing the left arm over the right knee.

- Keep your hips on the mat and look over your right shoulder.

- Hold the stretch for thirty to sixty seconds, breathing through your nose with deep rhythmic breaths.

- Repeat on the other side.

Midback Stretch

- From a standing position, fold your body forward with bent knees so that you can grab under your toes with your hands.

- Slowly straighten your legs until you reach maximum comfort, ideally straight, but without locking your knees.

- Round your back in a cat stretch and feel your mid-torso expand.

- Breathe deeply through your nose.

- Hold for thirty to sixty seconds. Repeat.

pedaling means your muscles are not contracting or extending to their fullest extent. Consequently, the working muscles become tighter, which in turn causes them to become shorter. Without stretching, overuse injuries and tightness in areas such as the low back, hamstrings, and knees can result.

When it comes to stretching the upper body, focus on options that incorporate lateral movements, such as twisting and bending in the opposite direction from which you find yourself sitting on a bike. Remember to incorporate the muscles of the fingers, forearms, chest, neck, upper and lower back, and torso. The following selection is not comprehensive, and you may need to research additional sources to complement these stretches.

Aim to stretch for five to ten minutes before and after every ride. Or designate a time every day to stretch. The recommended time to hold each stretch is thirty to sixty seconds. Your proprioceptors need at least thirty seconds to relax and release tension. Anything less offers little to no benefit. If it feels good, stretch longer. Just remember not to overstretch and stop if you feel acute pain.

Chest/Arm Stretch

- You need pre-existing flexibility to perform this form of chest/arm stretch. Otherwise, consider using a doorway and one arm to simulate the movement.

- Stand or kneel and grasp your hands low, behind your back. Lift your hands higher in back of you.

- Have a partner assist by lifting your arms higher, or carefully use a desk or counter yourself.

- Keep your head high and back straight and breathe deeply through your nose.

- Hold for thirty to sixty seconds. Repeat.

Neck Stretch

- Stand tall with feet shoulder-width apart and shoulders retracted. Engage abdominals and stabilize your core.

- Let your left arm hang down the side of your body. Hyperextend your wrist so that your palm faces down.

- With your right hand, grasp your head.

- Gently pull your ear toward your shoulder and press your left arm down toward the floor. Breathe deeply through your nose.

- Hold for thirty to sixty seconds. Repeat on both sides.

LOWER-BODY STRETCHES

Learn key stretching techniques to keep your legs, hips, and lower back supple and flexible

Stretching will improve flexibility, help with your cycling performance, and speed recovery between workouts. Focus on your buttock muscles, hip flexors, quadriceps, hamstrings, calves, inner thighs, outer thighs, and your illiotibial (IT) band when stretching the lower body. Use your bike as a prop to assist you with basic stretching. It is recommended that you

seek additional resources for more comprehensive stretching options in addition to the samples below.

The IT band is a fibrous reinforcement on the outside of the leg that connects the hip to the knee. Cyclists and runners are prone to iliotibial band syndrome (ITBS), which has been associated with knee pain. Unfortunately, the IT is difficult to

Hamstring Stretch

- In a wide stance, place your hands on the top of the bike, one on the saddle, the other on the handlebars.

- Keep your legs straight, without locking your knees, and bend forward until your upper body is parallel to the floor.

- Keep your weight on your midfoot and heels.

- Reach forward and continue dropping your chest deeper, feeling the stretch in the hamstrings, back, shoulders, and arms.

- Hold for thirty to sixty seconds. Repeat.

Quad Stretch

- Stand next to the bike with your feet shoulder-width apart. Place your right hand on the saddle.

- Bend the left knee and grab the left foot with the left hand.

- Keep your hips square. Continue lifting the foot higher

toward your buttocks, keeping the thigh as vertically straight as possible.

- Push your left hip forward, or pull your knee back for an extra stretch.

- Hold for thirty to sixty seconds. Repeat both sides.

148

stretch unassisted. Ask a physical therapist to demonstrate specific stretches that target the IT band. A good sports massage therapist will know how to work the IT band and also may be able to recommend additional stretches.

A foam roller is a good way to work on your IT band at home. You can buy one at a specialty store or online. Place the roller on the floor and roll the side of your upper leg gently back and forth. You may need to support some of your body weight with your hand and other foot if your IT band is particularly sensitive.

OFF-THE-BIKE FITNESS

Glute Stretch

- Stand next to the bike with your feet shoulder-width apart. Grab the saddle and handlebars.

- Place your right foot, right ankle side down, on top of your saddle (or top tube if flexibility is challenged). Let your knee fall out to the side, rotating at the hip.

- The left leg should be as straight as possible.

- Lean forward to increase the stretch to the buttocks and hips.

- Hold for thirty to sixty seconds. Repeat both sides.

Calf Stretch

- With your feet shoulder-width apart, place your hands on the top of the bike and lean the bike toward you.

- Step back with your left leg and place your toe on the floor. Slowly push your left heel to the floor. Hold this position for a moment and

then lunge forward with your right knee, lifting your upper body forward away from your left calf.

- Keep your left heel on the floor.

- Hold for thirty to sixty seconds. Repeat both sides.

STRENGTH TRAINING FOR CYCLING

Lifting weights will not cause you to develop extra bulk or decrease aerobic performance

There was a time when many cycling coaches and athletic trainers discouraged weightlifting for cyclists. The general consensus was that lifting weights would cause cyclists to develop bulk and decrease performance on the bike. Eventually, research won over misinformation.

Research has shown that strength training is good for your bones, your muscle strength ratios, and your connective tissue. You can improve your lactate threshold and become more efficient physically on and off the bike. Lifting weights allows you to train weak areas of the body with specificity and can be helpful in preventing overuse injuries, which are common in cycling.

Lunges

- Place dumbbells over your shoulders.

- With torso erect, step right leg forward. Do not let your knee pass beyond your toes, as this compromises the integrity of the joint.

- Make sure your weight is evenly distributed between both legs. The right thigh is parallel to and the left thigh perpendicular to the floor. Your knee should not touch the floor.

- Lunge only as low as comfortable.

- Repeat on the other side.

Squats

- Stand tall with your feet shoulder-width apart, shoulders retracted, and abdominals engaged. Hold dumbbells over shoulders.

- Toes and knees should be facing forward and aligned.

- Squat until thighs are parallel with the floor. Keep weight back on heels and knees behind toes. Avoid letting your knees buckle in or bow out.

- Rise by initiating the motion from your buttocks and lead vertically from your head.

Consider strength training year-round. Squats, lunges, and step-ups are excellent compound movements that work your lower body. Be sure to incorporate hamstring-specific and calf exercises (not shown) into your program.

Aim to lift weights three days per week in the off season and one to two days during the season. Two to three sets of twelve to fifteen repetitions of compound exercises and the same for specific muscle work, like hamstrings and inner and outer thighs, will keep you balanced and strong.

Step-ups

- Stand behind a bench or platform, dumbbells in hand.

- Retract your shoulders and engage your abdominals.

- Place right foot on the bench and transfer weight to your left heel. Keep hips square to the floor.

- With your upper body erect, push your weight into your right heel.

- With an erect upper body, lower your left foot to the floor while keeping weight on your right heel.

- Repeat on the other side.

Side Lunges

- Side lunges are a dynamic, athletic, lateral movement recommended for cyclists.

- Stand with your legs and feet together. Retract your shoulders and engage your abdominals. Keep your feet pointed straight out in front of your body during the movement. Step to the left side while keeping the right foot stationary.

- Do not lock out the knee and keep your upper body as upright as possible. The left knee will be aligned over your foot and behind your toes. Repeat on the other side.

COUNTERBALANCE EXERCISES

Poor position on the bike may indicate a lack of fitness in your core and stabilizer muscles

Take a moment to notice what people look like on a bike. Are their shoulders rolled forward with rounded back? Do their necks protrude out and look strained? Are their bellies hanging loosely without support? Unfortunately, these are common sights for a number of cyclists because they have neglected to train the muscles needed to ride with more stability.

A weak core, combined with neglected muscles and joints, causes painful riding experiences. The devil is in the details. Strengthen your midsection to sit properly on the saddle. A strong core will help with back strain and fatigue. Core strength improves power and cycling efficiently.

Pull-down exercises build strength in the upper back and

Core Exercise

- Use a fitness or stability ball for this exercise by sitting first on the ball. Walk your feet forward until your hips are off the ball and your lower back is resting on it.

- Place both hands behind your head, keeping your elbows wide.

- Without moving the ball or dropping your hips, curl your upper body toward the ceiling, maintaining tension throughout the crunch.

- Change arm and body position for variations.

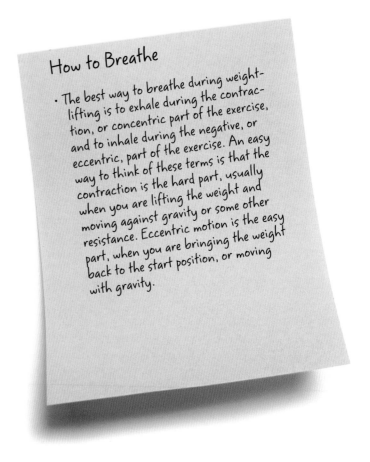

How to Breathe

- The best way to breathe during weight-lifting is to exhale during the contraction, or concentric part of the exercise, and to inhale during the negative, or eccentric, part of the exercise. An easy way to think of these terms is that the contraction is the hard part, usually when you are lifting the weight and moving against gravity or some other resistance. Eccentric motion is the easy part, when you are bringing the weight back to the start position, or moving with gravity.

shoulders. The latissimus dorsi (lats) are the largest muscles in the back. Building strength in the lats can help stabilize the shoulder joint while in motion. If the shoulder blade is unstable, too much pressure is placed on the rotator cuff. In addition, pull-down exercises educate your muscles so that on your bike, you can mentally cue yourself to drop your shoulder blades into your back pockets for proper scapular stabilization. Doing this helps keep the neck neutral and your shoulders relaxed during a ride.

Scapular Retraction

- Use an elastic toner/ resistance band for this exercise. Anchor an elastic toner overhead. Facing the anchor, grab the handles, palms forward and arms overhead.

- Retract your shoulders and engage abdominals.

- Keeping your torso tall, pull equally on both handles by bending your elbows. Lower hands to chest level.

- Keep hands, lower arms, and toner in alignment.

- Avoid overarching your back or moving your arms out of the vertical plane.

Support Muscles

- Internal rotation exercise:

- Use an elastic toner/resistance band for this exercise. Anchor an elastic toner at elbow height. Stand facing the anchor.

- Grasp the handle with your left hand, palm in. Keeping the elbow bent and fixed to the left side of your waist, rotate your lower arm out to the side. Initiate movement with the shoulder.

- Repeat with the other arm.

- Always stretch after training the rotators.

INDOOR CYCLING

Use a cycling trainer to work out during inclement weather and to fine-tune your technique

An indoor cycling trainer is recommended to maximize training. A trainer can be stored easily at home and pulled out when the weather or time of day prevents riding outdoors.

The advantage to using your own bike is consistency of the fit, as opposed to a stationary bike with limited adjustments. On your bike, your seat height, handlebar position, component specifications, and frame geometry are exactly what you are used to, increasing the transfer to real-life cycling.

Another profound component of riding your own bike is the q-factor. The q-factor is the distance between the pedals, compared to the width of your hips. If you are accustomed to your own bike, which has a particular bottom bracket width,

KNACK CYCLING FOR EVERYONE

Trainer

Place book under wheel for level riding

CompuTrainer

- An indoor trainer can be used with your personal bike. Trainers use air, magnetic, or fluid resistance in addition to some resistance from the bike's gears. Air and fluid resistance provide progressive resistance for the most roadlike feel.

- Resistance is not provided

by overtightening the roller pressure against the rear wheel, which will simply wear out your tire.

- Attach bike by clamping the trainer to the rear wheel skewer. Place a small block/book under the front wheel to position the bike horizontally (not shown).

- CompuTrainer is an indoor cycling trainer with an ergometer that allows you to measure wattage, heart rate, and cadence.

- An interactive video screen displays famous road and triathlon courses. CompuTrainer films the courses so that you experience real

race simulation. GPS mapping software makes you feel you are on the course.

- Advanced features include an aerodynamic drag factor software algorithm that adjusts to individual riders' body geometry and riding position.

the manner in which your hips and knees line up over the pedals is established.

Getting onto an indoor cycling bike or riding a fabricated gym machine changes this q-factor and can create a biomechanical challenge, sometimes leading to excessive soreness and injury.

Which indoor trainer is right for you depends on your needs and goals. Classic models that allow you to simply attach the rear wheel to the machine are very convenient. Add a heart rate monitor or connect your own cycling computer to the bike, and you'll have tools to track your performance and supervise your cardiovascular system.

High-tech CompuTrainers provide so much fun, interactive instruction that indoor cycling becomes more pleasurable. Let's face it: Spinning along the road to nowhere isn't really an adrenaline rush. So, if you are using a trainer to prepare for a race or other event, consider spending the extra money to get a product that will facilitate exhausting the long hours indoors.

Rollers

- Rollers develop a smooth, round pedal stroke, comfort at a high cadence, and balance. Recommended for intermediate to advanced level cyclists.

- Set up rollers next to a counter or wall for stability. At first, it will feel a bit like riding on ice. Hang onto the counter until you feel comfortable putting both hands on the bars.

- Look up and ahead for balance. As you get comfortable, try shifting, drinking from your water bottle, and sitting up no-handed for extra challenges.

Indoor Cycling Class

- Indoor cycling bikes are typically fixed gear. Some models incorporate a freewheel, allowing the wheel to spin without pedaling.

- Instructors lead a class of forty to sixty minutes using music as a prop, simulating various riding conditions.

- Great for individuals who need motivation and enjoy social networking.

- Not recommended as an accurate crossover to real cycling.

155

COMPLEMENTARY CROSS-TRAINING

Stay fit, add variety, and rejuvenate your mind with workouts that complement cycling

Cross-training is a combination of two or more types of physical activity. Cross-training helps keep you interested in exercise, giving your mind, muscles, and joints a break from monotonous stresses. Cross-training activities may simulate a similar cycling endurance effort or provide complementary fitness. Yoga, Pilates, and strength training are forms of cross-training that complement cycling year-round.

We encourage you to participate in any sport you enjoy as an adjunct to cycling. Some sports, however, are much better than others for maintaining cycling-specific fitness. Sports that target muscles needed for cycling, as well as cardiovascular-challenging workouts, will transfer more easily when

Yoga and Pilates

- Yoga dates back over five thousand years and is considered a spiritual practice by many. Yoga improves concentration, coordination, and flexibility. It can calm the nervous system, lower blood pressure, and relieve stress.

- Inverted poses are beneficial for reversing gravity after sitting on a bike. These poses enhance heart function, too.

- Pilates is a widely accepted practice that stretches and strengthens your core body muscles, improving posture and blood circulation.

- Each discipline is ideal to balance a cycling program.

Trail Running

- Trail running complements cycling by providing a weight-bearing endurance activity.

- Dirt paths are easier than pavement on your body. The uneven terrain is good for your ankles, balance, and agility. Running uphill is a motion similar to pedaling for effective crossover fitness.

- The time efficiency and lack of a wind chill factor make trail running a great cold-weather cross-training option for cyclists.

you get back onto your bike.

The caveat, however, is that you need to plan your training so that you don't experience overtraining symptoms. These occur when you consistently train too much, or too often, or when you fail to get enough recovery in between workouts. Overtraining can cause chronic fatigue, insomnia, injury, illness, and changes in appetite. This is a rarity for recreational athletes, but if you find that you are getting slower on your bike, are struggling during workouts, or are lacking enthusiasm, seek professional advice from a coach or an athletic trainer.

Skate Skiing

- Skate skiing is a variation of the classic cross-country ski technique.

- Cyclists cross-train during winter months with skate skiing because the motion of the skis mimics the pedal motion used on a bike.

- Major muscles used in cycling, including the quads, hips, glutes, and core, are worked out during skate skiing.

- The cardiovascular exertion is comparable to that of cycling, providing heart and lung endurance gains that transfer over to cycling.

Snow-shoeing

- Snow-shoeing is an affordable option that adds variety and intensity to winter training. It is easy on the joints and ligaments and is considered a low-impact sport.

- Deep snow works the glutes and hip flexors, and more so when climbing. This transfers over to more power in your pedal stroke when riding a bike.

- Hard-packed snow allows you to run with snowshoes, which help you increase turnover speed in the legs.

157

TRAINING PRINCIPLES

Training smart is as important as training hard; know the difference to capitalize on progress

Riding without a training plan can cause burn-out, boredom, and frustration. The body strengthens by applied stress and adaptation. If you ride at the same level of effort or on the same routes, without introducing new challenges, you will never improve. These miles are referred to as "slop" or "junk" miles because they bring little to no fitness improvement. To

get stronger, use systematic training.

Most pro cyclists use a winter preparation period (October through December) to maintain fitness, followed by prerace season preparation (January and February) to build endurance and unstructured anaerobic threshold training. Next, an early race season period (mid-February through April)

Building Endurance

- Base miles are easy aerobic rides and provide the foundation for cycling fitness.

- Ride at a pace during which your heart rate is at 65–75 percent of its limit.

- Greater endurance improves your short, intense intervals later.

- Work up to an endurance ride that is as long as your upcoming race or event. Calculate the hours it will take you to complete the event, not the miles, and use this as your training goal.

Threshold Intervals

- Lactate threshold (LT) intervals last four to thirty minutes.

- The best way to determine your LT is by testing in a lab. Alternatively, do a thirty-minute time trial at maximum effort. Your average heart rate or power for that effort will give you a good

idea of your effort at lactate threshold.

- Subjectively, without the use of a monitor, threshold intervals are efforts outside of your comfort zone, where your breathing is labored, but you are able to maintain the effort for some time, albeit uncomfortably.

develops endurance, anaerobic threshold, and high-intensity efforts, culminating in peak fitness during the race season (April to October.)

Customize your training program based on your individual ability, training history, outside responsibilities, and goals. Ask yourself questions, such as "How often can I work out?" and "What is my athletic background?" and "When do I want to peak?" and "What are my strengths and weaknesses?" Seek out a coach or training plan that allows you to personalize your own training program.

Here's a well-respected schedule for weekly race-season training: **Monday** is rest day, which may include a short, super-easy ride. **Tuesday** is sprint and interval training. **Wednesday** is medium-distance training with moderate intensity. **Thursday** is a long endurance ride. **Friday** is a recovery ride, or an easy spin if you are racing on **Sunday** or an off/travel day. **Saturday** is an endurance ride with some sprints and interval efforts. **Sunday** is race day! If you are not racing, then another endurance ride is recommended.

Strength Intervals

- Strength intervals develop cycling-specific strength for climbing and are referred to as "weightlifting on the bike."

- Find a steep hill and ride in an uncomfortably hard gear that results in an inefficiently slow cadence for four to eight minutes. The idea is to maintain constant loading on the muscles throughout the pedal stroke.

- Recover by spinning back down the hill and flatter terrain for an equal amount of time or slightly longer.

Speed

- Sprints last ten to twenty-five seconds and use 100 percent effort. They train your fast-twitch muscles and your body's ability to use ATP.

- Harder gears develop muscle recruitment and explosive power. Flat, straight, or slightly downhill roads develop leg speed.

- Sprint for an object, such as a street sign as an end point goal.

- Fully recuperate after each sprint until your heart rate is at or below 65 percent of its limit.

COACHING

To fully capitalize on systematic cycling training, seek out a qualified coach

They say numbers don't lie. If you keep an accurate account of your cycling training, there is no way to fudge the facts. Heart rate, training days, time on the bike, and other physiological data when written out are quantifiable. Take that information, let a third party look it over, and the information is further strengthened.

We have an ability to fool ourselves. Memory is unreliable. Even with a cycling journal, we might ignore the data. A coach or an online training plan that offers outside analysis can prevent this from happening.

How do you find a good coach? Referrals and word-of-mouth are the best option. Look for an accredited individual

Online Coaching

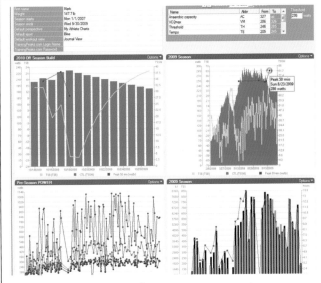

- Online coaching is one of the most popular forms of training. Packages allow you to speak to the online coach on a regular basis while inputting data online.

- Advantageous for individuals who do not have access to hands-on coaching and more affordable than one-

on-one attention.

- Consider an online option with phone coaching sessions, too. A real person will be able to adapt your training for unplanned events, like getting sick or suffering work stress and other fine-tuning.

Personal Coaching

- Prior to hiring a personal coach, research the individual's credentials. Is the coach certified through a governing body? What particular expertise does the person have? Ask for references and speak with other clients.

- Some coaches offer packages that include regular one-on-one sessions on or off the bike.

- If you can't afford a monthly plan, a one-time personal coaching session can provide the foundation to get you moving in the right direction.

with a cycling background. Speak with others who have worked with a particular coach and determine if his or her style will fit in with your desires. Of course, check price, too.

Online coaching at first glance seems impersonal. Nevertheless, online options are cost-effective and offer just the right amount of feedback and accountability to keep you on track toward achieving your goals. Plus, they are ideal for those of you living in remote areas without face-to-face options.

· · · · · · · · · · · · · GREEN ● LIGHT · · · · · · · · · · · · ·

Go backward. If you've got a favorite loop that you ride often, reverse directions for a more challenging workout. Chances are the route has become second nature, and your muscles and body have adapted to the nuances. Most riders enjoy the ego-stroking feeling of having prowess on a familiar training session. Changing the routine is vital to improving performance.

One-on-one

- One-on-one practical skills coaching can be a great way to make quick, significant improvements in your ability. The individualized attention means you will get to work on your weaknesses and ask questions.

- One-on-one skills training does not have to be from an accredited coach. Experienced riders, friends, and friends of friends can make excellent teachers. Even simply following a top-notch bike handler will improve your skills as you mimic his or her technique.

Motor Pacing

- Motor pacing is a training tool during which you ride in the draft behind a motorcycle or scooter. This allows you to ride at a higher speed than on your own and develops rhythm and speed.

- Used for sprint, interval, and endurance training, it is most advantageous for anaerobic threshold training because you can ride at a high heart rate for long periods of time.

- Make sure it's legal where you live. And know that your driver (coach/trainer) is proficiently skilled to hold a steady pace.

TRAINING

BOOKS & CLINICS

Read books for the theoretical knowledge of the sport; use camps for practical application

Make a point to read a couple of cycling books prior to embarking on the sport. Better than magazines, books provide a more complete profile of what cycling is all about. Conceptual knowledge provides a great foundation for the sport and gets you thinking before you head outside. Magazines are a great way to stay on top of what's new and exciting

in the sport. Recommended reads are listed in the resource directory of this book.

Although books provide the theoretical knowledge, practical experience is considered the finishing school. You would never read about flying an airplane and expect to be able to do so without practice. The same applies to cycling. Camps

Training Books

- Books are available for a variety of cycling disciplines. Browse the local bookstore if you like to flip through pages and see if it has what you are looking for.

- Online shopping is worthwhile because the catalog

of choices may be greater, but books are difficult to preview. Ask for referrals from friends and coaches.

- Subscribe to a cycling newspaper or magazine that has tips and articles. The information is typically fresh and up-to-date.

Clinics

- Clinics can be a full day of training or a multi-hour session. There are free and paid options available.

- Typically offered through bike shops, cycling clubs, and recreation centers.

- Clinics may start with a short lecture in which key points are discussed, followed by a group ride to practice the topic at hand.

- Once-per-week clinics can keep you progressing through a multitude of skills and drills.

and clinics are an excellent choice for new riders. Find one that caters to beginners, and you'll be surrounded by like-minded, enthusiastic compatriots. Being with others who are at your level is encouraging and provides an opportunity to meet future riding partners.

Skills clinics and camps are not just for beginners. Experienced riders can take their skills to the next level and get out of a riding rut. Practicing with deliberation, instead of just riding, is a powerful tool to improvement. Going back to basics, so to speak, should be practiced by all athletes.

Camps

- Typical camps run multiple days. You will eat, drink, and sleep bikes for the duration.

- In addition, camps are fun and bring together like-minded individuals. The support and encouragement from others quickly improve your skills, as well as your risk-taking.

- Choose a camp operated by someone who is both a reputable rider and has the ability to teach well. Remember that some folks have talent but can't seem to communicate their knowledge to others.

MAKE IT EASY

You are going to need to blow your nose when cycling. Two options are available: (1) Use a tissue or handkerchief or (2) learn the farmer's blow. The farmer's blow is when you plug one nostril with your hand and blow heartily out the other nostril. Make sure no one is behind you, lean out to the side of your bike a bit, and let 'er rip.

Why Cyclists Shave Their Legs

- If you have a sliding crash on asphalt, the hair on your legs can contribute to the ripping off of more skin (called "road rash"). Hair makes cleaning the wound harder and is uncomfortable when changing bandages.

- The leg grippers on shorts can make the hair ball up and rip off your legs while riding.

- Massage, which cyclists get often, is more comfortable with smooth skin.

- Shaved legs show off muscle definition and feel good on clean sheets.

163

TECH TRAINING TOOLS

Don't be left in the Dark Ages; today's sophisticated devices use technology to your advantage

Devices that monitor your heart rate, pedaling cadence, power output, and other performance indicators are readily available on the retail market. Some products are extremely complex while others are reasonably simple. It's how you use the information that determines their usefulness for training.

Heart rate monitors (HRMs) were amongst the earliest electronic-based training tools that provided data necessary to improve athletic performance. A strap worn over the chest sends a signal to a display (typically a watch or bike computer) that shows your heart rate in beats per minute (bpm).

HRMs provide an objective measurement of how hard your body is working. Heart rate also can tell you when your body is

Heart Rate Monitor

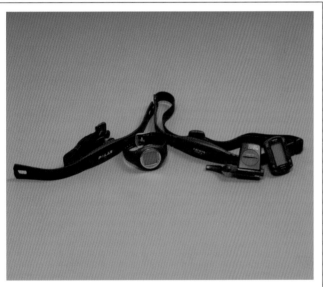

- Heart rate monitors allow you to stay in your target zone.

- To determine your maximum heart rate without sophisticated testing, subtract your age from 220.

- You can also get a good idea of your maximum heart rate

- by wearing a monitor during a race or long, all-out sprint.

- An established guide is 60–70 percent of maximum heart rate equals endurance training; 70–80 percent of maximum heart rate equals threshold training; 80–90 percent of maximum heart rate improves VO2.

Power Meter

- Power meters provide an objective measurement of your real power output.

- Compared with a heart rate, power output is immediate, whereas it takes time for your heart rate to climb to the desired zone. Power output can decline while heart rate remains constant

- over time due to fatigue.

- The most commonly used power meters measure power with a torque-measuring crankset or hub that replaces your current equipment and a handlebar-mounted screen for reviewing the information.

unwell, when you are symptomatic of overtraining, and when you are well-trained. The proliferation of this tool resulted in more accurate training plans, assessment, and, ultimately, improved performance for elite and recreational cyclists.

While HRMs measure the physiological effect of your effort, power meters measure the power you deliver to the wheels. A power meter works by measuring the force that moves the bike forward multiplied by the velocity. No matter what your heart rate reads during a training ride, the true test of how strong you are is determined by power to the pedals.

Regardless of technological equipment that measures your physical and mechanical exertion, your subjective effort will remain key training information. For example, if your heart rate is elevated, but you feel like you are not working that hard, this can indicate stress or a lack of adequate rest. Objective data alone is not enough. Hence, for the ultimate effective training plan, a combination of information will give you the most complete picture.

Electromuscle Stimulation

- Electromuscle stimulation, also called "EMS" or "eStim," generates electrical impulses that trigger an action potential in muscle nerve fibers (motor neurons).

- Twitches performed by EMS are the same as a muscle contraction generated by the body's nervous system in response to regular exercise.

- EMS has been demonstrated to perform more work with less oxygen in your Type I (slow-twitch) muscles. This strength gain can improve your endurance cycling.

Contour Sport EMS Technology

- The brain typically recruits approximately 40 percent of the muscle fibers and cannot discern between fiber types. The brain also has a "limiting switch" that always keeps some of the muscle in reserve for emergency purposes. Contour Sport EMS can accomplish three things that are outside of the brain's capabilities:

- Recruit and synchronize more of the muscle fibers in any muscle group than traditional exercise.

- Create more muscle activity in muscles being worked.

- Target specific muscle fibers, depending on the frequency: slow-twitch, fast-twitch, and very fast-twitch fiber.

PHYSIOLOGICAL TESTING

Sport science testing procedures tell you how to maximize training by using zones

Pick your parents well. That's the number one way to ensure impressive athletic ability. The rest is up to you and how well you apply yourself. Your physiological capabilities can be greatly improved with training, with the exception of your VO2 maximum (your aerobic engine), which is limited by genetic potential. If you are unfit, chances are you can improve your VO2 max through training volume and intensity more than an individual who is already in excellent condition. This actuality is most likely due to the fact that fit athletes are already at their genetic potential.

An average VO2 is 40–47 mL/kg/min for a male of thirty to thirty-nine years and 34–41 mL/kg/min for a female of the

Simplified Training Zones

- Zone 1 = Active recovery (warm up/cool down).

- Zone 2 = Base or basic endurance (conversational pace/feels easy).

- Zone 3 = Tempo (moderate effort that feels like training).

- Zone 4 = Subthreshold (moderate to hard but manageable effort).

- Zone 5 = Suprathreshold (hard effort that can be sustained only for short periods).

- Zone 6 = VO2 (intense maximal or near-maximal effort).

- Zone 7 = Anaerobic capacity/sprint.

Lactate Profile

- A lactate profile test measures your body's responses to exercise intensities.

- Test protocol typically involves a ten- to fifteen-minute warm-up, four-minute stages of gradually increasing intensity, and a cool-down. You will not reach a maximal effort

- during a lactate profile test, although it may feel very uncomfortable.

- Values that are taken into account include heart rate, rate of perceived exertion, blood lactate levels, and the intensity at which you reach the lactate threshold (LT).

same age range. Olympic athletes are in the range of 65-plus for men and 59-plus for women. Lance Armstrong, for example, is reported to have a VO2 max of 85 mL/kg/min, which explains a lot about his prowess on the bike. When you get tested, don't be discouraged if you don't have a super-high VO2 max. Many other factors come into play. For example, someone with a super-high VO2 may not win a gold medal because the individual lacks the mental toughness.

Lactate threshold (LT) is your most trainable zone and the most important for being able to sustain long, hard efforts. LT changes over the course of a year, depending on your fitness level. Although your heart rate at LT may stay approximately the same, your power output and speed will drop during the off-season and when you are not training your LT. Gains occur when you do structured interval workouts near your LT.

Physiological testing in a laboratory is the most accurate measure of the physiological determinants of your endurance performance. A facility such as the Boulder Center for Sports Medicine in Colorado follows strict test protocols and provides expert analysis.

Maximum Oxygen Uptake

- VO2 max (aka "maximum oxygen uptake") is the fastest rate at which your body can use oxygen to make energy.

- The higher your VO2 max, the better you are equipped to be an elite endurance athlete.

- A performance lab is needed to ascertain your VO2 profile, which shows your oxygen consumption measured against exercise intensity until it plateaus as your muscles fatigue.

- Testing lasts ten to fifteen minutes and requires an all-out effort.

Results Graph Sample

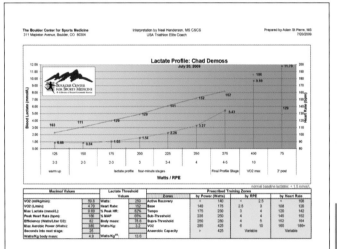

- This is an actual graph from Chad DeMoss, a Colorado athlete who volunteered to undergo testing at Boulder Center for Sports Medicine.

- He achieved a VO2 of 59.8 mL/kg/min, a good rating. His peak heart rate was 186 beats per minute (bpm).

- With this data, Chad can design a training plan using his heart rate zones and his power in watts.

- The recommendation is that Chad reevaluate in three to six months.

ORGANIZED RIDES

Cycling events and organized rides are great for challenging yourself and meeting other cyclists

Organized rides come in many forms. They can be charity events, century distance rides, or 20-kilometer tours through cityscapes. Typically, they are organized by race directors who arrange food and water and first aid stations and map out a safe route. They also require a permit, which is why riders pay a registration fee and sign waivers.

Multi-day tours are a great way to explore a new area. Instead of plotting your own route and having to deal with transporting your gear either via your bike or a vehicle, an organized tour will take care of these logistics. Riding point-to-point routes allows you to cover more terrain than you might if planning on your own. Some tours, such as Ride the

Organized Rides

Charity Rides

- Organized rides or tours may be single-day or multi-day supported events. You need only pay your entry fee, and the logistics are taken care of for you.

- Typical benefits include aid stations with food and water along the route,

police officers to ensure safety at intersections, course marshals to direct you, and a sag wagon for transporting gear.

- Single-day events often have multiple distances to choose from to accommodate different ability levels.

- Charity rides generally incorporate all of the attributes of an organized ride or tour, except the added bonus of supporting a charity.

- Some charity rides donate a portion of your entry fee to the charity, and others

ask you to raise a certain amount of money, with prizes for the individual or team raising the most.

- These events have the added inspiration of letting riders meet participants who are the beneficiaries of the charity.

Rockies in Colorado, offer camping or hotel lodging options.

Tours that follow major bike race routes in Europe are a popular way to explore an area and get a taste of what the pros experience. Some tours are small group affairs run by private outfitters; others are public events that also raise money for charities. Most organized rides are held on roads, but there are off-road options as well. See the chapter on cycling vacations for more ideas.

Cycling Festivals

- Cycling festivals are often weekend-long events that incorporate many cycling-related activities.

- Festivals may include races, organized rides, bike demos, exhibitors, food, and entertainment.

- Festivals may be organized around a keystone event, cause, or theme. Appealing destination locations are common.

- Mountain bike racing began in the spirit of festivals as a way to distinguish the sport from its more traditional road racing cousin.

Club Rides

- Cycling clubs come in different shapes and sizes. Often there will be a focus on a particular type of riding or rider.

- Cycling clubs organize their own informal rides. These rides may or may not be open to nonclub members.

- You can find cycling clubs in your area via the same sources as organized rides. Ask around in the cycling community for the inside scoop on different clubs before joining to make sure the club is a good match for you.

OUT OF THE NORM

There seems to be no limit to what can be done while riding a bike

You are probably starting to notice that cyclists come together in many organized ways to enjoy the sport. Organized rides or tours and racing are the most common and straightforward events. But the possibilities do not end there. Cycling events that cater to a particular sub-subculture of the sport may be harder to find but still gain a dedicated following.

Some cycling events double as a form of advocacy or demonstration. Other events combine cycling with sporting aspects. Still, others are just for the fun and spirit of a particular theme or type of riding.

Critical Mass began in 1992 in San Francisco, California, as a way to bring attention to cyclists' rights. Typically, a mass of cyclists follows a designated route through an urban area, often blocking traffic and effectively taking over the roads.

Critical Mass

- Held the first Friday of every month in cities worldwide.

- Part protest, part social gathering, part parade, and part loosely organized ride, these rides have sparked support, controversy, debate, and opposition.

- Cycling advocacy groups and others concerned about the subversive impression of Critical Mass have organized Critical Manners rides in some cities. Cyclists ride through the streets, obeying all traffic laws and perpetuating friendly interaction with motorists.

Bike Rodeo

- Bike rodeos often incorporate safety and bike-handling skills. Participants gain points for each event; the highest score wins.

- Common events include a safety check, helmet inspection, zigzag course, stop on a dime, ride in a figure-eight without putting a foot down, and a simulated newspaper route.

- Bike rodeos combine fun competition with skills-learning opportunities for an educational cycling event.

Some participants intentionally block side street traffic, allowing the mass to proceed through red lights. This practice is called "corking." There is no formal leadership or structure to Critical Mass rides, sometimes referred to as an "organized coincidence," which makes it hard to accurately identify the intended message of the ride, if there even is one.

ZOOM

Artistic cycling is a lesser-known sport but incredibly impressive to watch. Individual, paired, or four- or six-person teams perform acrobatic tricks on specialized bikes. The bikes are fixed gear with no brakes. The handlebars are turned up and attach directly to the steer tube. Participants are given a fixed length of time to perform figures and tricks and awarded points by six judges.

Bike Polo

- A team sport that mimics equestrian polo using bikes instead of horses. Players use a long-handled mallet to hit a ball into the opposing team's goal. There are penalties for dabbing your foot to the ground.

- Mallets can be purchased or made out of household items.

- Played on a grass field using mountain bikes or on hard surface courts. Some players prefer fixed gear bikes for the game.

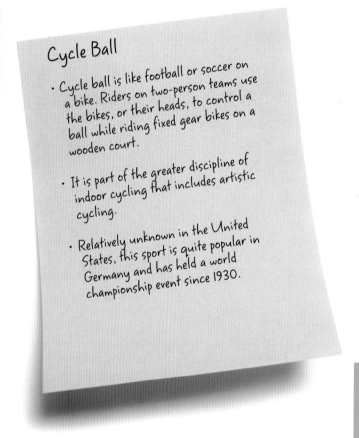

Cycle Ball

- Cycle ball is like football or soccer on a bike. Riders on two-person teams use the bikes, or their heads, to control a ball while riding fixed gear bikes on a wooden court.

- It is part of the greater discipline of indoor cycling that includes artistic cycling.

- Relatively unknown in the United States, this sport is quite popular in Germany and has held a world championship event since 1930.

171

ROAD RACING

Road racing is a sport that combines individual effort with team tactics

For some, road racing is the natural next step after buying a road bike and riding recreationally. For others, road racing is a secret society they long to join but aren't sure where to begin. Many wonder if they are good enough to try a race.

If cycling generally has its own vocabulary, road racing has its own dialect. There's no wonder that new entrants are intimidated. Any given race flyer lists numbered categories, informs that race support is "wheel in/wheels out," and threatens that the "yellow line rule" will be strictly enforced. In reality, you don't need to know a special handshake or have a predetermined threshold of fitness to try your first race. Most road races have categories based on ability, so you will

Road and Circuit Races

- A road race is a mass start event and can be one large loop, a point-to-point, or several medium-length circuits.

- Often race support follows each category with extra wheels in case someone gets a flat tire or has a mishap.

- "Wheels in/wheels out" means you must put your own spare set of wheels in the race support vehicle.

- "Neutral support" means wheels are provided (to be returned after the race).

Criteriums

- A criterium is a mass-start event run on a 1–5-kilometer closed (to traffic) course.

- Racers complete as many circuit laps as possible during the allotted time. First to cross the finish line wins.

- The referee counts down five laps to go, holding up placards.

- "Primes" are special prizes offered on a particular lap. A prime lap and the last lap of the race are signified by a ringing bell.

generally be grouped with like-fitness individuals. These categories are usually based on a number system, with the lowest number being the most experienced (that is, Category 1) and beginners being grouped into Category 4. Some larger races will further differentiate groups by age.

For starters, it is helpful to know what kinds of road races are available. Pick an event that sounds appealing and suits your strengths. Stage races and omnium races are multi-day races. Each day's race, called a "stage," counts toward the overall winner. The winner of a stage race is determined by the lowest combined time. An omnium uses points awarded for a rider's placing in each stage to determine the winner. Omnium races are called the "pentathlon of cycling."

Road racing is unique in that it simultaneously incorporates individual effort with complex team tactics. During a race, you might work together with someone to form a breakaway and then sprint against that person for the win. You do not need to master tactics when starting out, but pay attention and learn from those who are more experienced.

Time Trials

- A time trial is an individual race against the clock. No drafting or any other form of working together is allowed.

- Racers start at set intervals, for example, every thirty seconds.

- Special time trial bikes that are built for speed and aerodynamics are often used.

- Team time trials are raced in a similar fashion, except with a small team of riders whose members work together to go as fast as they can.

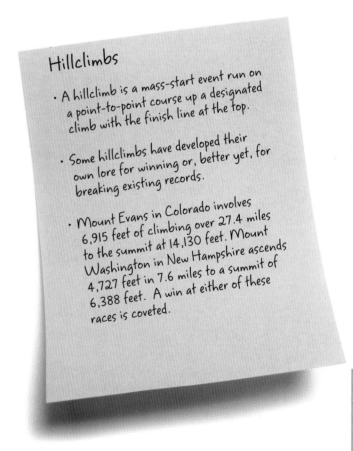

Hillclimbs

- A hillclimb is a mass-start event run on a point-to-point course up a designated climb with the finish line at the top.

- Some hillclimbs have developed their own lore for winning or, better yet, for breaking existing records.

- Mount Evans in Colorado involves 6,915 feet of climbing over 27.4 miles to the summit at 14,130 feet. Mount Washington in New Hampshire ascends 4,727 feet in 7.6 miles to a summit of 6,388 feet. A win at either of these races is coveted.

173

MOUNTAIN BIKE RACING

Even though you compete against others, the ultimate contest is between you and the mountain

Although a relatively new sport, mountain biking has spawned several specialty off-road events in a short amount of time. The Union Cycliste Internationale (UCI) is the international governing body for road, track, cyclocross, BMX, trials, and mountain biking. Currently, the UCI designates world champion titles for cross-country, downhill, four cross, and trials. A world champion is also recognized for the marathon event, which is a longer version of cross-country. Similar to alpine ski racing, mountain biking has a world cup race series of eight races each for cross-country, downhill, and four cross. Only the cross-country event has Olympic medal status, gained in 1996.

Originally, mountain bike races required all riders to be self-

Cross-country

- A mass-start event that may consist of one large loop, a point-to-point course, or several shorter loops.

- The best courses have a combination of singletrack, doubletrack or fire roads, technical sections, undulations, climbs, and descents.

- Olympic distance cross-country races last approximately two hours for the professional category. Marathon events may be 60 to 120 kilometers in length.

- Hardtail, full-suspension, and 29-inch wheeled mountain bikes are used.

Observed Trials

- Riders negotiate an obstacle course during a time limit.

- Competitors get points for dabbing (putting a foot down), resting a part of the bike on the ground or an obstacle, going outside the course boundary, and exceeding the time limit.

- The rider with the lowest points wins.

- There are two trials categories. Stock uses a relatively unmodified mountain bike. Trials bikes must have wheels no smaller than 20 inches and brakes on each wheel.

sustainable. This meant that racers had to carry equipment for changing a flat or fixing any mechanical problem during a race. Outside help of any kind was prohibited. The UCI modified this rule a couple of years ago to allow outside technical assistance within a certain zone on the course. Beyond this zone, riders may receive help only from another rider on the same team. Riders must finish with the same bike frame and number plate. However, for the local racing level and for practicality, you should always be prepared to fix your own mishaps in a mountain bike race.

Downhill

- A time trial-format race run on a point-to-point course, with the finish line at the bottom.

- Incorporates large drop-offs and other extreme, technical elements.

- Downhill racers use specialty full-suspension mountain bikes with over 5 inches of travel in the front and rear.

- Racers often wear protective gear such as a full-face helmet, arm and knee pads, and chest protectors.

Four Cross

- Inspired by BMX racing. The event pits four riders at a time on a fast downhill course that includes jumps and berms.

- Four cross replaced dual slalom in the UCI World Cup series in 2002. Dual slalom used a head-to-head format that resembled dual slalom ski racing.

- Racers use full-suspension or hardtail bikes with a single chainring and frame design to optimize cornering and acceleration. Bikes are light, nimble, and aggressive.

ADDITIONAL COMPETITIVE EVENTS

Competitive cycling is limited only by what is possible on a bike; possibilities are endless

Other types of bike racing exist as stand-alone events instead of fitting into a larger genre. A specific locale or season makes these events less likely to be combined with other types of bike racing.

Track racing is perhaps one of the oldest forms of competition in the sport. Gaining huge popularity in the 1890s, track racing uses fixed gear bikes with no brakes. Races are run on an oval track with banked sides, called a "velodrome." Velodromes may be indoor or outdoor and are usually made of concrete or wood. Track racing is still a big draw in the summer Olympics, with the Kierin, Madison, Points, Pursuit, and Sprint events contested.

Track Racing

- Fixed gear bikes with no brakes are raced on an oval track with banked sides, called a "velodrome."

- Velodromes range from 250 to 400 meters in length. Track events include time trial formats, tactical head-to-head sprint matches, and team events.

- The Madison event has a relay format in which riders grab hands to transfer the overtaking teammate's momentum to the next rider.

- The first world championships were held in 1895.

Cyclocross

- Mass-start, timed event lasting an hour or less.

- Under UCI rules, courses use a 2.5–3.5-kilometer closed loop that may include up to six obstacles requiring dismounting, such as sand pits, logs, steep run-ups, and barriers.

- Riders are allowed to get technical help in a designated pit area, including a full (clean) bike.

- Uses bikes with drop handlebars, 700c wheels, and slightly knobby tires. Disc brakes and flat handlebars are forbidden, according to UCI rules.

Cyclocross developed in the 1940s as a way for European road racers to stay fit in the autumn and winter months. As the sport gained popularity, racers chose to focus on this discipline in and of itself. Cyclocross incorporates running dismounts and remounts of the bike in order to jump over human-made barriers or natural obstacles. A technique for shouldering the bike while running is also part of cyclocross-specific skills. Due to the time of year, muddy, wet, cold conditions are synonymous with cyclocross. This spectator-friendly sport is also known for its beer-fueled, cowbell-wielding, animated fans who are devoted to the sport.

In the late 1960s, young Californians who couldn't afford to participate in motocross imitated the sport on their bicycles. BMX was born. BMX races use a 350-meter circuit with jumps, banked corners, and other challenges. Riders compete in heats of eight, with the top four moving to the next round. BMX has gained worldwide popularity. The first world championships were held in 1982. In 1993, BMX was included under the governing umbrella of the UCI. BMX racing attained full medal status at the 2008 Olympics in Beijing.

BMX

- Mass-start, timed event run in heats of eight riders. The top four riders advance to the next heat.

- Uses rigid-frame bikes with 20-inch wheels. Bikes must have a working rear brake; a front brake is optional.

- There are restrictions regarding tire size, handlebar width, accessories, and protruding parts.

- Also may feature a 26-inch-wheeled "cruiser" class.

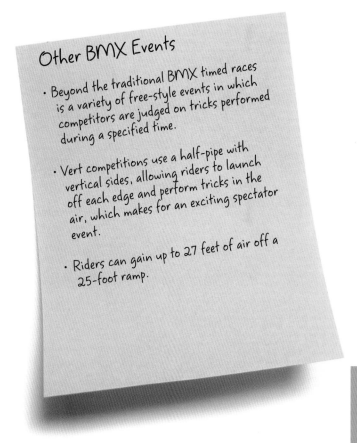

Other BMX Events

- Beyond the traditional BMX timed races is a variety of free-style events in which competitors are judged on tricks performed during a specified time.

- Vert competitions use a half-pipe with vertical sides, allowing riders to launch off each edge and perform tricks in the air, which makes for an exciting spectator event.

- Riders can gain up to 27 feet of air off a 25-foot ramp.

ENDURANCE EVENTS

For some, the mental and physical challenge of covering ultralong distances is appealing

Endurance racing combines fitness with mental fortitude. Endurance cyclists, often riding alone, must not only develop the ability to maintain a constant fast pace for many miles, but also keep their mental focus and drive.

Proper hydration and nutrition pose a special challenge for long-distance athletes. The usual fare of energy drinks and bars is not enough to sustain riders during such long periods of effort. Determining what food is desirable and provides sustenance without upsetting the digestive system requires much trial and error during training rides. Ultimately, the wrong choice of food can prevent even the fittest athlete from finishing.

Race across America

- The Race Across America (RAAM) traverses the country, covering just over 3,000 miles and climbing over 100,000 feet.

- Participants race individually or in two-, four-, or eight-person teams and require a support caravan.

- The race is one really long time trial. There is no drafting, and the clock doesn't stop until riders reach the other side of the country.

- Racers balance sleep and time off the bike against ride time for maximum efficiency.

Brevets

- Also called "randonnée"; an organized ride that requires riders to complete a designated but unmarked route in a specified amount of time.

- The route passes through checkpoints where riders have a card verified and can receive outside help.

- Otherwise riders must be self-sufficient.

- Typical lengths are 200, 300, 400, and 600 kilometers.

- Paris-Brest-Paris, a 1,200-kilometer out-and-back course, began in 1891 and is held every four years.

Events that last for longer than daylight hours require a light system. Look for a set-up that combines high-power illumination with lightweight, long-lasting battery life. Practice riding at night before an event and determine how long your batteries will last. A backup light system should be employed, especially for mountain biking events.

In Ironman distance triathlons, racers who are on the course after dark are required to carry a glow stick provided by race organizers. This is done for safety because many courses are not closed to traffic.

Twenty-four-hour Races

- Twenty-four-hour mountain bike races gained popularity as an alternative and fun racing option.

- Support crews are critical. Due to the remote location of some races, entire tent cities emerge.

- Participants can race individually or in relay-style teams.

- The format has been extended to a triathlon. Racers complete as many short-course laps in twenty-four hours as they can.

Ironman Triathlons

- First held in Hawaii in 1978, triathletes swim 2.4 miles, bike 112 miles, and then run a full marathon (26 miles).

- The fastest men and women complete these tasks in eight or nine hours.

- For many, just to finish is a huge accomplishment.

- Shorter-distance, more-accessible triathlons exist, but the Ironman maintains the status as the ultimate race in this discipline.

CYCLING EVENTS

KIDS' BIKES

A child gains more from a bike than coordination, balance, and agility

A bicycle teaches children balance and coordination. Riding builds agility and teaches a child to think critically. Problem solving for a young mind is enhanced. And mostly, a bike develops a sense of independence, confidence, and pure joy. The question for parents should be not whether to get a bike for their children, but rather which bike is best for them.

The current consensus about the best first bike has shifted. No longer is a tricycle the bike of choice. Today, push bikes are the preferred choice for two- to four-year-olds. Essentially these bikes are pedal-free. The child sits on the saddle and uses her feet, positioned on each side of the bicycle for balance. This setup allows the child to have complete control to

Tricycle

- Tricycles have three wheels: two in the back and one in the front. They are typically used by children between the ages of two and four.

- The wider the wheel base, the less likely the bike will tip over easily.

- Some come with direct drive (no chain), and the child resists the pedals to stop. Others have hand brakes. Wheels can be plastic or inflatable.

- Steel frames are more durable than plastic. Steel rusts, so keep the bike out of the rain.

Push Bike

- Push bikes are also called "balance bikes," "striders," and "run bikes." They have no pedals, chains, or gears. Push bikes are recommended for children between two and five years old.

- Some push bikes have adjustable seats, handlebars, and brakes.

- On a budget? Make your own push bike by removing the pedals, cranks, bearings, bottom bracket, and chain from a pedal bike. Save the parts so that later you can rebuild the bike.

shuffle forward and backward, while learning to balance on only two wheels. A word of caution for those of you living in a hilly area: Always keep a hand on your child's push bike. Even if the push bike has brakes, you can't be sure they will be used.

A child will learn balance much faster on a push bike than on a bike with training wheels. Training wheels force a child to sit crooked on the saddle and can develop a sense of false confidence, making it harder to transition to a traditional bike.

After your children progress past a push bike or a bike with training wheels, let them experience a bike with personality. By "personality" we mean frills, colors, and panache! Kids will be more excited to ride a bike they like, even if the reason they like it has nothing to do with how it rides. (By the way, adults are kind of like this, too.) This energetic desire may be the foundation for a lifetime of cycling passion.

Training Wheels

- Training wheels are after-market additions to a traditional pedal bike to assist with balance. The idea is to help the child transition to riding without them.

- Training wheels, however, do not teach a child balance. The design forces children to be off-balance.

- They typically self-adjust and thrust their hips and upper bodies off center.

- Training wheels have been around for so long that using them may be a matter of habit rather than good sense.

Girls-specific Bike

- Two-wheel bikes with pedals and brakes are appropriate for kids who have developed balance and can ride on their own.

- A girls-specific bike isn't as much about design geometry as about aesthetic appeal.

- Marketing companies assume that young girls prefer pastel colors, flowers, and fringe and that young boys are drawn to flames and primary colors.

- Let your child decide on the bike. If he likes the bike, he will ride it more and that is the objective..

BIKE SEATS & TRAILERS
Choose a means of transporting your child that suits adults' riding skills first and foremost

Children who are not capable of riding distance can still join adults on casual rides. There are child bike seats, trailers, and tag-alongs that allow for family outdoor recreation. As an adult, you should assess your own riding skills prior to selecting a carrier for your child. If you find that you have difficulty with balance and that your bike-handling skills are lacking,

do not use a bike-mounted seat, or a tag-along, for your child. This is a very serious matter.

Riding a bike with your child should be a positive experience. Wait until your child is at least one year old and can properly support her head while wearing a helmet before you take her for a ride. Typically, a child up to five years old

Child Bike Seat

- Rear-mounted children's bike seats are positioned behind the adult's saddle, over the rear wheel.

- Front-mounted seats are mounted on the top tube, behind the handlebars.

- Rear child seats can be dangerous in an accident

because the child would fall almost 3 feet to the ground.

- Seats are challenging for the adult to balance, especially starting and stopping.

- Seats support children between one and four. Weight recommendation is approximately 38 pounds.

Tag-along Bike

- A tag-along is ideal for kids between five and ten years of age. It will help them learn balance and keep them engaged.

- The trailer bike handles best with a mountain bike.

- Various brands have features that include gears,

suspension seats, and alloy wheels that won't rust.

- When riding, remember that the additional length of the trailer may make tight turning challenging. Consider the extra weight when stopping, too. Carry an extra tube for the tag-along in case you have a flat.

can be hoisted onto a bike seat or trailer, but always check the manufacturer's recommended weight limit.

Kids love the feeling of rolling along. Quite often they will fall asleep, too. Mostly they will learn very early about the positive benefits of exercise and bicycling. Always choose a safe place to ride. When you are testing the set-up for a bike trailer or other child-carrying options, look for a park or smooth trail where there are no cars or heavy foot traffic.

Trailer

- Bike trailers can carry one or two small children and up to 100 pounds. Check manufacturer's weight recommendation.

- Some trailers cannot be mounted on bicycles with disc brakes or oversized tubes, so check the compatibility prior to purchasing.

- The major concerns regarding safety are that the low profile makes trailers hard to be seen by motorists. Use an orange flag on a pole of three-and-one-half to seven feet tall.

- Also, trailers may flip over when you turn abruptly.

Head Injuries

- Always put helmets on your children when toting them on a bike seat, a tag-along, or a trailer. Set an example and wear one yourself.

- Scrapes and broken bones heal, but traumatic brain injuries do not.

- Cognitive challenges may develop after a brain injury. Balance and memory can be impaired. In addition, speech, comprehension, sensory abilities, and emotions may be disturbed.

- The highest rate of bike-related head injuries is among boys ages ten to fourteen.

KIDS' BIKE FEATURES
Children care about how many gears they have on a bike

What do you look for when buying a kid's bike? The price, size, and fit should be first on the priority list. Depending on the type of riding you expect your child to do, these factors will make a difference.

Is the kid into dirt jumping and riding up and down trails? If so, a BMX bike or a mountain bike with lots of gears and fat tires may be the best option. If your child is more apt to be riding in the neighborhood on paved sidewalks and paths, a one-speed or three-speed with coaster brakes may be the ticket. If the bike has any gears, then hand brakes, as opposed to coaster brakes, are part of the equation. This shouldn't be a problem so long as your child is old enough and capable of performing the mechanical skills necessary to use the braking mechanism.

Wheel Size

- Children's bikes are measured by wheel sizes. A range includes 12-inch (not shown), 16-, 20-, 22-, and 24-inch wheels.

- Most importantly, the bike should fit the child. When seated, a child should be able to straddle the bike flat-footed, but not be scrunched up.

- After children outgrow their bikes, they transition to adult bikes with 26-inch, 27-inch, or 700c wheels. These bikes are sized by the length of the seat tube.

Hand Brakes

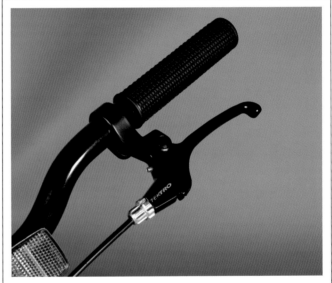

- Coaster brakes and hand brakes are found on kids' bikes.

- Using coaster brakes, the child pedals backward to stop the bike. Hand brakes are just like adult rim brakes and use a lever on the handlebars to stop the bike when squeezed.

- Make sure your child's hands are strong enough to stop the bike with a hand brake. Also, ensure that the brakes are in good working order.

Coaster brakes can be a challenge for young children not versed in bike handling. Young children often take their feet off the pedals in anticipation of stopping and falling over and find themselves with no braking options. The best of both worlds would be to purchase a singlespeed bike with both coaster brakes and hand brakes.

Next on the list are graphics, color, and style. This is where you get to have fun and find a bike that resonates with your child from a personality perspective. Don't assume that what you find attractive is what your child will like.

Kids' bikes would cost hundreds and thousands of dollars if they came with the same high-end components as adult bikes. These options do exist for those parents with a hefty disposable income, but regardless of how much you spend, the bike will still be quickly outgrown. Most commonly kids' bikes have heavier, less-expensive equipment and weigh more than you would expect for such small frames.

Gears

- Kids' bikes have from as few as one to as many as twenty-one gears. BMX models usually have a single gear.

- A greater number of gears improves the way the bike pedals, especially with varying terrain. Kids love to use the shifters—another gadget for them to try!

- Gears can also complicate the riding experience. Take some time to teach your child how to appropriately change gears.

- Multi-geared bikes have hand brakes as opposed to coaster brakes.

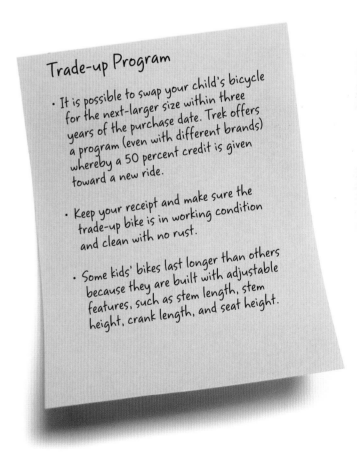

Trade-up Program

- It is possible to swap your child's bicycle for the next-larger size within three years of the purchase date. Trek offers a program (even with different brands) whereby a 50 percent credit is given toward a new ride.

- Keep your receipt and make sure the trade-up bike is in working condition and clean with no rust.

- Some kids' bikes last longer than others because they are built with adjustable features, such as stem length, stem height, crank length, and seat height.

MAKING IT SAFE & FUN

A preride checklist helps teach responsibility and gives kids a sense of importance

Even if your children do not know how to read, you can prepare a checklist for them to use before each ride. You can draw images or cut out photos from magazines to remind children of important matters and how to get ready. Put this list in the garage, or wherever the bikes are stored. Have fun with the outline and let your children help you create it.

The preride checklist should have the basic clothing needed, accessories, how to determine if the bike is in good working order, and positive references. For little kids, the list will be quite basic. But, if your children are capable of riding solo, and if they can tell time (that is, when they need to be home for dinner), then the list can be more elaborate.

Kids' Helmets

Chin strap should be tighter

- A helmet is designed for safety. Make sure it fits.

- The helmet should be snug when placed on the head. It should sit level, covering most of the forehead. If it's about 1 inch from the eyebrows, that's perfect.

- Side straps form a V around the earlobe. The chin strap should be tight enough to be snug, but not pinching. If you can fit multiple fingers through the strap and the child's chin, it's too loose.

- Rock the helmet back and forth and side to side to make sure it doesn't move.

Kids' Clothing

- Cycling clothing that looks like adult performance wear is available for kids (not shown). You will find padded bike shorts, technical fabric jerseys, and little cycling gloves.

- Kids are typically fine without a chamois. Many don't like the feeling of a pad anyway. Perhaps it's too many years in diapers?

- Make sure that kids are comfortable and can move freely. Their clothing should not constrict or inhibit them, nor be likely to get caught in moving bike parts.

Here are some considerations:

What to wear and bring—helmet, glasses, cycling clothes, proper shoes, gloves, sunscreen, water, snack, pump and flat tire kit (if appropriate), money, I.D. with parents' contact information, watch.

Preride bike check—wheels are tight and secure in frame, quick release levers closed (or bolts tight), handlebars are tight, tires are inflated and have no cracks, brakes work, crank and pedals turn and are tight, gears work, chain has lube.

ZOOM

Helmets are not expensive. Models can be purchased from discount stores for less than $20. Look for organizations that donate helmets if price is still a factor. Helmets 4 Safety gives away multisport helmets to children. The program is supported by a grant from the Integra Foundation and the American Society of Plastic Surgeons (ASPS).

Kids' Shoes

Remember to tuck in shoelaces

- Flip-flops, sandals, or closed-toe shoes?

- For safety reasons, closed-toe, flat-soled shoes are your best choice. Asphalt is an abrasive surface, and when combined with bike riding, it can be a recipe for cuts and stubbed toes.

- If kids are wearing sneakers, tuck the shoestrings under themselves so that the laces don't get caught on the bike.

- Small SPD shoes are available, and children as young as five years old can learn to clip in.

Positive Experience

- Ultimately, you want your kids to have fun while learning responsibility.

- It will mean the world to your kids if you are with them during a bike ride.

- When crossing the street, teach kids to look both ways and have them walk their bikes.

- Give them positive choices for options when playtime is over. Which would you rather do: Go home and enjoy a snack, or go home and take a nap?

KIDS' SKILLS

With competence comes confidence: Help your child learn to ride better and be safe

Bicycles are fun to ride. The enjoyment factor is multiplied when kids are really good at it. Just like adults, if kids are not competent at something, chances are they will quit or lose interest. The opposite, of course, is true, too; positive reinforcement begets increased participation.

Regardless of how much pride or enthusiasm children experience, they need to understand that bicycle riding comes with responsibility. Bikes are considered vehicles and subject to many of the same traffic rules and regulations as motor vehicles. So, when children are on a sidewalk, in a park, on the street or road, they should follow the law. This practice is for everyone's safety.

Neighborhood

- Riding in a suburban neighborhood can be a positive experience. Other children are around, residents are aware of children at play, and typically neighborhoods have nice sidewalks.

- When riding on the sidewalk, teach children to look beyond obstacles that restrict vision, such as trees, bushes, fences, and parked vehicles.

- Always stop before crossing the street and look both ways for traffic. Small children should walk their bikes across pedestrian crossings.

Bike Path

- Multi-use paths are a great place to ride because there is no traffic, but they are not playgrounds.

- Prepare your children to ride on a bike path. They should know basic hand and voice signals, be able to pay attention and have comprehension of other users, know right from left, and have some bike-handling skills.

- Necessary bike skills are being able to weave and pedal slowly, knowing how to stop, and knowing how to take one hand off the handlebars without swerving.

Depending on the age of the children, their awareness of and ability to learn these laws will vary. But then again, toddlers should not be riding in traffic, right? Learning practical skills and participating in bike rodeos are the best ways to teach your children proficiency that transfer over to the road. Make sure to reinforce why your kids are learning the skills. If there is no bike rodeo in town, invite a few friends over and set up your own. Think of a kids' bike rodeo as an obstacle course with purpose.

Balancing and Falling

- Kids are going to fall off their bikes. It's just a fact of life. So, teach them how to fall and what to do to get back onto their bikes.

- Use the lawn or a park with soft grass. Show your children how to tuck and roll. Even if children put their arms out, teach them how to then let them retract and tuck their shoulders under them and roll to dissipate the force of the falls.

- In real-life situations, after they fall, assuming that there are no serious injuries, encourage them to get back onto their bikes.

Camps and Clinics

- Sending kids to a bike camp or clinic is worth the investment of time and money. Just like sending them to ski school, kids are more engaged and tend to listen to instructors with rapt attention.

- Indoor cycling facilities and YMCAs in your area may have kid-specific classes.

- At a bike rodeo, kids learn a variety of skills, such as riding in a straight line, weaving through cones, slowing for balance, stopping, and using hand signals.

YOUTH RACING

They say competition isn't about winning, but rather about how you play the game

The competition of sport builds character and skills applicable to many other situations. Learning how to accept the disappointments of defeat—and the joys of victory—at an early age and how to turn those disappointments into positive experiences is an important tutorial in life. Often successful adults trace their wisdom and success to competitions in their youth.

Participation in cycling offers benefits to youth on multiple levels. They earn attention and respect for their personal attributes and abilities. This is very important. Self-esteem, self-confidence, and a healthy body image develop, too. Socially, kids learn better communication through the group dynamic, including leadership and team spirit. Kids must

Motto for Youth Cycling

- The Black Sheep Junior Cycling Club encourages youth, regardless of socioeconomic level, to learn, train, and compete on an even playing field. The club sums up its objective with words we can all live by. The club should produce and contain members who:

- Are informed, curious, constructive, and creative;

- Know how to think critically, to evaluate issues, and to distinguish truth from error; and

- Possess an appreciation of the cultural and aesthetic values of life.

Youth BMX

- Youth BMX is most notable for teaching kids bike-handling skills, providing head-to-head competition, and developing explosive strength.

- BMX tracks are dirt and have a starting gate, straightaways, jumps, and berms.

- The sanctioning organization is the American Bicycle Association (ABA).

- BMX is an Olympic sport and part of the Youth Olympic Games (ages fourteen to eighteen).

follow rules to compete. These lessons are internalized so that the importance of following order is understood.

Kids who are racing bikes will tell you that they are happy and having fun. Furthermore, when it comes to the bikes themselves, it's a real buzz for kids to be so much a part of the sleek, powerful, mechanical potential of the two-wheel machine. Taking care of a bike and keeping it in race-shape requires responsibility. Ultimately on race day, when it performs well, it's another source of empowerment and self-sufficiency.

Youth racing clubs teach skills like road riding, mountain biking, BMX, track riding, racing proficiency, and basic mechanic maintenance. Typically, a club hosts regular training rides either after school or on weekends. During the season, clubs assist with race day participation.

It is important to note that certain restrictions apply to the gears for young riders. These restrictions are in place to protect the health of the racers. When the integrity of developing ligaments, tendons, joints, and muscles is compromised, the potential for long-term damage is increased.

Junior Road Racing

- The Black Sheep Junior Cycling Club has more than forty junior racers, ranging in age from nine to twenty-three years old. It is the fastest-growing junior cycling team in Colorado.

- Certain gear ratios are restricted to youth road racing, and riders are subject to tests for compliance on the road and track.

- Ages eighteen and under are considered juniors. Some races run age categories in two-year increments, from eight years old and up.

Junior Mountain Bike Racing

- Mountain bike racing at the elite level is a discipline that demands keen bike-handling skills and a high level of physical fitness.

- Racers get the opportunity to ride challenging mountain courses, often on the same track as their heroes.

- Under 23 (U23) is a world championship category that is highly contested at state, national, and international levels.

- Youth series races are held for riders ages ten and under on very basic courses. Kids get an award, such as a medal or a ribbon for participation.

191

CAR ROOF RACKS

Specifically designed racks make transporting your bike easy without sacrificing interior space

Travel with your bike can take many forms. The most common scenario is using a vehicle to transport your bike to a riding area. Transporting your bike via car can challenge your efficiency. One bike may fit just fine in the back of a wagon with the seats down, but this arrangement doesn't leave much room for anything else. Your bike may fit in a large

trunk by removing both wheels, but then what about the bikes that belong to your passengers?

Fortunately, this problem is easily solved. Bike racks for your vehicle come in several types and allow you to carry as many bikes as passengers in one car by attaching the bikes externally. Each type of rack has its own advantages and

Fork Mount Rack

- The bike mounts to the rack via the fork and the rear wheel.

- Advantages: Attachment is stable; bike is easy to lift; rack is secure; bike is out of the way; locking system is incorporated into the fork clamp; can carry up to four bikes.

- Disadvantages: Some mountain bikes with heavy suspension need an adapter for the fork; bikes drag and decrease gas mileage; narrow roofs may limit number of bikes that can be carried; driver can forget about rack and drive into garage.

Front Wheel Holder

- A forklike front wheel holder solves any problem about what to do with your front wheel.

- Stagger the front wheel holder in between the bikes.

- Make sure the wheel is latched securely to avoid flying wheels after you are driving at speed. Run a bungee cord through the wheel or, better yet, angle the holder forward so the wind pushes the wheel into the holder instead of out of it.

disadvantages, which we have identified.

Roof racks are the most commonly used option by avid cyclists. These racks mount to the roof of the car, thus leaving the car's interior free to carry passengers and gear. This type gets the bike up and out of the way and keeps it safe from fender-benders. The main disadvantages of this type are the decreased gas mileage from the air drag of the bikes and the danger of forgetting that the rack is on the roof and driving into a garage, which can result in major damage to the bike, the rack, and your car.

GREEN ● LIGHT

Lock your bike. A parked car with a bike mounted to an exterior rack can be an easy target for thieves. Theft has also occurred during heavy traffic in urban areas when a thief will grab the bike off the car while the car is stopped at an intersection. Secure your bike with a rack locking system or run a cable through the wheels and frame.

Upright Roof Rack

- The full bike mounts to the rack without taking the wheels off. An arm attaches to the down tube or wheels to secure the bike.

- Advantages: Does not require removing the front wheel; bike is out of the way.

- Disadvantages: More difficult to lift the bike and secure rack at the same time; causes drag and decreases gas mileage; narrow roofs may limit number of bikes that can be carried; driving-into-the-garage brain fart.

Locking System

- Lock the cross bars to which the bike trays are mounted to prevent someone from taking the entire rack off the roof.

- Locking systems can be added to fork mount racks and upright racks. A lock cylinder is sold separately.

- A thief with minimal tools may still be able to take the rest of the bike by disassembling the fork or wheels. For extended time away from your vehicle, never leave your bike on the roof.

CAR REAR RACKS

With your bike strapped to the back of your car, be mindful when backing up

An alternative to roof racks is bike racks that mount to the rear of the vehicle. Your vehicle type may dictate what kind of rack you can use. For example, roof racks don't work on a truck because the roof isn't long enough for the two secure mounting points. Aerodynamic rooflines do not provide anything for a roof rack to mount to.

Strap racks are a common, easy way to transport your bike. These racks are easily installed on and removed from the car and are a less permanent option than roof racks. Different designs work with sedans and hatchbacks. The main drawbacks of this type are the inability to access the rear door while the rack is in use and the lack of a built-in

Strap Rack

- Advantages: No effect on gas mileage; no need to remove wheels; easy access to bikes; easily removable from car.

- Disadvantages: If bikes are not secured, they can scratch the car and each other; easy access for

thieves and difficult to lock; bikes get covered with road grime coming off rear wheels; need adapter for use with most full-suspension mountain bikes; can't open the trunk or boot after bikes are on rack; extends length of car.

Hanging Hitch Rack

- Advantages: No effect on gas mileage; no need to remove wheels; easy access; easily removable from car; holds bike away from vehicle, so no risk of scratching.

- Disadvantages: Easy access to thieves and difficult to lock; bikes get covered with road grime coming off car; need adapter for use with most full-suspension mountain bike; can't open the tailgate after bikes are on rack; extends length of car.

locking system, providing easy access to thieves. Make sure to carry a long cable and padlock if you plan on leaving the car unattended.

Both strap racks and hanging hitch racks hold the bikes by sliding the top tube onto horizontal bars. This task can be challenging for small frames and full-suspension mountain bikes because adapters attach to the stem and seatpost, making a vertical virtual top tube from which to hang the bike. A rear mount system will increase the length of your vehicle, which is important to remember when backing up.

Truck fork mounts work in the same way as a roof fork mount. The fork clamp can be attached to a removable board placed in the bed of the truck or directly bolted to the bed itself. These mounts will also work with a truck topper. For an open-bed truck, the fork mounts can be attached to the edge of the bed. Fork mounts can incorporate a locking system similar to the roof rack version. Nevertheless, additional cables to secure the frame, rear wheel, and loose front wheel are recommended.

Tray Hitch Rack

- Advantages: No effect on gas mileage; no need to remove wheels; easy access to bikes; entire rack can be removed from hitch; holds bikes away from vehicle, so no risk of scratching; locking capabilities similar to those of upright roof rack.

- Disadvantages: Easy access to thieves; bikes get covered with road grime; can't open the tailgate after bikes are on rack; extends length of car and can bottom out on dips in road.

Truck Fork Mounts

- This photo shows the fork clamp type mounted to the front edge of the bed. Mounting the forks to the sides results in a more space-efficient system.

- Advantages: Secures bike to prevent scratching or dam-age to bed or bike; minimal road grime spray; mounting the bike upright allows room for other cargo; no decrease in gas mileage.

- Disadvantages: Bikes are easily accessible to thieves.

PACKING YOUR BIKE
Flying with your bike is worth the extra work after you get to your destination

When flying or shipping your bike, a special case or box is needed to pack the bike. Special cases for flying provide protective padding.

Some disassembly is required to fit the entire bike into the case. The following parts will need to be removed: wheels, skewers, seatpost (with saddle still attached), pedals, and handlebars. Make sure that you know how to put it all back together and that you bring the proper tools for doing so.

If you are flying, first check the airline policy for sporting equipment. Bike cases are considered oversize luggage, and there is usually a fee to fly with a bike. Unfortunately, fees range from $50 to $200 each way. Policies tend to change

Hard Case

- Hard-shell cases offer the most peace of mind about the abusive environment of luggage handling and compartments.

- These cases, such as the Trico brand shown here, use large pieces of foam to sandwich the bike. Compression straps squeeze the bike between the foam, minimizing interior movement.

- The disadvantage of hard cases is storing and transporting the case (and your bike, once built) after you arrive at your destination, especially if several people are traveling together.

Soft Case

- Soft-shell cases offer excellent protection while offering a bit more flexibility for storage.

- Some soft cases include a framework on which to mount the bike and special internal compartments for the wheels.

- Look for cases that have built-in roller wheels and a strap for towing. These make for easier maneuvering to and from the airport.

- Most cases will fit across the back seat of a four-door sedan or cab.

frequently, and airline personnel may not always be sure of the latest, so knowing the policy ahead of time will allow you to plan better and also ensure that you do not get overcharged.

You will also need to make sure that the overall weight meets the airline requirements. Although most cases will afford room to pack other items such as shoes, helmet, tools, and some clothes, be careful of weighing down the case too much. Shipping companies have similar restrictions, so do your homework before you begin to pack.

Packed Bike in Case

- Rags, clothing, and packing material will provide padding and ensure that the bike does not scratch itself in transit.

- Put the necessary tools for reassembly into a water bottle or wrap them in a rag and include them with your bike.

- Rigid plastic spacers fit in the fork and rear dropouts to prevent bending.

- Be careful to arrange the handlebars in a way that does not put too much pressure on the brake levers and shifters.

Packed Bike Detail

- The handlebars will need to be removed. Removal is easiest with a removable face plate on the stem. The bike may fit best by removing the handlebars and stem together off the steer tube.

- You also may want to remove the rear derailleur, especially if it sits precariously close to the edge of the case. Wrap it in a rag and secure it inside the frame with a zip tie.

- Carry extra zip ties.

COUPLING & FOLDING BIKES
Bikes made especially for traveling are a great option for your cycling adventures

Options exist to let you avoid the increasing costs of taking a bike on airline flights. Traveling with a bike that can be packed compactly is more convenient and less expensive. Essentially, two bikes fall into this category: coupling bikes and folding bikes.

Coupling bikes have special joints allowing the frame to be disassembled. This means the bike can be packed into a smaller case by separating the front and rear triangles. Two popular options use couplings to break down a full-size bike. Coupling bikes that resemble folding bikes in wheel size and frame style are also available for the ultimate combination of compactability and quality ride.

Built Coupling Bike

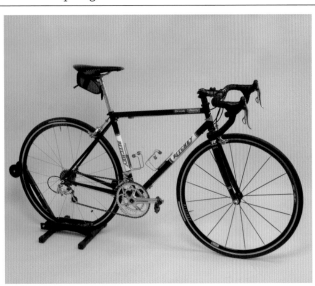

- A fully built coupling bike looks and rides like a regular bike.

- Coupling bikes also come with smaller wheel styles to allow for even more compact packing.

- The dimensions typically do not incur an airline's extra baggage charge.

- A smaller case means easier maneuverability to and from the airport and a better fit in the trunk of a vehicle.

- Practice packing and reassembling the bike before you go.

Packed Coupling Bike

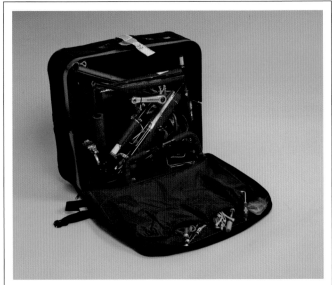

- Follow the manufacturer's packing suggestions. Use plenty of padding, such as clothing or foam piping, around the frame and parts to avoid scratching or other damage. Larger-size bikes may require more disassembly than smaller bikes.

- Cases come in hard-shell, backpack, and hybrid construction versions.

- S and S Machine makes compression members that are PVC piping put crosswise inside a hard case to distribute pressure to the outside of the case.

Ritchey's line of Break Away bikes uses its patented design. The Break Away frame joins in two places on the seatpost and down tube. The seatpost slides through the two parts, using the seatpost itself to align the pieces. The second joint is a discreet coupler clamp on the down tube, right above the bottom bracket. Ritchey makes a steel, titanium, and singlespeed road version, a titanium and steel cross version, and a titanium hardtail mountain bike version of the Break Away. The bike comes with its own travel case.

S and S Machine Company makes Bicycle Torque Couplings, which are lugged joints that can be installed in a bicycle frame. Some frame builders offer this option at manufacturing, and others can install the couplings on an existing bike frame of steel, titanium, or carbon fiber.

Folding bikes provide a convenient option for traveling and small space scenarios. Their clever design allows the bike to be broken down and folded on the fly, requiring no special tools. Folding bikes have the added advantage of being allowed on public transportation systems when full bikes are not.

Built Folding Bike

- Folding bikes are perhaps the most versatile traveling option.

- Good designs will have the same pedal, saddle, and hand positions as a full-size, fixed-frame bike.

- Smaller wheels are stronger and mean faster acceleration, lower rolling resistance, and better aerodynamics.

- But smaller wheels do not absorb bumps in the road. For this reason, some folding bikes include a suspension for a smoother ride.

Packed Folding Bike

- Some folding bikes are compact enough to fit into the overhead bin on an airline.

- In urban areas, being able to bring your folding bike onto public transportation is an invaluable option.

- Some folding bikes are designed so that the chain is completely covered when you are riding and when the bike is folded to make sure your hands stay clean in the process.

- It takes approximately one minute to fold the bike—with practice, just twenty seconds.

PUBLIC TRANSPORTATION
Commuting on your bike is easy but may require more planning

Mixed-mode commuting combines several modes of transportation on one trip. If your commute is too long to cycle the entire way, your bike still may be the most convenient method to get to and from the train or bus station. Some stations have special bike lockers that can be rented for those who use a bike to get back and forth to the station, but who don't need to take their bike with them. If you do take your bike along, there are often limitations on when or how bikes may be taken onto public transit, so first check transit websites or the local authorities to make sure you are prepared and have all the pertinent information.

This situation is where the folding bike really shines. Most transit authorities that limit transporting full-size bikes in some way allow folding bikes with minimal or no restrictions.

KNACK CYCLING FOR EVERYONE

Bus Luggage Compartment

- If a bus has no special bicycle racks, you may be able to stow your bike in the luggage compartment.

- Ask the driver before opening. Place your bike so that it rests on the pedal with the chain side up to prevent damage to the derailleurs.

- If you are loading multiple bikes, it may be more efficient to take the front wheels off and lay them on top of the bike frame.

Bus Bike Racks

- Some buses have exterior racks for bicycles.

- Look for a demo rack in the station to familiarize yourself. Otherwise, if you are unsure, ask the bus driver.

- It is your responsibility to make sure your bike is properly secured.

- As you exit the bus, remind the driver that you have to unload your bike.

- Leave the rack ready for use by the next rider if they are waiting. Or, return the rack to the position in which you found it.

Even when full bikes are allowed, space limitations may result in your needing to wait for the next train or bus to get to where you are going.

With congestion clogging more city centers and with increasing concern about pollution and greenhouse gas emissions from vehicles, many municipalities are instituting or strengthening cycling-friendly initiatives. For example, Transport for London has organized free group commuter rides to encourage more people to commute to work. Transportation authorities can be a great source of support and information beyond just the rules.

As a side note, you should always bring a lock when commuting. Even if you do not plan to stop along the way, you never know. Situations, such as the need to take a bathroom break or the desire to grab the newspaper and a cup of coffee, arise. A simple combination cable lock will suffice for a quick stop.

Trains

- Some trains allow you to roll your bike on and provide designated spots for storing them. There may be a limit on the number of bikes allowed, so get to the station early.

- Other trains allow bikes only when they are packed as luggage, much like on an airline.

- Whether bikes are allowed or not may depend on the time of day and direction of the train. This restriction is due to the extra space that bikes take up during rush hour.

Underground Railways

- The New York subway system allows bicycles but provides suggestions such as using particular stations, standing in particular places on the train, and avoiding rush hour.

- San Francisco, California's BART allows bikes with some restrictions. Folding bikes must be folded before you board or enter a crowded station.

- Bikes are generally not allowed on the London Underground with the exception of limited off-peak hours and only at particular stations. Folding bikes are allowed on the tube with no restrictions.

PACKING LIST

Make a packing list of the must-remember items; save a copy for future use

When packing for your cycling trip, take time to think about what items are necessary. Forgetting an item can ruin a trip or, at minimum, result in an unnecessary expenditure. Beyond the basics, how you are getting there, what the climate will be, and what type of riding you will be doing will dictate what accessories are needed.

Even if you travel in the warmer months, a few small extra items will prevent your being uncomfortable on an unexpected cooler day. Arm warmers, knee warmers, and a light wind jacket take up little space and extend your cycling wardrobe into cooler weather. If you are heading to the mountains, remember that higher elevation means colder

For Your Person

- The bare minimum for cycling excursions (and this applies to short trips from home) includes shorts, shoes, a helmet, a jersey, glasses, gloves, socks, and a wind jacket.

- If you are particular about energy food, pack your favorite brand to be safe. Remember a water bottle or hydration pack.

- Depending on weather, don't forget rain gear and sunscreen. Arm and knee warmers are an easy-to-pack option for cooler weather.

For Air Travel with a Bike

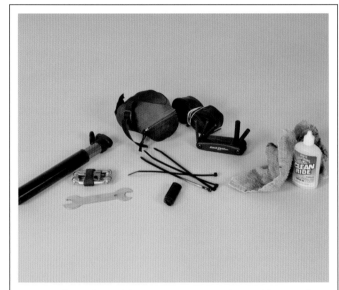

- You will need a pedal wrench, Allen wrench set, lube, minipump, rags, and flat-tire changing tools.

- Zip ties and a short length of duct tape rolled onto itself can be handy and help with repacking.

- Do not bring CO_2 cartridges because they are illegal on flights and will be confiscated by the airline and increase the chance that your bag will be searched.

- Remember a shock pump (not shown) if riding a full-suspension bike.

air and quickly changing weather patterns.

If you will be using your bike for transportation, think about the items you usually use when commuting. A lightweight foldable bag that is comfortable for cycling and a bike lock allow you to stop and enjoy the scenery or pick up a souvenir.

Packing light and efficiently is of utmost importance when you fly or take extended trips. Be sure to have only the necessary tools for reassembling your bike and take the lightest versions of these tools (that is, a multi-tool instead of a full-size Allen set). Consider that some items, such as jerseys, are easily rinsed and dried. Shorts, on the other hand, do not dry quickly, so one pair per riding day is a good idea.

When traveling by car, you can usually afford to take heavier items. A full tool set and spare parts for commonly broken bike parts can save a trip, especially if you are camping or in a remote area. It is always a good idea to make a written list of the items you want for a trip. Save the list for future reference and continue adding and subtracting, as needed.

For Car Travel with a Bike

- Take advantage of the added space of car travel and bring a full tool box.

- A floor pump, spare tire(s), and extra common-sized bolts should be added.

- If you are mountain biking, take a shock pump and commonly broken spare parts.

- Don't forget the cooler with snacks and drinks.

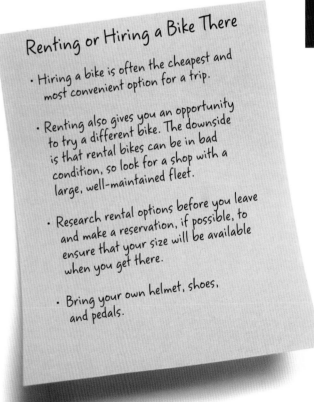

Renting or Hiring a Bike There

- Hiring a bike is often the cheapest and most convenient option for a trip.

- Renting also gives you an opportunity to try a different bike. The downside is that rental bikes can be in bad condition, so look for a shop with a large, well-maintained fleet.

- Research rental options before you leave and make a reservation, if possible, to ensure that your size will be available when you get there.

- Bring your own helmet, shoes, and pedals.

WHO'S GOING?

Cycling vacations burn calories, exercise your mind and body, and provide a sense of satisfaction

Combining fitness with a vacation is the ultimate in traveling with purpose and creating a feeling of physical and emotional satisfaction. Too often trips that involve an overindulgence of drinking, eating, and sitting leave you more miserable after the vacation than before. If you burn calories at some point during your holiday and keep the metabolism revved up,

you'll feel justified in more local cuisine indulgence.

When you bike through a town or across scenic landscapes, you will see things much more intimately than in a car. Yet, you'll be able to cover more ground while biking than while walking or hiking. The ability to be close to nature is a big selling point.

Solo

- Cycling solo is a wonderful experience. You'll notice that your perceptions are exceptionally acute when you are alone. Sunsets and scenery have greater personal detail.

- People tend to invite you into their lives more readily when you are alone. Per-

haps it's easier to approach and feed a single person? Your encounters may be full of generous offers of unexpected companionship and meals.

- Nevertheless, listen to your instincts and avoid situations that feel unsafe or wrong.

Couples

- Vacations are a make-or-break experience for many couples. A partner's good personality traits can be accentuated and bring two people closer together, or the opposite may happen.

- When riding individual bikes, the stronger rider needs to be patient.

- Consider a tandem bike, which balances fitness levels.

- With a partner, you'll be able to share experiences and recall them together later.

A number of companies can help you plan cycling vacations. Day trips, multi-day supported vacations, and adventure destinations are available. This chapter covers various options.

Prior to deciding where to go and what to do, determine who's going and how you visualize the experience. Are you looking for a personal journey alone, or would you rather hook up with a group? Do you want to spend time with your significant other in the outdoors? Is your family able to ride bikes during all or part of a vacation? After you answer the question of who's going, the rest is fun planning.

Friends

- If you're looking to laugh a lot and celebrate a group dynamic, go on a cycling trip with buddies.

- Ride together prior to the trip so that everyone is aware of each other's abilities. Groups of like-fitness riders are great for the ultimate shared experience.

- If you have a variety of speeds in the group, make sure no one is left behind or alone.

- Sharing the cooking, cleaning, and planning responsibilities on a camping trip is great for building camaraderie.

Family

- A family cycling vacation is not about getting fit. Leave your ego at home and don't push each other past physical and emotional limits.

- Make sure you take plenty of snacks and stay hydrated. Stop often to look around and experience the moment.

- Make the trip a life lesson about respect, togetherness, and positive experiences.

- The distance covered during the day should depend on the age and ability of the children.

TRIP TYPE

Don't miss the opportunity to spend time exploring life on a bike

Some people feel that every day on the bike is a minivacation. Riding your bike is truly an escape. Bottom line: Enjoy riding your bike and have fun with the options for doing so. Make it a goal to try a different type of trip each year. Some trips require little planning; others require reservations and commitments. Whatever you gravitate toward, break out of the routine on your bike.

Day trips and multi-purpose trips are the easiest to plan. It's often a matter of perspective. You can create a vacation feel on a weekend close to home, for example. Just dedicate a portion, or the whole day, to this idea. Choose a location that you want to visit or connect with a guide or friend who knows an interesting locale. Get on your bike and explore.

Cycling can be combined with other activities for extra fun

Day Trip

- Day trips can be incorporated into a business trip, a holiday, or an excursion close to or away from home.

- The main focus of this style of outing is sightseeing and pleasure. You do not have to carry excessive supplies.

Typically, a camera, snacks, water, and a small backpack will suffice.

- Day trips to nearby towns are great for eating out. Be sure to carry money and a lock for your bike.

Multi-day Supported

- Road and mountain bike tours for any level of bike rider are offered by companies like Western Spirit Cycling and Escape Adventurers.

- A selection of locations and styles accommodates individuals, families, groups, and so forth.

- Led by a guide, multiday supported trips take the work out of vacationing. The guide leads you on beautiful routes, cooks your meals, cleans the dishes, and shares knowledge about the area visited.

and interest. If a particular sport tickles your fancy, figure out how to participate in this sport by riding your bike, too. There is something epic about riding from point A to point B and following up the ride with another jolt of fun. Some of our favorite holidays involved day trips over singletrack passes, culminating with a big meal at a cozy mountain house. That's multi-purpose eating and drinking at their finest.

During the writing of this book, we met Joel on the coast of California (image on preceding page). He had finished university and decided to ride, unsupported, across the country.

Talking with him magnified the importance of living life to its fullest and taking advantage of moments when we are able to enjoy such a journey.

If traveling alone seems daunting, tour companies provide supported vacations that will thrill, pamper, and satisfy your curiosity.

Multi-day Unsupported

- Traveling on a multiday trip without outside assistance requires planning.

- Carry supplies for sleeping, cooking, navigating, handling emergencies, and coping with weather conditions.

- Credit card touring is finding lodging along the route.

- If you are traveling with a group, you have the option of bringing a sag vehicle to carry supplies and take turns driving. This allows for more creature comforts and changes the scope to semi-unsupported.

Mixed-purpose Trip

- When you want to squeeze in as much action as possible, couple your cycling trip with another sport.

- The challenge is getting the equipment and timing organized. If you drive to the beach, take your bikes so that you can do a loop from there. Make sure to

store your valuables safely and be wary of thieves who prey on unattended cars.

- Always carry running shoes for hiking, walking, or running after a ride. The motion stretches the legs and helps recovery.

207

CULTURAL LOCATIONS

Take advantage of history, culture, and architecture by choosing an enriching destination

Less is more. That's the best advice you can take with you on a vacation. Don't try to fit in too much, or else you'll be scattered and frazzled. Often slowing down to appreciate the simple pleasures makes us remember the trip with more fondness.

This advice also applies to packing. A wise traveler once said, "Take half as much stuff as you think you need and carry twice as much money!" (Good luck mastering the second element of that advice.) In any case, vacationing with purpose and focus takes some planning and practice.

Culturally interesting urban or historical locations are ideal for travelers who are looking to enhance their social and

Urban

- In case you haven't noticed, driving a car through a big city can be frustrating. Gridlock is a problem. Walking takes a long time compared to riding a bike, and skateboarding isn't practical for most.

- Put on your helmet, grab a bike with plenty of gears

and a comfortable riding position, and get to know the city.

- Wear comfortable touring shoes or walking shoes and bring a lock so you can enter museums and restaurants and step away from the bike whenever the mood strikes you.

Vineyards

- Vineyards provide rolling hills, scenic views, and plenty of stopping points to enjoy the fruits of the vine. Remember that drinking alcohol while cycling is not wise nor legal if you surpass the local limits of alcohol consumption.

- Bed-and-breakfasts, boutique rentals, and vacation rentals by owner are great overnight accommodation options.

- Drink plenty of water between tastings and eat a wholesome snack every few hours to keep energy levels up.

worldly perspectives. Pick one to three locations to see each day and use your bike to take you there. The best routes will be bike-friendly and take you off the beaten path. Carry a good map and use caution when going into an area that is questionable. However, don't be so overcome with self-inflicted fear that you miss out on the local scene. Often getting lost results in finding an area you would have otherwise missed. Smile as often as possible; it's contagious.

If you are taking a point-to-point trip, such as a pilgrimage route, or are taking a ride through wine country, understand that it takes preparation. Tour companies can arrange these trips for you. These companies carry your bags to prearranged hotels or campgrounds, leaving you free to ride unburdened. If you decide to ride on a more spiritual mission, research like minds and travelers who can offer advice and encouragement about the route.

Coastal

- Port towns, islands, and coastal villages are treasure destinations for those who enjoy the ocean.

- The benefit of riding by the coast is that the weather is typically cooler than inland.

Ocean breezes provide just the right amount of air flow to make a bike ride pleasant. The downside is that when the wind picks up, it can hinder bike handling and pedaling.

Cultural/Historical

- Pilgrimage routes, cathedrals, Roman ruins, towers, bridges, and monuments all fall into the cultural/historical category of bicycle tours.

- Consider following a classic road racing route through France, Spain, Italy, or Belgium.

- Choose a travel guidebook that has up-to-date information and some cultural and historical background. To truly learn the culture, ride with a local guide. That person will be able to share history and take you places not listed in the books.

209

ACCESSIBLE SCENIC LOCATIONS
Get away from the daily grind by finding a quiet road out of town

If you look hard enough, you'll find a valid excuse to keep your bike at home and to avoid venturing out into new locations. It's our job to convince you that you can do better.

The United States has 84 million acres of national parks protected from human development and pollution. There are over two thousand ski resorts worldwide, and every country has a small town or rural area where you can ride a bike. That

said, U.S. annual family vacations have decreased by 28 percent, and national park attendance has fallen steadily.

Accept that your cell phone may not work in the mountains and that you may not have a television. Concerns about budgets, driving, and packing can be surmounted with some creativity. Failing to take time for sun and fun is detrimental to your mental and physical health.

National Parks

- The United States national park system comprises 391 areas. The parks were created by an act signed by President Woodrow Wilson on August 25, 1916.

- Be respectful when riding through national parks; you are sharing the trails, roads, and surroundings with

other tourists and animals. Bikes are allowed on roads and designated trails only. Follow the golden rule and leave no trace when you visit the parks.

Mountain Ski Resorts

- If you have not spent time on a ski slope in the summer, you're missing out.

- Ride your bike on the wide range of singletracks, doubletracks, and fire roads up and down the mountain.

- If the ski resort has chair lifts operating, you can

attach your bike and catch a lift to the top. Then enjoy a sweet ride downhill.

- Wear the appropriate helmet and gear and make sure your bike is capable of handling the long descents.

Sunlight triggers skin to make vitamin D, which helps fight cancer. Studies have shown decreased crime in urban areas after trees are planted. People tend to socialize more outdoors, which is why many cultures use downtowns to walk and visit in the afternoon and evenings.

Plan your cycling vacation this year and prepare yourself for vitamin G—G for "Green"! Trails, rivers, wilderness areas, lakes, national forests, and scenic byways will all be at your disposal up close and personal on a bike.

ZOOM

Assuming that you are competent on a bike and do not need to mentally concentrate on the basic skills, riding sharpens the mental processes. As you pedal rhythmically and your heart pumps vital oxygen through your body, the stimulus prompts your brain. Personal questions are often answered, speeches are mentally completed, and the solutions to problems can become clearer.

Rural

- Country rides offer quiet simplicity. Barns, horses, pastures, and agricultural fields are a Zen-like backdrop for riding.

- The disadvantages, however, should not be overlooked. Typically, the roads are not smoothly paved, tend to be narrower, and may have no shoulder.

- If you are traveling with another person, be sure to ride single file because the "locals" with pickups and trailers may not take too kindly to swerving around you.

Budget Travel

- If you are looking for a budget trip, take your bike to a ski resort in the summer. Overnight accommodations, restaurants, rental shops, and retail stores tend to be less expensive during the off-season.

- Practice the fine art of negotiation if you are unable to afford the asked price. Be courteous, clever with your reasons, and respectful. If you don't ask, you'll never know, right?

- The website, pedaling.com, details self-guided road and mountain bike trails with maps, cue sheets, and trail descriptions.

ADVENTURE LOCATIONS

Don't be intimidated by remote destinations, but be prepared physically and mentally

Having a certain level of fitness, bike-handling ability, and overall comfort on a bike is recommended for adventure locations. You certainly can find adventure locations that will accommodate basic skill levels, but you probably can't take advantage of the experience as profoundly as could an intermediate or advanced rider. Having greater proficiency

enhances the experience.

That said, you can ride yourself to increased fitness and improved skill sets. However, making a commitment to do so might depend on your personality and comfort level.

Make sure that your companions are similarly prepared and realistic about their capabilities. It's infuriating when someone

Tropical

- Think Maui, Hawaii, and Costa Rica when you think tropical.

- Locations for hardcore road riding, touring, cyclocross riding, mountain biking, and cruising are optional.

- To enjoy trips in humid climates, drink plenty of

water, take bug spray, and pack repair gear for the bike.

- Self-guided tours or guided tours are available. If exploring without assistance, stay on marked trails and respect the sensitive environment.

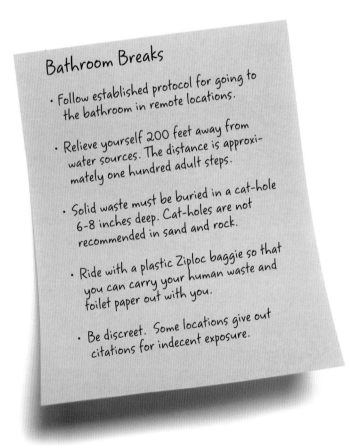

Bathroom Breaks

- Follow established protocol for going to the bathroom in remote locations.

- Relieve yourself 200 feet away from water sources. The distance is approximately one hundred adult steps.

- Solid waste must be buried in a cat-hole 6-8 inches deep. Cat-holes are not recommended in sand and rock.

- Ride with a plastic Ziploc baggie so that you can carry your human waste and toilet paper out with you.

- Be discreet. Some locations give out citations for indecent exposure.

gets in over her head and suffers. Doing so affects the rider individually and can have negative consequences on others. Don't hesitate to have a frank conversation before you leave to avoid anyone having unrealistic expectations and souring the trip or, worse yet, a friendship.

Save your pennies if you plan on combining adventure with cultural experiences. Locations such as Tibet and Nepal, which claim to have the world's longest downhill rides, are expensive and require extra days for travel.

Ancient Trails

- Europe has ancient trails that are worn out and overgrown with vegetation. Riding them can thrill the senses.

- Greece offers routes that pass ancient sites and gorges. Old World trails and cobblestone villages are a good starting point for planning.

- Peru has thousands of miles of trails and dirt tracks but lacks good maps to show you where to go, requiring a bit more research.

Backcountry

- The Kokopelli trail and White Rim in Utah offer a great back-country mountain bike riding experience.

- Fruita, Colorado, and Moab, Utah, offer fantastic spring and autumn riding, with a number of excellent single-day rides.

- Rim Tours, Western Spirit, and Escape Adventures are companies that specialize in backcountry cycling trips.

- If organizing your own trip, note that National Park Service campsites require a permit.

CYCLING HISTORY

The bicycle has maintained similar form and spirit while experiencing incredible advances

In spite of many advances during the Industrial Revolution, a successful bicycle design as we know it was somewhat elusive.

Karl von Drais, a German baron, made several attempts before his "running machine" gained some attention. The draisine, or "velocipede" as it was called, had two inline wheels, a steering mechanism for the front wheel, and a seat in the middle. The rider propelled the velocipede with her feet, much the way a child propels a kid's push bike today.

The term "bicycle" was introduced in the 1860s in France and quickly gained acceptance. At that time, the next major advance took place. Frenchman Pierre Michaux unveiled

Nineteenth-century Cycling

- The high-wheeler of the 1870s is often seen as a symbol of the early bicycle movement.

- The high cost and challenge of mounting and dismounting the high-wheeler limited its use.

- Highly popular in Britain, races drew large crowds, and recreational cycling clubs emerged.

- Cyclists logged impressive rides to show the possibilities of the bikes, such as the 700-mile trek from London to John O'Groats in 1873, taking two weeks to cover the distance.

The Golden Age

- The safety bicycle used similar-sized wheels and a lower seat height, reducing the dangers of the high-wheeler.

- The Rover, created by John Kemp Starley and introduced in 1885, included a chain drive and is credited as the first modern bicycle.

- Other developments quickly followed, including the addition of a seat tube and the double-triangle frame design.

- The pneumatic tire—the combination of a tire and an air-filled inner tube—was developed by Scotsman John Dunlop in 1888.

a two-wheeled vehicle propelled by pedals and a crank attached directly to the front wheel. The machine's high cost and some public skepticism initially prevented the vehicle from becoming the transportation panacea for the common person. But Michaux offered riding lessons, and despite the cost, the bicycle caught the world's attention.

Michaux's claim as the inventor was actually disputable. He claimed to have a patent in early advertisements, but no such patent existed. In fact, the only bicycle patent was filed in the United States in 1866 by Pierre Lallement, who had spent time working in various workshops in France before coming to the United States in 1865. Lallement brought his iron bicycle with him but failed to initiate the new industry as he had hoped. Michaux's business partners, brothers Marius, Aimé, and René Olivier, were the driving force behind the development at Michaux's shop—and later sued Michaux. At the trial, René testified that the inventor of the machine was not Michaux, but rather a workman whom he did not identify by name. Regardless, the bicycle craze had begun and soon spread well beyond France.

Tour de France

- The first Tour de France was run in 1903, sponsored by the newspaper *L'Auto* to encourage cycling fans to read the paper. The race's main supporter today is still a newspaper.

- The race has been run every year since, with the exception of 1915–1918 and 1940–1946 for World Wars I and II.

- The winner is determined by a combined time of all stages. Separate awards are given to the King of the Mountains, the Points Competition, and the Best Young Rider.

Bicycle as Transportation

- The bicycle is the primary mode of commuting in India, China, and many European countries.

- Bicycles are the most efficient self-powered means of transportation. They are both biologically and mechanically sound.

- You can also carry an impressive amount of weight or cargo on a bike.

- Pneumatic tires, spoke-tensioned wheels, and ball bearings for cars came from bikes.

MOUNTAIN BIKE HISTORY

Mountain biking enjoyed a colorful beginning that was, in many ways, uniquely American in spirit

The concept of off-road cycling gained traction in the 1970s. Mountain biking was born out of the desire of some counter-culture northern Californians who raced their balloon-tired bikes down the trails of Marin County. Around the same time and some 1,800 miles away, the hippie residents of Crested Butte, Colorado, found that old cruiser bikes were a practical way of getting around on the rutted dirt roads of town.

In 1976, the Marin County crew held the first downhill races on a 2-mile-long fire road with a 1,300-foot elevation loss named "Repack" because riders needed to repack their coaster brake hubs after each run. The same year in Crested Butte, a small group of cyclists, along with a follow vehicle

Mountain Bike Hall of Fame

- The Mountain Bike Hall of Fame and Museum was founded in 1988 to record the history of mountain biking.

- The quaint old building on Elk Avenue in downtown Crested Butte, Colorado, houses memorabilia, photos, vintage bikes and components, and press clippings.

- Each year three to seven persons or groups are inducted into the Mountain Bike Hall of Fame. The list of inductees honors the developers, champions, advocates, and influencers of the sport.

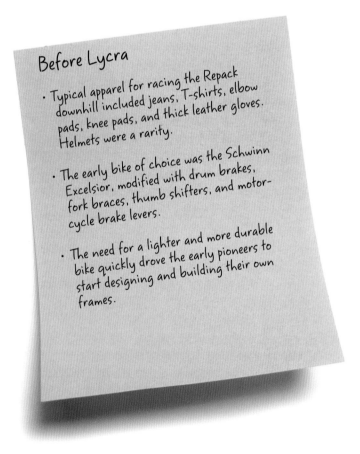

Before Lycra

- Typical apparel for racing the Repack downhill included jeans, T-shirts, elbow pads, knee pads, and thick leather gloves. Helmets were a rarity.

- The early bike of choice was the Schwinn Excelsior, modified with drum brakes, fork braces, thumb shifters, and motorcycle brake levers.

- The need for a lighter and more durable bike quickly drove the early pioneers to start designing and building their own frames.

(someone had to carry the keg), made the trek over 12,700-foot Pearl Pass to Aspen. These two cultures converged in 1978 at the third annual Pearl Pass Tour, when five of the northern Californians brought their latest manifestations of off-road cycling machines to Crested Butte. The *Crested Butte Pilot* covered the story and aptly headlined one photo, "I wish they all were California klunkers."

In 1979, three pioneers of the sport—Gary Fisher, Charlie Kelly, and Tom Ritchey—started the first company dedicated to off-road bike production. The first mountain bike to achieve wide circulation was Specialized's 1981 Stumpjumper.

Charlie Kelly would become a founding member of the National Off-Road Bicycle Association (NORBA) in 1983 and help write the first set of rules for the sport. Tom Ritchey would continue designing and building bikes, forming his own company and innovating mountain bike-specific parts, as well as inventing the Break Away frame. Gary Fisher formed Fisher Mountain Bikes, which was sold to Trek in 1993; Fisher remained involved in design and marketing.

First World Champions

- The first mountain bike world championships took place in Durango, Colorado, in 1990, crowning men's and women's cross-country and downhill champions.

- Women's and men's cross-country winners were Americans Juli Furtado and Ned Overend, respectively.

- Men's and women's downhill winners were Greg Herbold from the United States and Cindy Devine of Canada, respectively.

European Influence

- It did not take long for Europeans to catch the mountain biking buzz. With road and cyclocross racing already huge sports in Europe, it was only a matter of time before Europeans dominated the dirt as well.

- Europeans compete in regional, national, and international competitions.

- The European championships are held every year in a different location. It is not uncommon for about five hundred cyclists and technical staff from twenty-three countries to participate in the championships.

BICYCLE ART

Be it artistic or utilitarian, bicycle art provides a medium for conversation

When they are not being ridden or when they have surpassed their riding life, bicycles and their parts have performed other functional tasks—and even been turned into art. The array of bicycle paintings, posters, and photographs is equally impressive and satisfies abstract to impressionistic tastes.

Some bicycles are considered art themselves. Indeed, some fanatics spend more time caring for and staring longingly at their machines than they do riding them. Some folks turn their love of the sport into a collector's pastime by accruing rare parts and maintaining a stable of bikes that follows some historical or personal theme.

Perhaps we shouldn't poke too much fun at these

Vintage Posters

- The booming bicycle trade of the 1890s conveniently coincided with the Golden Age of Illustration.

- Bike manufacturers commissioned illustrators to create advertisements.

- The colorful posters, made possible by recent innovations in lithography, are still popular art pieces today. Some of the ads are quite sultry.

- Posters come in small and extravagant sizes. They will surely create a conversation piece hanging in your home or office.

Collectors' Bikes

- A limited edition Optibike (OB1) is hand numbered and custom fitted for the owner. Only twenty-four are produced per year. The base model costs approximately $14,000.

- This bike is fully loaded, with ultralight carbon fiber components, state-of-

the-art GPS navigation, a fully-integrated PDA, and a patented Motorized Bottom Bracket.

- A lithium ion battery lets you ride with powered-assistance for more than two hours.

enthusiasts because what new owner of a bicycle hasn't uttered to at least one friend, "Check out my new bike" with a proud smile? No matter how utilitarian the goal, no matter how many other bikes you have owned before your new one, the freedom and joy that the bicycle embodies are present in every single one.

What to do with the old bike, though? How about donating it to an artist? Designers turn recycled steel and aluminum bicycles, rims, handlebars, and frames into high-quality tables, bar stools, and chairs.

Furniture

- A creative flare, some spare parts, and some welding skills can result in interesting bike-inspired furniture.

- Bike mechanic and artist Andy Gregg of Bike Furniture combined his talents to make modern design-inspired chairs, tables, and loveseats from recycled steel and aluminum rims, handlebars, and frames.

- Accessories, such as coat racks and mirrors, are also available.

Trinkets

- Small parts and bits of gears can be recycled for all kinds of useful and decorative trinkets including belts, bags, bottle openers, wind chimes, and jewelry.

- Creative bike shop employees seem to find increasingly clever uses for unused bike parts.

- The most interesting recycled tube use: A young man in a certain London bike shop used old tubes to make S&M whips.

ROAD ACCESS
Cyclists have the same legal responsibilities as drivers, even though bikes aren't cars

The bicycle craze of the late nineteenth century quickly presented the problem of what to do with all those reckless riders careening all over the streets. The answer, for better or for worse, was to legally treat bicycles much the same as motorized vehicles. Some heralded this answer as a victory. Equating bicycles with vehicles was a signal that bicycles and their riders were taken seriously.

If you spend much time getting around on two wheels, you will notice a sense of entitlement by motorists, as if cyclists should consider themselves lucky to be able to use the roads at all. Yet, most cyclists pay the same road taxes as do motorists and probably drive a vehicle as well, not to mention have

Bike Lanes

- Separate bike lanes have the most impact on new or potential riders by lowering the hurdle to enter the bicycle commuting realm.

- However, adversaries of bike lanes believe the lanes push aside bikes to make room for cars in contradiction to the status of bikes as vehicles.

- Practically speaking, bike lanes are nice, but their presence or lack thereof probably doesn't weigh considerably in route choosing by the avid commuter.

Sharrow

- The shared-use arrow, or sharrow, communicates to drivers (and cyclists) that cyclists may be present on the road and are permitted to ride in the lane.

- The arrow encourages cyclists to ride on the street instead of the sidewalk and to ride farther in the lane.

- The sharrow first appeared in the United States in the early 1990s on Denver, Colorado, streets.

- A study in San Francisco, California, determined the sharrow has a positive impact on the behavior of both cyclists and motorists.

jobs, families, and friends just like everyone else. This simple reality does not seem to occur to motorists who are in a hurry and who would rather conveniently typecast every cyclist as an annoying threat to their individual pursuit of driving.

The challenge with treating bikes like cars is that bikes are not like cars in many ways. Bikes are quicker and more agile than cars in some situations, and slower in others. Cyclists enjoy much better the ability to see and sense what is happening around them while easily being overlooked by drivers. Bikes are allowed in places where cars are not. Cyclists can merely hop off their bikes and become pedestrians.

Consider the differene between car and bike when approaching a stop sign. On your bike, you approach the sign slower and may have greater visibility, making coming to an absolute stop often unnecessary, practically speaking. Nevertheless, it is illegal to not stop in most jurisdictions, and some cities enforce this law vigorously. However, Idaho recognizes the practical reality of bikes and allows cyclists to treat red lights like stop signs and stop signs like yield signs.

Signage

- Signage communicates messages to cyclists and motorists.

- Messages include share the road, ride single file, and don't pass cyclists in the traffic circle.

- A sharrow might be a more effective and noticeable way to communicate the presence of cyclists and the need to share the road.

- Sharing the road works both ways. As a cyclist, do your part to ride single file and respectfully.

Bike Paths

- Designated bike paths often follow railways, canals, rivers, or creeks, placed away from or below traffic.

- A cyclist is able to zip along away from cars and traffic lights, intersections, and stop signs.

- Off-street bike paths that are away from trafficked streets are coveted. Homes near these paths fetch a higher sale price in cities.

- Because these paths may be away from busy streets, you will need to pick up a map to locate these hidden, yet nearby treasures.

TRAIL ACCESS

If you don't have money to donate to worthy causes, give your time and service instead

As new mountain bike riders, we spent the early 1990s riding as many trails, remote locations, and sweet surroundings as we could find. In retrospect, we were riding through a lot of private property. Allow us a moment to formally apologize to the landowners for our ignorant behavior. We know better now.

How did we ultimately find out that we were trespassing?

Barbed wire fences, NO TRESPASSING signs, piano wire strung across trails, and an occasional gun found its way into our fields of vision. Although landowners have a legal right to exclude others from their land, they do not have a right to inflict intentional harm upon trespassers. The duty a landowner owes to a known trespasser is merely to warn or make

No Bikes Allowed

No Trespassing

- NO BIKES ALLOWED signs can be found in urban settings, as well as on trails. Typically, shopping centers and outdoor malls prohibit bikes, skateboards, and inline skates.

- Mountain parks and open space trails may prohibit

bikes on all or some trails, so pay attention to signs.

- Signs or placards will have a clearly marked bicycle with a red slash through it.

- "No bikes" laws are strictly enforced, and fines can be steep for violators.

- Trespassing is legally defined as an act of physical invasion of another's real property. It does not matter whether you know the land belongs to someone else.

- If you find yourself unintentionally on private property, owners should simply ask you to leave. They cannot

arrest you or hold you on their property.

- Depending on the jurisdiction, criminal trespassing is committed if you intentionally enter or remain on private land that is fenced or otherwise designed to exclude intruders.

222

safe any artificial, dangerous, concealed, and known hazards. In other words, a trespasser's injury from human-made booby traps can invoke liability on the landowner.

Public land is another matter. Thanks to the International Mountain Bike Association and local trail advocacy groups, programs bring bike advocates and land managers together in productive partnerships. These groups have helped reverse early blanket closures so that mountain bikes are allowed. This is why riders in Colorado are still able to enjoy 30 miles of sweet singletrack on the Monarch Crest Trail, or ride the Kokopelli trail from Colorado to Utah.

IMBA understands that not all trails should be open to bikes. It also believes in and works toward creating bike-only trails and shared-use trails that work best for the needs of most users. They minimize environmental impact and are economical.

If you enjoy mountain biking, we strongly encourage you to support these organizations by donating either money or time. Membership dues are often the life blood of nonprofit organizations. Volunteering is a feel-good way to help make a difference, as well as meet some new friends.

U.S. Land Use Legislation

- Almost all states have statutes that limit the liability of landowners who permit people to enter their land for recreational uses.

- Some states grant immunity to liability if the recreational use is permitted without payment.

- Landowners cannot escape liability from willful, wanton, and intentional acts. In other words, landowners who put piano wire across a trail and cause injury to a trespasser can be held liable for the act.

- Other countries have more liberal public access rights under the "freedom to roam" theory.

Trail Building

- Local trail advocacy groups often sponsor trail-building days when you can donate your sweat and muscles to creating and maintaining trails.

- A well-designed trail takes time and careful consideration. Erosion patterns, precipitation, surface type,

and types of users all factor into how a trail is built.

- Proper construction means the trail will last forever with minimal degradation.

- Use a resource book from IMBA or attend a training session to learn proper construction and maintenance.

PARTING THOUGHTS

Sunrise rides, afternoon escapes, evening serenity: The chance to reflect is waiting for you

Set a goal for yourself today. Decide on a cycling experience and an event and start preparing for it right now. Don't look at what you can afford or what you think you are capable of accomplishing. Think of what you truly desire. Put your desire down on paper, meaning write it down. Focus on it. Give yourself a definitive date for when it will be done. Then make

the dream turn into reality.

Our real-life experience has taught us that doing this really works, even when the ideas didn't seem achievable. A simple way to make immediate objectives come true is to commit to a charity ride by signing up and paying a registration fee. This very act can generate so much excitement. If the social scene

Inspiration

- Early morning rides start your day off with positivity. Typically, there is less traffic, which provides the quiet needed to think and reflect.

- Your metabolism will get fired up from an early workout, meaning you'll burn more calories during the day.

- You'll feel inspired. Webster's dictionary defines "inspiration" as the action or power of moving the intellect or emotions.

- And to think you can have that while riding a bike!

Motivation

- The more you do and the higher you jump, the greater the motivation to keep going. It's one of those life juxtapositions.

- An example of this fact can be seen in X-Games competitions and sports, in general. Faster, higher,

stronger, and better are human forces that drive world records.

- The achievement of finishing a bike ride embeds itself in you, making the next experience possible and often easier.

isn't for you, pick a distance goal to ride alone. Plan a trip with your bike or decide if it's time to enter a competition.

If competing has already captured your attention, take it to the next level—especially if you detect a talent or characteristic that makes you valuable to others. You might find that you are a great support team member and can help others win races. Or have a niche that is vital to team success. If you are "marketable" and have the capability of generating media attention independently of how many races you win, you have value.

Becoming a professional athlete is not as hard as one may think (given that you have the physiological talent). Then again, it's not easy either. If becoming a pro is your goal, and you dedicate 100 percent of your energy to it through training, self-promotion, common sense, perseverance, and determination, then it is possible. Remember that we all have to pay our dues. Enjoy the journey. The moment you become bitter and have selfish expectations, the doors close quickly.

Bliss

- "Stop and smell the roses" is a common saying that reminds us that we should take time to relax, enjoy, and appreciate life.

- When riding any trail with or without flowers, remind yourself of this blissful thought.

- For those of you who think it's contradictory that you can relax and feel serene while engaging in the physical exertion of pedaling a bike, we challenge you to do so and see for yourself.

Riding into the Sunset

- Our final words of wisdom before you ride off into the sunset:

- Be sure you know the basics about your bike and that you have done your preparation, including a preride bike check.

- Have an idea of where you're going so you know how to get there.

- Be sure you are dressed appropriately and have your must-carry-on-every-ride items.

- In this sunset scenario, remember a light.

RESOURCES

Resource Directory for All Your Cycling Needs

The cycling industry has an abundant selection of resources. The web is rife with information, products, and services. To further your cycling passion and gather more information, we encourage you to read books, blogs, and magazines. The resources listed here will point you in the right direction for exceptional publications, products, and services. We have also listed links to some cycling advocacy groups so you can get involved and give back to the sport. Even if they are not located in your area, they will be able to help you find a local chapter in your area.

Bicycle Manufacturers

3D Bikes www.v2racing.com
Bianchi www.bianchiusa.com
Brown Cycles www.kidztandem.com
Coupling/Folding Bikes
   Ritchey www.ritcheylogic.com
   S and S Machine www.sandsmachine.com
   Brompton www.brompton.co.uk
   Moulton www.moultonbicycles.co.uk
Cervélo www.cervelo.com
Freedom Rider www.freedomryder.com
Fugi www.fujibikes.com
Gary Fisher www.fisherbikes.com
Giant www.giant-bicycles.com
Gios www.gios.it
Gyro Bike (kids) www.thegyrobike.com
Intense www.intensecycles.com
Look www.lookcycle-usa.com
Marin www.marinbikes.com
Moots www.moots.com
Redline www.redlinebicycles.com
Ridley www.ridley-bikes.com
Ritchy www.ritcheylogic.com

Salsa www.salsacycles.com
Santa Cruz www.santacruzbicycles.com
Scott www.scottusa.com
Seven www.sevencycles.com
Surly www.surlybikes.com
Tomac www.tomac.com
Trek www.trekbikes.com

Clothing

Castelli www.castelli-us.com
Craft www.craft-usa.com
Descent Athletic www.descenteathletic.com
Fox Racing www.foxracing.com
Louis Garneau www.louisgarneau.com
Nike www.nike.com
Patagonia www.patagonia.com
Pearl Izumi www.pearlizumi.com
Shebeest www.shebeest.com
Skirt Sports www.skirtsports.com
SmartWool www.smartwool.com
Sock Guy www.sockguy.com
Sugoi www.sugoi.com
Troy Lee Designs www.troyleedesigns.com
Under Armour www.underarmour.com
Wigwam www.wigwam.com

Components

Avid www.sram.com/en/avid/
Campagnolo www.campagnolo.com
Cane Creek www.canecreek.com
Chris King www.chrisking.com
Magura www.magura.com
Shimano www.shimano.com
SRAM www.sram.com

Computers and GPS

Cateye www.cateye.com
Garmin www.garmin.com
Mavic www.mavic.com
Sigma www.sigmasport.com
Suunto www.suunto.com

Cycling and Running Shoes

DC BMX http://bmx.dcshoes.com/
Keen www.keenfootwear.com
Newton Running www.newtonrunning.com
Northwave www.northwave.com
Pearl Izumi www.pearlizumi.com
Shimano www.shimano.com
Sidi www.sidisport.com
Specialized www.specialized.com

Eyewear

Bolle www.bolle.com
Fox Racing www.foxracing.com
Giro www.giro.com
Oakley www.oakley.com
Rudy Project www.rudyproject.com
Smith Optics www.smithoptics.com
Specialized www.specialized.com
Zeal Optics www.zealoptics.com

Helmets

Bellsports www.bellsports.com
Bern www.bernunlimited.com
Giro www.giro.com
Pro-tec www.pro-tec.net
Yakkay www.yakkay.com

Lights

Cateye www.cateye.com
DiNotte www.dinottelighting.com
Jetlites www.jetlites.com
NiteRider www.niterider.com
Princeton Tec www.princetontec.com

Organizations and Press

Alliance for Biking & Walking www.PeoplePoweredMovement.o
Bicycle Radio www.bicycleradio.com
Bicycling Australia Magazine www.bicyclingaustralia.com
Bikes Belong www.bikesbelong.org
Competitor Magazine www.competitor.com
Cycle Sport www.cyclesportmag.com
Cycling News www.cyclingnews.com
Cycling Weekly www.cyclingweekly.co.uk

Dirt Mountain Biking Magazine www.dirtmag.co.uk
Dirt Rag www.dirtragmag.com
Elite Racing www.competitor.com
Growth Cycle www.growthcycle.net
Inside Triathlon www.competitor.com
International Mountain Bicycling Association www.imba.com
League of American Bicyclists www.bikeleague.org
Mountain Bike Magazine www.mountainbike.com
National Bicycle Dealers Association www.nbda.com
Project Rwanda www.projectrwanda.org
Super Human Magazine www.superhumanmag.com
Triathlete Magazine www.competitor.com
USA Cycling www.usacycling.org
VeloGear www.competitor.com
VeloNews www.competitor.com
VeloPress www.competitor.com
World Bicycle Relief www.worldbicyclerelief.org/grassroots

Pedals

CrankBrothers www.crankbrothers
Look Cycle www.lookcycle-usa.com
Shimano www.shimano.com
Speedplay www.speedplay.com
Time www.timesport.fr

Performance Food

Accelerade www.accelerade.com
Bear Naked www.bearnaked.com
Champion Nutrition www.championnutrition.com
Clif Bar www.clifbar.com
Cytomax www.cytosport.com
Endurox www.accelsport.com
Enervit www.enervitusa.com
GU www.guenergy.com

Hammer Nutrition www.hammernutrition.com
Honey Stinger www.honeystinger.com
LaraBar www.larabar.com
PowerBar www.powerbar.com
Sharkies www.sharkeiesinc.com
Sport Beans www.sportbeans.com

Products and Accessories

Camelbak www.camelbak.com
Contour Technology www.thecontour.com
Crank Brothers www.crankbrothers.com
Klean Kanteen www.kleankanteen.com

Park Tool www.parktool.com
Pedros www.pedros.com
Saris www.saris.com
Silca www.silcapompe.it
Timbuk 2 www.timbuk2.com

Recommended Books

A Dog in A Hat by Joe Parkin
Andy Pruitt's Complete Medical Guide for Cyclists by Andy Pruitt, EdD, with Fred Matheny
Bicycle Diaries by David Byrne
Bike & Brew America by Todd Bryant Mercer
Bike Racing for Juniors by Kristen Dieffenbach and Steve McCauley
Cyclocross by Simon Burney
Graham Watson's Tour de France Travel Guide by Graham Watson
Greg Lemond's Complete Book of Bicycling by Greg Lemond
Heart Zones Cycling by Sally Edwards and Sally Reed
Mountain Bike Maintenance by Guy Andrews
Optimum Sports Nutrition by Dr. Michael Colgan
Racing Tactics for Cyclists by Thomas Prehn, with Charles Pelkey
The Cyclist Training Diary by Joe Friel
The Cyclist's Manifesto by Robert Hurst
The Cyclist's Training Bible, 4th Ed. by Joe Friel
The Cyclist's Training Manual by Guy Andrews and Simon Doughty
The Mountain Biker's Training Bible by Joe Friel
The Time-Crunched Cyclist by Chris Carmichael and Jim Rutberg
Training and Racing with a Power Meter by Hunter Allen and Andrew Coggan, PhD
Training Plans for Cyclists by Gale Bernhardt
Zinn & the Art of Mountain Bike Maintenance by Lennard Zinn
Zinn & the Art of Road Bike Maintenance by Lennard Zinn

Saddles

Fizik www.fizik.com

Selle Italia www.selleitalia.com
WTB www.wtb.com
Selle San Marco www.sellesanmarco.com

Shops and Services

Bike Fit www.wobblenaught.com
Boulder Center for Sports Medicine www.bch.org
Cycle Chic www.cyclechic.co.uk
Excel Sports www.excelsports.com
Naturally Caffeinated www.naturallycaffeinated.com
Peter Kraiker Photography http://studiofstop.com
Race for Tara www.racefortara.com
REI www.rei.com
The Fix Bike Shop www.thefixbikes.com
University Bikes www.ubikes.com
Western Spirit www.westernspirit.com

Technical Equipment

Blackburn www.blackburndesign.com
Cyclops www.cyclops.com
Computrainer www.computrainer
Contour www.thecontour.com
Kreitler www.kreitler.com
Kurk Kinetics www.kurkkinetics.com
Polar www.polarusa.com
SRM www.srm.de/usa/index/

Tires

Continental www.conti-online.com
Hutchinson www.hutchingsontires.com
Kenda www.kendausa.com
Maxxis www.maxxis.com
Michaline www.michalinebicycletire.com
Victoria www.victoriatire.com

Training and Coaching

Alison Dunlap Adventure Camps www.alisondunlap.com
Bike Skills www.bikeskills.com
Boulder Center for Sports Medicine www.bch.org
Carmichael Training Systems www.trainright.com
Contour Technology www.thecontour.com
FasCat Coaching www.fascatcoaching.com
Jimena Cycling www.jimenacycling.com
Per4mance Coaching Training www.totalcyclist.com
Trailmaster Coaching www.trailmastercoaching.com

Travel and Racks

Bike Pro www.bikeprousa.com
Rocky Mounts www.rockymounts.com
Thule www.thuleracks.com

Trico www.tricosports.com
Yakima www.yakima.com

Vacation and Tours

Bicycle Tour of Colorado www.bicycletourcolorado.com
Escape Adventures www.lasvegascyclery.com
Outdoor Adventure www.BOC123.com
Ride the Rockies www.ridetherockies.com
Tour d'Afrique www.tourdafrique.com
Vail Mountain Bike Camps www.vailmountainbikecamps.com
Western Spirit www.westernspirit.com

REFERENCES & BIBLIOGRAPHY

References and Bibliography

David A. Herlihy, *Bicycle: The History* (Yale University Press: New Haven, London) (2004).

Robert Hurst, *The Cyclist's Manifesto* (Falcon Guides) (2009).

Greg Lemond & Kent Goris, *Greg Lemond's Complete Book of Cycling* (Perigree 1990) (1987).

Kieron Humphrey, "From Bush to Bike—A Bamboo Revolution," BBC News, July 1, 2009, http://news.bbc.co.uk/2/hi/africa/8125274.stm (describing Zambikes, a bamboo bike company in Zambia); also see Calfee Design website, www.calfeedesign.com/BambooOverview .htm.

David Derbyshire, "A Pint of Beer Is Better for You after a Workout Than Water, Say Scientists," *Daily Mail*, November 7, 2007, www.dailymail. co.uk/news/article-491236/A-pint-beer-better-workout-water-say-scientists.html.

Major City Transit Bike Policies

San Francisco: Bay Area Rapid Transit, "Bike Rules," www.bart.gc guide/bikes/bikeRules.aspx.

New York City: Metropolitan Transportation Authority, "Bicycle Safe in the Subway," www.mta.info/nyct/safety/bike/index.html.

London: Transport for London, "Bikes on Public Transport," www .gov.uk/roadusers/cycling/11701.aspx.

GLOSSARY

Abs: Rectus abdominus muscles.

Aerobic Exercise: Also called cardiovascular training (cardio), aerobic exercise conditions the heart and the respiratory system. Cardio increases your capacity to work, burns fat, and helps keep it off your body.

Agonist: A muscle that causes specific movement via its own contraction. Agonists are also referred to as "prime movers" since they are primarily responsible for generating a specific movement.

Antagonist: A muscle that acts in opposition to the specific movement generated by the agonist and is responsible for returning a limb to its initial position. Antagonistic muscles are found in pairs called "antagonistic pairs." These consist of an extensor muscle, which opens the joint, and a flexor muscle, which does the opposite.

Attack: A sudden acceleration to elude another rider or group of riders.

Bonk: Total exhaustion caused by lack of sufficient food during a long race or ride.

Brake Bosses or Posts: Part of the bicycle frame that rim brakes mount to.

Break, Breakaway: A rider or group of riders that escape from the main group and try to stay away until the finish.

Bridge: To leave one group of riders and join another group that is farther ahead.

Bunny Hop: To jump the bike, without dismounting, over a log or a big rock on a mountain bike, or over a pothole or a curb on the road.

Calorie: A calorie is the metric unit of heat measurement. When used in relation to nutrition, it refers to the energy value of food, or the amount of energy used when performing an exercise.

Cardiovascular System: The body's system that moves nutrients, gases, and wastes to and from cells using blood in the veins and arteries of the circulatory system. This system also helps fight diseases and stabilizes body temperature.

Cardiovascular Training (Cardio): Also called aerobic exercise, or cardiovascular conditioning. Cardio conditions the heart and the respiratory system. It increases your capacity to work, burns fat, and helps keep it off your body.

Cassette, Cluster, Block: Collection of gears mounted on the rear wheel.

Chain Stay: Bottom piece of the rear triangle of a bicycle frame, from the rear dropout to the bottom bracket.

Chain Tensioner: A device used on singlespeed bicycles that adjusts the chain tension.

Chainrings: Larger gears mounted to the cranks and bottom bracket.

Chainsuck: When the chain becomes caught between the chainstay and the rear wheel, whether due to mud buildup or poor frame design.

Chasegroup, Chasers: Riders who are trying to catch a breakaway group.

Circuit Race: A multi-lap event on a course usually two miles or more in length.

Compound Movement: Exercises that work two or more muscle groups simultaneously.

Concentric Contraction: A muscular contraction where the muscle shortens (contracts) as you move it.

Cool-down: The final phase of a workout. Cool-downs are used to slow your heart rate and help transition your body to its regular rhythm.

Core: Also called core muscles, the core includes the major muscles of the abdomen, mid and lower back.

Criterium: A multi-lap event on a course usually a mile or less in length.

Cross-Country: A mountain bike race, either point-to-point or over a long circuit, contested over trails, jeep roads, singletrack, etc.

Cross-Training: A combination of two or more types of physical activity. Cross-training helps keep you interested in exercise, giving your mind, muscles, and joints a break from repetitive stresses. It also facilitates recovery of the muscle groups not being worked.

Derailleur: The mechanism that moves the chain from one chainring or sprocket to another.

Domestique: A team rider who will sacrifice individual performance to work for a designated teammate.

Down Tube: Bottom diagonal tube of a bicycle frame.

Downshift: Shifting to an easier gear.

Drafting: Riding closely behind another rider to save energy by using that racer as a windbreak.

Drivetrain: Umbrella term for the group of parts that are directly involved with transferring your pedal-power to forward motion, i.e., cranks, chainrings, derraileurs, cogs, chain.

Dropout: Where wheels insert into bicycle frame.

Dumbbell: A weight that can be held in one hand.

Eccentric Contraction: A muscular contraction where the muscle lengthens (extends) as you move it.

Echelon: A staggered line of riders, each downwind of the rider immediately ahead. Can move considerably faster than a solo rider or small group of riders.

Elastic Toners (Toners): Resistance tubing of elastic nature used to build strength and muscle tone.

Electro Muscle Stimulation (E-Stim): An electrical device that uses electrical current (stimulation) to make muscle fiber contract. E-stim, also known as EMS, is used in the medical rehabilitation of wasted muscles and for physical training.

Endo: To crash by going over the handlebars.

Endurance Training: Exercising to increase stamina and endurance.

Feeding: A member of the team's support crew in a designated area on the course hands up a small bag containing liquid and food to riders during the race.

Field: The main group of riders. Also known as the "pack," "bunch," or "peloton".

Field Sprint: A sprint at the finish among the main group of riders.

Flyer: A surprise attack, usually done alone.

Force the Pace: When one rider increases the tempo to cause the group to ride harder.

Free Weight: A weight, such as a barbell or dumbbell, that is not constrained or attached to another device.

Gap: The distance (usually measured in time) between individuals or groups. Gaps are "opened" and "closed."

Gear, Cog, Sprocket: Individual toothed gear.

Glutes: Gluteus maximus muscle.

Gram (g): Unit of mass equal to 1/1000 th of a kilogram. 1 oz = 28 g and 1 lb = 454 g.

Granny Gear: The third and smallest chainring on a mountain bike, combined with the biggest sprocket. This is the lowest gear, used for extremely steep climbs.

Hammer: Riding hard, going all out.

Hammered: Exhausted, beaten to a pulp, wiped out.

Hanging On: Barely maintaining contact at the back of the pack.

Head Tube: Front tube of a bicycle frame into which the steerer (of the fork) inserts.

Heart Rate Monitor (HRM): An electrical device that measures your heart rate by sensing the electrical impulses produced by your heart. Heart rate monitors are usually incorporated in a wristwatch and use a chest strap to sense the impulses.

Hike-a-bike: A section of trail with inadequate traction, or too-steep pitch, that forces cyclists to dismount and push or carry their bikes up the grade.

Hook: To suddenly move to the side, forcing the following rider to slow down to avoid running into the front rider's bike.

IMBA: International Mountain Bicycle Association, the Colorado-based advocacy organization that monitors trail access issues.

Jump: A quick acceleration usually developing into a sprint.

Kick: A final burst of speed that provides acceleration for the sprint.

Kilogram (kg): International unit of mass. 1 kg = 35 oz or 2.2 lb.

Lead-out: An intentional sacrificing tactic whereby one rider races at high speed to give a head start to the rider on his wheel. That rider comes around the leader at an even faster speed for a finishing sprint.

Mass Start: Any race in which all the racers start at the same time.

Massage: The practice of soft tissue manipulation using pressure, tension, motion, or vibration. Massage is used to work on muscle, tendons, ligaments, skin, joints, lymphatic vessels, and the gastrointestinal system. Massage can be applied with the hands, fingers, elbows, forearms, and feet.

Maximum Heart Rate (MHR): Your Maximum Heart Rate is the highest rate at which your heart can possibly beat. It can be estimated by subtracting your age in years from 220.

Mechanical: A mechanical problem with the bicycle.

Metabolism, Metabolic Processes: Metabolism is the group of chemical reactions that occur in your body to maintain life. These metabolic processes allow you to grow and reproduce, maintain tissues and organs, and function effectively.

Meter (m): International unit of length. 1 meter = 39.4 inches.

Naturally Caffeinated: A state of high energy, enthusiasm, and enjoyment of life. A term used to describe individuals who energize their bodies and their lives through movement, activity, and healthy living.

Neutral Stance: Also known as the anatomical position. Used as a reference when describing parts of the body in relation to each other. Neutral stance is standing erect with the head, eyes, and toes pointing forward, feet together, with arms by the side. The palms of the hands also point forward.

Neutral Support: If a rider crashes or has a flat tire during a road race or time trial, a mechanic riding in a follow vehicle will provide a new wheel or do other adjustments to get the rider quickly back into the race. During mountain bike races, riders are responsible for doing their own repairs; receiving assistance from another person results in disqualification.

NORBA: National Off-Road Bicycle Association, the licensing body responsible for mountain bike racing in this country; functions under the umbrella of USA Cycling.

Overtraining: Training too much or too often or when you fail to get enough recovery in between workouts.

Paceline: A string of riders that moves at high speed by each individual taking turns setting the pace, and riding in the draft of the others the rest of the time.

Pannier: A bag that is mounted to a bicycle and hangs alongside the wheel(s).

Peloton: A pack of racing cyclists.

Pole Line: The innermost line on the velodrome surface. This line is used to measure the length of the track.

Pretzel or Taco: To wreck a wheel.

Protein: A complex organic compound essential for the chemical processes that sustain life. Dietary protein is consumed in foods such as meat, fish, and eggs.

Pull: To take a turn at the front of the group, maintaining the same speed of the group.

Rails: Part of the saddle that attaches to the seatpost clamp.

Rainbow Jersey: The coveted rainbow-striped jersey awarded to world champions in each of cycling's disciplines.

Range of Motion (ROM): The distance between the fully flexed position and fully extended position of a joint or muscle group.

Repechage: Usually used in sprint competitions, this term describes a round of the competition in which losers of previous heats are matched against each other. The winner of the repechage gains re-entry in to the main competition.

Reps: The number of repetitions of an exercise movement in a "set." One rep is a complete exercise cycle, for example one biceps curl.

Resistance Training: A form of training where muscular effort is performed against an opposing force. The goal of resistance training is to gradually and progressively overload the musculoskeletal system so it gets stronger.

Seat Collar: Clamp that tightens the seatpost into the seat tube of the frame.

Seat Stay: Part of the bicycle frame that connects the seat tube to the rear dropouts.

Seat Tube: Vertical tube of a bicycle frame into which the seatpost inserts.

Set: A group of repeated exercises, or reps, for example a set of twelve biceps curls.

Singletrack: A path or trail wide enough for only one rider at a time.

Sitting In: Drafting, or sitting closely behind the rider immediately in front.

Slipstream: The area of least wind resistance behind a rider.

Snakebite: Most common type of flat tire. Caused by hitting an obstacle so hard that the innertube is pinched against the rim. Results in a double puncture that resembles two fang holes. Also called a "pinch flat."

Stabilizer Muscles: The smaller peripheral muscles that provide stabilization and support for your joints and movements.

Strength Training: The use of resistance to build the strength, muscular endurance and tone of skeletal muscles. There are many different methods of strength training, the most common being the use of metal weights or elastic/hydraulic forces to provide resistance.

Suspension: A system designed to absorb shock on a mountain bike. mountain bikes can have motorcycle-like front forks, or "full suspension" with shocks front and rear. Front suspension has also been used by some road racers who must tackle severe cobblestone-paved courses in Europe.

Switchback: A tight, zigzag turn on the face of a mountain. Can be negotiated either uphill or downhill.

Take a Flyer: To ride off the front suddenly.

Target Heart Rate: The minimum and maximum heart rate in beats per minute (bpm) between which you want to train. Target heart rate range varies depending on your training goals.

Technical: A section of trail fraught with obstacles that test a rider's bike-handling skill, balance, and finesse.

Time Trial: A race in which riders or teams start individually and race against the clock. The winner is the individual or team covering the course in the fastest time.

Top Tube: Horizontal (or slightly sloping) top tube of a bicycle frame.

Track Bike: A bike with a "fixed" singlespeed gear and no brakes.

Track Stand: A sprint maneuver in which neither rider wishes to lead, resulting in both remaining motionless and balancing on the track.

Transverse Abdominis: The group of muscles running laterally from your sides to the front of your body.

UCI: Union Cycliste Internationale, the international governing body of cycling.

Upshift: Shifting to a harder gear.

USA Cycling: USA Cycling, America's National Governing Body for cycling, which is responsible for establishing the selection criteria for the U.S. Olympic Cycling Team.

Velodrome: An oval track made of concrete or wood with banked sides, used for track racing.

Warm-up: Light exercise used to increase body temperature, blood flow, respiration, and metabolic processes in preparation for more intense training.

Wheel Base: The distance from the front hub to the rear hub.

Wheel Sucker: A person who sits in the draft of another while road riding and does not help work.

Yoga: A system of exercises practiced as part of a Hindu philosophy to promote control of the body and mind.

INDEX

INDEX

INDEX